EMPIRE AND APOCALYPSE

The Bible in the Modern World, 12

Series Editors
J. Cheryl Exum, Jorunn Økland, Stephen D. Moore

Editorial Board
Alison Jasper, Tat-siong Benny Liew, Hugh Pyper, Yvonne Sherwood,
Caroline Vander Stichele

EMPIRE AND APOCALYPSE

POSTCOLONIALISM AND THE NEW TESTAMENT

Stephen D. Moore

SHEFFIELD PHOENIX PRESS

2006

Copyright © 2006 Sheffield Phoenix Press

Published by Sheffield Phoenix Press
Department of Biblical Studies, University of Sheffield
Sheffield S10 2TN

www.sheffieldphoenix.com

A CIP catalogue record for this book
is available from the British Library

Typeset by Forthcoming Publications
Printed by Lightning Source

Hardback ISBN 978-1-905048-85-4
Hardback ISBN 1-905048-85-8

Paperback ISBN 978-1-905048-86-1
Paperback ISBN 1-905048-86-6

ISSN 1747-9630

CONTENTS

ACKNOWLEDGMENTS

The scholarly debts incurred during the decade or so in which this slim book has been gestating and coagulating are too numerous to itemize in full, but I wish to acknowledge the following dialogue partners in particular. First, my former colleagues on the steering committee of the New Testament Studies and Postcolonial Studies Consultation of the Society of Biblical Literature launched in 2000 — Laura Donaldson, Kwok Pui-lan, R.S. Sugirtharajah, and, above all, Fernando Segovia, whose encouragement has been so vital to me. Second, Catherine Keller, my visionary colleague at Drew Theological School, whom I was privileged to assist in organizing a colloquium entitled 'Com/promised Lands: The Colonial, the Postcolonial, and the Theological' in 2002, followed by a conference entitled 'An American Empire? Globalization, War, and Religion' in 2003. Third, Musa Dube, Richard Horsley, Tat-siong Benny Liew, and Jeff Staley, all of whom have also been important to this book through the inspiration and provocation of their work and the warmth of their collegiality. And last but certainly not least, the members of my PhD seminar from Spring 2006 who joined me in wrestling with representations of empire across the New Testament: Lynne Darden, Grant Gieseke, Malebogo Kgalemang, Ho Sung Kim, Okjoo Kim, Ok Pil Kim, and Seong Hee Kim.

    Lynne Darden also deserves my gratitude in another capacity, that of my research assistant. Were it not for her diligent labors, this short book that has been too long in the making would still not have seen the light of day. I wish to express my thanks, too, to David Clines, Co-Director of Sheffield Phoenix Press, for believing in this book even before seeing it (an act upon which Jn 20.29 pronounces a blessing), to Cheryl Exum for warmly welcoming it into The Bible in the Modern World series, and to Duncan Burns whose work on the proofs was all the more impressive for the fact that it is practiced amid the Sybaritic distractions of the South of France. And lastly my gratitude and more to Jane and Olivia for cheerfully enduring the days and nights when I was entombed, Lazarus-like, in my study (and probably smelling just as bad).

An earlier version of Chapter 2 appeared in Catherine Keller, Michael Nausner, and Mayra Rivera (eds.), *Postcolonial Theologies: Divinity and Empire* (St Louis: Chalice Press, 2004), while an earlier version of Chapter 4 appeared in Stephen D. Moore and Fernando F. Segovia (eds.), *Postcolonial Biblical Criticism: Interdisciplinary Intersections* (New York: T. & T. Clark International, 2005). A portion of Chapter 1, meanwhile, appeared in an earlier version in A.K.M. Adam (ed.), *A Handbook of Postmodern Biblical Interpretation* (St Louis, MO: Chalice Press, 2000), and further portion of Chapter 1 appeared in an earlier version in Moore and Segovia (eds.), *Postcolonial Biblical Criticism*. I am grateful to Chalice Press and T. & T. Clark International (Continuum) for permission to reprint this material in revised form.

PREFACE

The morning the Twin Towers fell, I found myself mute before the remnant of my Mark class. The fact that the carnage had occurred a scant two dozen miles to the east of us accounted in no small part for my aphasia; but what compounded it was the chapter of Mark that providence, fate, chance — or the course syllabus, at any rate — had dealt us for discussion that morning. Mark 13 begins: 'And as he came out of the temple, one of his disciples said to him, "Look, Teacher, what wonderful stones and what wonderful buildings!" And Jesus said to him, "Do you see these great buildings? There will not be left here one stone upon another, that will not be thrown down."' To this day I'm not sure how I should, or could, have responded to this lurid provocation to preach — unless the present book be regarded as a belated rejoinder to it. For the book is animated by the simple conviction that the nexus of Christianity and empire requires nuanced strategies of reading — precisely the kind of reading ordinarily denied us in the public domain, whether its object of analysis be September 11, the Bible, or America itself.

Nuanced reading in turn requires delicate tools. The primary conceptual and analytic tools used in this book are those of postcolonial theory. The principal variant of postcolonial theory employed is that of Homi Bhabha. And the most explicit application of Bhabha's conceptual categories occurs in the final chapter of the book, my analysis of Revelation's relations to Rome.

This last chapter was, however, the first to be written. The first exegetical chapter of the book, that on Mark (see Chapter 2), was the second to be written, and makes less explicit appeal to Bhabha's concepts while still being indirectly informed by them. The last chapter, in chronological terms, that on John (see Chapter 3), appeals least directly to Bhabha or postcolonial theory more generally. Instead it attempts an analogue of what Bhabha, Gayatri Spivak, and other postcolonial theorists have done, which is to say that it brings poststructuralist critical sensibilities to bear on literature produced under empire (as does the final section of the chapter on Mark). This general tactic along with other related matters is treated at length in Chapter 4, which functions de facto as a second, 'advanced' introduction to postcolonial studies alongside the initial, and official, introduction in Chapter 1.

I would not have been content to write all three exegetical chapters, then, in the mode employed in the chapter on Revelation, with explicit indebtedness to Bhabha and, to a lesser extent, Spivak evident in every other page. Having said that, however, I have no desire to downplay the extent to which all three exegetical investigations are informed and enabled by a sensibility that owes much to Bhabha specifically—a predisposition to construe life under colonialism as characterized less by unequivocal opposition to the colonizer than by unequal measures of loathing and admiration, resentment and envy, rejection and imitation, resistance and cooption, separation and surrender. The 'truth' of this construal of the colonial condition—and the postcolonial condition besides—is one that I internalized long before encountering Homi Bhabha. It is a construal that perfectly captures the convoluted manner in which the postcolonial Ireland of the 1950s and 1960s in which I was raised related to British cosmopolitan culture. Either I am guilty, then, of projecting my own ambivalence toward empire onto early Christian texts themselves innocent of that trait, or else my cultural formation has sensitized me to elements in these texts that I might otherwise have overlooked. But that is to articulate two overly stark poles of what is, in fact, a complex spectrum. And to attempt to do justice to such complexities is, as indicated earlier, the prime exegetical aim of this book.

PART I

1

'AND SO WE CAME TO ROME':
MAPPING POSTCOLONIAL BIBLICAL CRITICISM

Territory

Now when I was a little chap I had a passion for maps. I would look
for hours at South America, or Africa, or Australia, and lose myself in
the glories of exploration. At that time there were many blank spaces
on the earth, and when I saw one that looked particularly inviting on a
map (but they all look that) I would put my finger on it and say,
'When I grow up I will go there'.

—Joseph Conrad[1]

An Outside Context Problem was the sort of thing most civilizations
encountered just once, and which they tended to encounter rather in
the same way a sentence encountered a full stop. The usual example
given to illustrate an Outside Context Problem was imagining you
were a tribe on a largish, fertile island; you'd tamed the land, invented
the wheel or writing or whatever, the neighbors were cooperative or
enslaved but at any rate peaceful and you were busy raising temples
to yourself with all the excess productive capacity you had, you were
in a position of near-absolute power and control which your hallowed
ancestors could hardly have dreamed of and the whole situation was
just running along nicely like a canoe on wet grass…when suddenly
this bristling lump of iron appears sailless and trailing steam in the
bay and these guys carrying long funny-looking sticks come ashore
and announce you've just been discovered, you're all subjects of the
Emperor now, he's keen on presents called *tax* and these bright-eyed
holy men would like a word with your priests.

—Iain M. Banks[2]

By the outbreak of the Second World War, European colonies and ex-
colonies encompassed 84.6 percent of the land surface of the globe
(Europe itself accounting for a sizeable chunk of the remaining 15.4

---

1. Joseph Conrad, *Heart of Darkness and Selections from The Congo Diary* (New
York: The Modern Library, 1999 [1902]), pp. 8-9.
2. Iain M. Banks, *Excession* (New York: Bantam Books, 1996), p. 61.

percent).[3] And although ensuing decades saw the decline of overt colonialism,[4] they also witnessed the escalation of a more insidious phenomenon that would soon be termed 'neo-colonialism', based on the global military, economic, and cultural supremacy of the former colonial powers and newly emergent superpowers.[5] It is against this impossibly expansive backdrop that postcolonial studies assumes its current significance as an academic enterprise, most notably as a subfield of literary studies (where its impact has been fundamental and formative), but also as a presence within a wide range of other disciplines, biblical studies included.

Whence the term 'post(-)colonial'? It appears to have been concocted by historians in the aftermath of World War II and first employed in such expressions as 'the post-colonial nation-state'.[6] Beginning around the late 1970s, literary critics began to adopt the term, although its usage in literary studies remained sporadic until the early 1990s when 'postcolonial studies' emerged into prominence.

The description 'a highly contested field' has become something of a cliché in literary studies, but it perfectly describes postcolonial studies nonetheless. Even the name of the field has been a hotbed of dispute.[7] What is the force of the 'post-' in 'post(-)colonial', particularly in formulations such as 'the post(-)colonial state', 'post(-)colonial consciousness' or 'post(-)colonial literature'? Does it imply a clean chronological and ideological break from the colonial 'past'? Such a conception of the post(-)colonial is now widely regarded as naive,

---

3.   See D.K. Fieldhouse, *The Colonial Empires* (London: Macmillan, 1989), p. 373.

4.   'Colonialism' is defined (minimalistically) by Edward Said as 'the implant-ing of settlements on distant territory' (*Culture and Imperialism* [New York: Alfred A. Knopf, 1993], p. 9). His corresponding definition of 'imperialism' is 'the prac-tice, the theory, and the attitude of a dominating metropolitan center ruling a distant territory' (*Culture and Imperialism*, p. 9).

5.   The term was coined by Kwame Nkrumah in his *Neo-Colonialism: The Last Stage of Imperialism* (London: Nelson, 1965). For more recent discussion of the term and concept, together with incisive analysis of the concepts of colonialism, imperialism, and postcolonialism, see Robert J.C. Young, *Postcolonialism: An His-torical Introduction* (Oxford: Blackwell, 2001), pp. 15-69.

6.   So Bill Ashcroft, Gareth Griffiths, and Helen Tiffin, *Post-Colonial Studies: The Key Concepts* (London and New York: Routledge, 2nd edn, 2001), p. 186.

7.   Early interventions in the 'what's in a name?' debate included Anne McClintock, 'The Angel of Progress: Pitfalls of the Term "Post-Colonialism"', *Social Text* 31 (1992), pp. 84-98; Aijaz Ahmad, 'Postcolonialism: What's in a Name?', in Román de la Campa, E. Ann Kaplan, and Michael Sprinker (eds.), *Late Imperial Culture* (London: Verso, 1995), pp. 11-32; and Bill Ashcroft, 'On the Hyphen in Post-Colonial', *New Literatures Review* 32 (1996), pp. 23-32.

inadequate, or utopian. It simply cannot account for the complex relations of domination and submission, dependence and independence, resistance and collusion that typically characterize the exchanges between colonizer and colonized not only during colonial occupation but also after official decolonization. Tracing and unraveling these often tortuous relations and affiliations accounts for some of postcolonial theory's most impressive achievements.[8] The unhyphenated term 'postcolonial', supposedly less suggestive of chronological or ideological supersession (it is surprising how much weight a hyphen can be made to bear), is now preferred by the majority of critics.

'Anti-colonial reading is not new', R.S. Sugirtharajah notes. 'It has gone on whenever a native put quill pen to paper to contest the production of knowledge by the invading power'.[9] Contemporary histories of postcolonial studies, however, customarily trace its intellectual roots to a disparate group of post-World War II critics and literary authors, each of whom lived the transition from colonialism to postcolonialism in his particular cultural context and engaged in sustained reflection on colonialism and its complex legacies, notably Frantz Fanon, Aimé Césaire, Chinua Achebe, C.L.R. James, Albert Memmi, and Ngugi wa Thiong'o.[10]

But the work of three further critics constitutes a more immediate resource for contemporary postcolonial studies: Edward Said, whose 1978 book, *Orientalism*, is now routinely seen as having been seminal for the field as an academic discipline;[11] Gayatri Chakravorty Spivak,

8. One thinks in particular of Homi K. Bhabha's *The Location of Culture* (London and New York: Routledge, 1994), which features prominently in Chapters 4 and 5 below.

9. R.S. Sugirtharajah, 'A Brief Memorandum on Postcolonialism and Biblical Studies', *Journal for the Study of the New Testament* 73 (1999), pp. 3-5 (3).

10. See, at minimum, Frantz Fanon, *White Skins, Black Masks* (trans. Charles Lam Markmann; New York: Grove Press, 1991 [French original 1952]); Aimé Césaire, *Discourse on Colonialism* (trans. Joan Pinkham; New York: Monthly Review Press, 2000 [French original 1955]); Chinua Achebe, *Things Fall Apart* (London: Penguin, 2001 [1958]); C.L.R. James, *Beyond a Boundary* (London: Stanley Paul, 1963); Albert Memmi, *The Colonizer and the Colonized* (trans. Howard Greenfeld; London: Earthscan, 2003 [French original 1966]); Ngugi wa Thiong'o, *Decolonizing the Mind: The Politics of Language in African Literature* (London: J. Currey, 1986). Ngugi is more of a contemporary of the other authors listed than the publication date of *Decolonizing the Mind* might suggest; his political plays and novels first began to appear in the early 1960s.

11. Edward W. Said, *Orientalism* (New York: Vintage Books, 2003); this twenty-fifth anniversary edition has a new Preface by the author. Further 'supplementary' reflection by Said on the concept of Orientalism — in a nutshell, the

whose 1985 manifesto, 'Can the Subaltern Speak?', has also been extremely influential (and controversial);[12] and Homi Bhabha, whose 1994 collection, *The Location of Culture*, has likewise been a major catalyst for the field.[13] In the work of all three critics, French structuralist/poststructuralist theory is a central resource for reflecting on colonialism and its complex aftermath: Said reads with Foucault, Spivak with Derrida, and Bhabha with Derrida, Lacan, and others.[14] To oversimplify somewhat, much contemporary postcolonial criticism may be broadly classified as 'poststructuralist', or, more narrowly, as 'deconstructive',[15] because it entails repeated demonstrations of how texts emanating from colonialist cultures — whether histories, travel narratives, or canonical works of literature (Shakespeare's *The Tempest*, say, or Defoe's *Robinson Crusoe*, or Conrad's *Heart of Darkness*) — are enmeshed in elaborate ideological formations, and hence intricate networks of contradiction, that exceed and elude the consciousness of their authors. The widespread 'poststructuralization' of postcolonial studies — the inevitable result, perhaps, of its primary embeddedness in a Western literary studies academy that has itself for decades been largely characterized by heady fusions of poststructuralist and political modes of reading — has been a source of concern in certain quarters, however, particularly those in which materialist philosophies,

---

discursive construction of the East by the West — includes his 'Orientalism Reconsidered', in Francis Barker *et al.* (eds.), *Literature, Politics and Theory* (London: Methuen, 1986), pp. 210-29, and 'Orientalism and Beyond', in Bart Moore-Gilbert, Gareth Stanton, and Willy Maley (eds.), *Postcolonial Criticism* (London: Longman, 1997), pp. 34-73. Said's oeuvre is extensive and varied; also of crucial significance for postcolonial studies, however, is his *Culture and Imperialism*.

12. The most ample version of this multi-version essay can be found in Cary Nelson and Larry Grossberg (eds.), *Marxism and the Interpretation of Culture* (Urbana: University of Illinois Press, 1988), pp. 271-313. Spivak's reflections on the subaltern, and much else besides, achieve 'final' form in her magnum opus, *A Critique of Postcolonial Reason: Toward a History of the Vanishing Present* (Cambridge, MA: Harvard University Press, 1998). Also significant for postcolonial theory are the collections Gayatri Chakravorty Spivak, *In Other Worlds: Essays in Cultural Politics* (New York: Methuen, 1987), and Spivak, *The Post-Colonial Critic: Interviews, Strategies, Dialogues* (ed. Sarah Harasym; London and New York: Routledge, 1990). In *A Critique of Postcolonial Reason*, however, Spivak archly renounces the label 'postcolonial' for the field she helped bring into being.

13. Further works by Bhahba are listed in the annotated bibliography at the end of this book. Nothing else that he has published to date, however, comes close to *The Location of Culture* in terms of influence.

14. I cover this terrain in more detail in Chapter 4, particularly in reference to Bhabha.

15. So Ashcroft, Griffiths, and Tiffin, *Post-Colonial Studies*, pp. 192-93.

such as Marxism, are still seen to provide a more practical basis for social and political action.[16]

Postcolonial criticism is not a method of interpretation (any more than is feminist criticism, say) so much as a critical sensibility acutely attuned to a specific range of interrelated historical and textual phenomena. Any example of postcolonial criticism that we might draw on for purposes of illustration is therefore bound to be arbitrary. A convenient (and not unrepresentative) example is nonetheless provided by Edward Said's 'Jane Austen and Empire', a much-cited section of his *Culture and Imperialism*. Said centers his analysis on Austen's *Mansfield Park*. The modest English estate of the title — the stage for a typical Austenian microdrama of manners and morals — happens in this case to be materially sustained by a second estate, a plantation in Antigua. To this far-off estate Sir Thomas Bertram, the owner of Mansfield Park, makes periodic journeys to manage his affairs there. Yet, whereas Sir Thomas's arrivals at and departures from Mansfield Park, and his conduct and actions while resident there, are matters of consequence in the novel, and as such are recounted in detail, as are events at Mansfield Park generally, the Caribbean plantation is but the object of a few passing references and none of the narrative is set there. Antigua, then, is entirely incidental to the action — yet absolutely crucial to it, since Sir Thomas's fortunes and those of his dependents (the cast of characters whom Austen has assembled at Mansfield Park, including the novel's heroine, Fanny Price) hinge on events at the plantation. The occluded relationship between the two estates, all but unexamined in previous criticism of *Mansfield Park*,[17] is a source of fascination for Said. 'How are we to assess Austen's few references to Antigua, and what are we to make

16. Some recent expressions of this critique include Epifanio San Juan, Jr, *Beyond Postcolonial Theory* (New York: St Martin's Press, 1998); certain of the essays in Crystal Bartolovich and Neil Lazarus (eds.), *Marxism, Modernity and Postcolonial Studies* (Cambridge: Cambridge University Press, 2002); and Benita Parry, *Postcolonial Studies: A Materialist Critique* (Postcolonial Literatures; London and New York: Routledge, 2004). For an instructive exchange on this topic in the context of biblical studies, see Roland Boer, 'Marx, Postcolonialism and the Bible', and David Jobling, '"Very Limited Options": Marxism and Biblical Studies in Postcolonial Scenes', in Stephen D. Moore and Fernando F. Segovia (eds.), *Postcolonial Biblical Criticism: Interdisciplinary Intersections* (The Bible and Postcolonialism, 8; New York: T. & T. Clark International, 2005), pp. 166-83 and 184-201, respectively.

17. I have been able to turn up only one exception, Moira Ferguson's '*Mansfield Park*: Slavery, Colonialism and Gender', *Oxford Literary Review* 13 (1991), pp. 118-39, a study with which Said appears to have been unfamiliar.

of them interpretively?' he muses.[18] Sir Thomas's Caribbean estate would have had to have been a sugar plantation sustained by slave labor, Said surmises, slavery not having been abolished within the British Empire until 1833, whereas *Mansfield Park* was published in 1814. The inhumanity of the slave trade, then, was precisely what made the exquisitely refined microcosm of Mansfield Park possible:

> All the evidence says that even the most routine aspects of holding slaves on a West Indian sugar plantation were cruel stuff. And everything we know about Austen and her values is at odds with the cruelty of slavery. Fanny Price reminds her cousin that after asking Sir Thomas about the slave trade, 'There was such a dead silence' as to suggest that one world could not be connected with the other since there simply is no common language for both. That is true. But what stimulates the extraordinary discrepancy into life is the rise, decline, and fall of the British empire itself and, in its aftermath, the emergence of a postcolonial consciousness. In order more accurately to read works like *Mansfield Park*, we have to see them in the main as resisting or avoiding that other setting, which their formal inclusiveness, historical honesty, and prophetic suggestiveness cannot completely hide. In time there would no longer be a dead silence when slavery was spoken of, and the subject became central to a new understanding of what Europe was.[19]

Translation

No empire earlier than those of modern Europe has featured thus far in this (admittedly compressed) account of postcolonial studies. The question therefore arises, is postcolonial studies really relevant to the Bible? An assumption that tends to permeate the literature of postcolonial studies itself is that colonialism is a phenomenon whose 'real' history begins only with the European colonization of the non-European world in the early modern period. And this assumption is not without substance. European colonization was qualitatively different from pre-capitalist colonial enterprises. European colonizers did more than extract tribute and other forms of wealth from subjugated peoples: they restructured the economies of those peoples, enmeshing them in a symbiotic relationship with their own, and thereby ensuring a constant two-way flow of human and natural resources (settlers, slaves, raw materials, and so forth) and a one-way flow of profits into their coffers.[20]

18. Said, *Culture and Imperialism*, p. 89.
19. Said, *Culture and Imperialism*, p. 96.
20. See Ania Loomba, *Colonialism/Postcolonialism* (London and New York: Routledge, 1998), pp. 3-4.

But although colonialism did acquire an unprecedented reach and devastating efficacy in the modern period, many earlier empires, not least those of the ancient Near East and the Mediterranean Basin, also engaged in colonization.[21] Postcolonial studies does pose a formidable 'translation' problem for students of ancient literature[22] — much the same sort of problem that contemporary literary theory, forged as it is primarily from analysis of modern and postmodern literatures, poses for the biblical critic — but ought not to be dismissed on that account, as the many successes of biblical literary criticism testify. Furthermore, postcolonial studies is by no means narrowly focused on the twin phenomena of colonialism and postcolonialism. A series of other, interrelated realia also fall comfortably within its orbit: imperialism, Orientalism, universalism, expansionism, exploration, invasion, slavery, settlement, resistance, revolt, terrorism, nationalism, nativism, negritude, assimilation, creolization, cosmopolitanism, colonial mimicry, hybridity, the subaltern, marginalization, migration, diaspora, decolonization, neocolonialism, and globalization — all intersected by the ubiquitous determinants of language, gender, race, ethnicity, and class. The relevance of many of these concepts to the biblical texts, considered even in their ancient milieux, hardly needs arguing.

Much traditional biblical scholarship, indeed, reads like postcolonial studies *avant la lettre*. That hallowed gateway to biblical criticism, for instance, the 'Old' or 'New' Testament introduction (whether the textbook or the course), derives much of its efficacy and allure from its ability to summon 'exotic' empires from the shadows of the biblical texts and parade them before the student: Egypt, Assyria, Babylon, Persia, Greece, Rome. So much biblical scholarship is already a reflection on imperialism, colonialism, and the resistance they inevitably elicit. The contributors to the seminal collection, *Paul and Empire*,[23] are thus able to draw almost exclusively on the resources of mainstream biblical studies to investigate its title topic; when interdisciplinary incursions are made, they are into such fields as classics, not postcolonial studies. Yet it stands to reason that the latter field would offer

21. For a sketch of Roman colonial practices, see pp. 99-101 below.

22. See further the incisive comments of Susan VanZanten Gallagher, 'Mapping the Hybrid World: Three Postcolonial Motifs', *Semeia* 75 (1996), pp. 230-33; and David Jobling, review of R.S. Sugirtharajah (ed.), *The Postcolonial Bible*, *Journal for the Study of the New Testament* 74 (1999), pp. 117-18.

23. Richard A. Horsley (ed.), *Paul and Empire: Religion and Power in Roman Imperial Society* (Harrisburg, PA: Trinity Press International, 1997).

significant conceptual and practical resources for focusing, sharpening, and nuancing such analyses.

The agendas for biblical scholarship suggested by postcolonial studies, moreover, are not limited to ancient texts and contexts. As is all too well known, the Bible in general, and specific biblical texts in particular, were used in both systematic and ad hoc ways to authorize the conquest and colonization of Africa, the Americas, parts of Asia, and even pockets of Europe itself, ranging from the strategic deployment of the Matthean 'Great Commission' in William Carey's immensely influential 1792 pamphlet, *An Enquiry into the Obligations of Christians to Use Means for the Conversion of the Heathen*,[24] to Oliver Cromwell's explicit assumption in 1649 of the role of the biblical Joshua in the mass slaughter of Irish 'Canaanites' during his subjugation of the Irish towns of Drogheda and Wexford.[25] Meanwhile, the colonized 'read back' to the empire with equal creativity, causing 'the white man's book' to turn and convict him in African, Indian, or Caribbean accents.[26] In addition to impelling us to resituate biblical texts in relation to their ancient imperial contexts, then, postcolonial studies also impels us to write further chapters, sections, and extended footnotes — but also programmatic prefaces and definitive afterwords — in the 'history of biblical interpretation'.

A third, perhaps less obvious, focus for postcolonial biblical criticism is suggested by the fact that the very period when critical biblical scholarship was being invented in Europe — principally, the eighteenth, nineteenth, and early twentieth centuries — was also the period when European colonization of the globe was in a phase of unprecedented, and eventually frenzied, ascent. Presumably, it is safe to say that the former process did not occur in a vacuum hermetically, or hermeneutically, sealed off from the latter. The task of tracing the

24. See R.S. Sugirtharajah, 'A Postcolonial Exploration of Collusion and Construction in Biblical Interpretation', in R.S. Sugirtharajah (ed.), *The Postcolonial Bible* (The Bible and Postcolonialism, 1; Sheffield: Sheffield Academic Press, 1998), pp. 91-116 (96-100).

25. See Robert Carroll, 'Cultural Encroachment and Bible Translation: Observations on Elements of Violence, Race and Class in the Production of Bibles in Translation', *Semeia* 76 (1996), pp. 39-53 (41-42).

26. See, for instance, R.S. Sugirtharajah, *The Bible and the Third World: Precolonial, Colonial, and Postcolonial Encounters* (Cambridge: Cambridge University Press, 2001), Chapter 3, which is entitled 'Reading Back: Resistance as a Discursive Practice', and contains African, Native American, and Indian examples. For African American slave hermeneutics, see certain of the essays in Part Two of Vincent Wimbush (ed.), *African Americans and the Bible: Sacred Texts and Social Textures* (New York: Continuum, 2nd edn, 2001).

affiliations and correlations between the two phenomena, however, is a formidably complex one that has scarcely begun.[27]

Navigation

I now turn to two exegetical illustrations of postcolonial biblical criticism to balance my earlier illustration of postcolonial literary criticism, Said's reading of Austen. Richard Horsley's 1998 essay, 'Submerged Biblical Histories and Imperial Biblical Studies', contained a brief but — in light of his 2001 book, *Hearing the Whole Story* — programmatic reading of Mark.[28] The reading begins with what, for my money at least, is the most electrifying page of postcolonial biblical criticism to date — a blistering critique of the entire history of Euro-American Markan scholarship, which argues that its tendency to accept as factual the traditions associating Mark with the imperial metropolis of Rome tacitly assigned this gospel a buttressing role in the legitimizing metanarrative of Western imperial Christianity; that its tendency to construe Mark as a passion narrative with an extended introduction depoliticized, and hence declawed, the gospel by emptying its peasant protagonist's Galilean mission of its social significance; and that its tendency to read Mark as a handbook for disciples assimilated the gospel to the excessively individualistic model of Western Christianity, further obscured 'the anti-imperial political plot of the Gospel', and reduced Jesus' confrontation with the Roman client rulers to 'incidental stage setting'.[29] In a reading that continues to bristle with provocative assertions, and eventually balloons into *Hearing the Whole Story*, Horsley proceeds to adumbrate an alterative understanding of Mark, one designed to enable its 'recovery...as a narrative of imperially subjected peasantries forming a movement of revitalized cooperative social formations based on their own indigenous traditions', and embodying resistance both to exploitative local

27. A beginning has been made primarily by Fernando Segovia; see, for example, his 'Biblical Criticism and Postcolonial Studies: Toward a Postcolonial Optic', in Sugirtharajah (ed.), *The Postcolonial Bible*, pp. 49-65 (58-63 *passim*). Shawn Kelley's *Racializing Jesus: Race, Ideology and the Formation of Modern Biblical Scholarship* (London and New York: Routledge, 2002), while differently focused, offers a full-scale model of how such analysis might proceed.

28. Richard A. Horsley, 'Submerged Biblical Histories and Imperial Biblical Studies', in Sugirtharajah (ed.), *The Postcolonial Bible*, pp. 152-73; Horsley, *Hearing the Whole Story: The Politics of Plot in Mark's Gospel* (Louisville, KY: Westminster John Knox Press, 2001). The essay treats Paul as well as Mark.

29. Horsley, 'Submerged Biblical Histories', p. 156.

authorities and alien imperial domination.[30] The Markan Jesus who
emerges from Horsley's essay, from *Hearing the Whole Story*, and from
his 2003 book *Jesus and Empire*,[31] is hardly a complete stranger; clearly
he has much in common with the historical Jesus fleshed out in
Horsley's earlier work,[32] as well as with John Dominic Crossan's
Jesus and other political Jesus constructs. But Horsley's reading in
postcolonial studies has apparently enabled him to bring his previous
portrait of Jesus in general, and Mark's Jesus in particular, into
sharper relief—specifically, elements of that portrait related to Roman
imperialism and anti-imperial resistance.[33] And implicit in Horsley's
reading of Mark is the notion that this gospel, properly understood,
is consistently anti-imperial in thrust, and hence a solid basis for
theological critique of hegemonic ideologies and institutions, whether
those of ancient Rome or the contemporary United States.[34]

A rather different, but equally important, postcolonial reading of
Mark is Tat-siong Benny Liew's *Politics of Parousia*, the argument of
which is sharpened and streamlined in a spin-off article of its own,
'Tyranny, Boundary and Might'.[35] The article begins by taking issue

30. Horsley, 'Submerged Biblical Histories', p.162.

31. Richard A. Horsley, *Jesus and Empire: The Kingdom of God and the New World Disorder* (Minneapolis: Fortress Press, 2003). The book's exegetical chapters alternate between the Gospel of Mark and the Sayings Gospel Q.

32. See especially Richard A. Horsley, *Jesus and the Spiral of Violence: Popular Jewish Resistance in Roman Palestine* (San Francisco: Harper & Row, 1987; reprinted Minneapolis: Fortress Press, 1993).

33. Horsley notes at one point in the essay that a postcolonial exegesis of Mark 'makes it appear much like the sort of history that recent subaltern studies are striving to construct of the Indian peasantry' ('Submerged Biblical Histories', pp. 156-57; cf. Ranajit Guha [ed.], *Subaltern Studies. I. Writings on South Asian History and Society* [Delhi: Oxford University Press, 1982]). Horsley's relationship to postcolonial studies, however, is complex, marked by disavowal as well as acknowledgment (see n. 52 below). Some of the reasons for his caution are apparent from his 'Subverting Disciplines: The Possibilities and Limitations of Postcolonial Theory for New Testament Studies', in Fernando F. Segovia (ed.), *Toward a New Heaven and a New Earth: Essays in Honor of Elisabeth Schüssler Fiorenza* (Maryknoll, NY: Orbis Books, 2003), pp. 90-105. There he criticizes postcolonial theory in blanket terms for what he sees as 'its steadfast rejection of metanarratives, its lack of interest in envisioning an alternative future' (p. 94).

34. For the latter, see both the introduction ('American Identity and a Depoliticized Jesus') and the epilogue ('Christian Empire and American Empire') to *Jesus and Empire*, as well as Richard A. Horsley, *Religion and Empire: People, Power, and the Life of the Spirit* (Minneapolis: Fortress Press, 2003), in which he turns his Jesus loose in earnest upon US foreign policy.

35. Tat-siong Benny Liew, *Politics of Parousia: Reading Mark Inter(con)textually* (Biblical Interpretation Series, 42; Leiden: E.J. Brill, 1999); Liew, 'Tyranny,

with interpreters who construe Mark purely or predominantly as a document for liberation.[36] It is not that Liew denies that Mark contains elements of an anti-colonial critique, but Liew is simply not content to stop there, arguing that Mark duplicates colonial ideology as much as (or more than?) it resists it. Liew takes up Homi Bhabha's highly influential concept of 'colonial mimicry',[37] but gives it a unique twist. Bhabha notes how colonial discourses regularly enjoin the colonized to internalize and replicate the colonizer's culture—to mimic it, in effect. But this strategy is fraught with risk for the colonizer, Bhabha contends, and replete with opportunity for the colonized, because such mimicry can all too easily slip over into mockery thereby menacing the colonizer's control. Liew sees Mark as engaged in colonial mimicry—not as active resistance to Roman hegemony, however, but as reduplication of Roman imperial ideology. Mark's characterization of Jesus is crucial in this regard. On Liew's reading, Mark is intent on replacing one absolute authority—that of the Roman Emperor—with another—that of Jesus Messiah. Mark's hegemonic characterization of Jesus achieves its apogee, according to Liew, in the motif of the parousia; then the victorious Christ will annihilate all competing authorities, replicating 'the colonial (non)choice of "serve-or-be-destroyed"' in the process, a (non)choice based upon the 'colonial rationalization' that certain people(s) are simply unworthy of autonomy, or even of life itself.[38] The problem, for Liew, is that by depicting the defeat of power by yet more power—power in hyperbolic measure—Mark is (inadvertently?) mimicking the 'might-is-right' ideology that props up colonialism and imperialism in the first place.

Horsley's and Liew's diametrically opposed readings of Mark graphically illustrate the two poles between which postcolonial biblical criticism currently oscillates. On the one hand, the biblical text is read as unequivocal and exemplary anti-imperial and anti-colonial

Boundary and Might: Colonial Mimicry in Mark's Gospel', *Journal for the Study of the New Testament* 73 (1999), pp. 7-31.

36. Liew, 'Tyranny, Boundary and Might', p. 7. His targets are Ched Meyers, Herman Waetjen, and Robert Hamerton-Kelly. Had *Hearing the Whole Story* been available to Liew, it is not hard to imagine that Horsley would have been on the list as well—especially after reading Liew's review of Horsley's book in the *Catholic Biblical Quarterly* 64 (2002), pp. 576-77, which bristles with questions and criticisms.

37. See Bhabha, 'Of Mimicry and Man: The Ambivalence of Colonial Discourse', in his *The Location of Culture*, pp. 85-92.

38. Liew, *Politics of Parousia*, p. 104, citing Said, *Culture and Imperialism*, p. 168.

resistance literature. On the other hand, the biblical text is read as covertly complicit imperialist and colonialist literature—or, more precisely, as literature that, irrespective of the conscious intentionality of its author, insidiously reinscribes imperial and colonial ideologies even while appearing to resist them. And it is between this Scylla and Charybdis—wishful projection on one side, excessive suspicion on the other—that the exegetical essays of the present volume attempt, however unsuccessfully, to navigate.

Mapping

How best to map the field of postcolonial biblical criticism more generally? The task is already a complex one, notwithstanding the fact that scarcely a decade has elapsed since the terms 'postcolonial(ism)' and 'Bible' were first conjoined within biblical studies. The complexity arises from the difficulty of postulating where precisely it is that postcolonial biblical criticism begins or ends. Depending upon the example being considered, postcolonial biblical criticism seems to emerge out of liberation hermeneutics, or extra-biblical postcolonial studies, or even historical criticism of the Bible, or all three at once.

The version of liberation hermeneutics out of which much post-colonial biblical criticism seems to flow is that relatively recent inflection of it variously termed contextual hermeneutics, vernacular hermeneutics, cultural exegesis, cultural interpretation, intercultural interpretation, or cultural studies.[39] Acutely attuned to the socio-cultural location of the biblical interpreter,[40] contextual hermeneutics may be said to relinquish the central (frequently Marxist-driven) focus on economics and the universal plight of the poor typical of classic liberation theology for a focus on the local, the indigenous, the ethnic, and the culturally contingent, with the aim of recovering,

39. See R.S. Sugirtharajah (ed.), *Vernacular Hermeneutics* (The Bible and Post-colonialism, 2; Sheffield: Sheffield Academic Press, 1999); Daniel Smith-Christopher (ed.), *Text and Experience: Towards a Cultural Exegesis of the Bible* (Sheffield: Sheffield Academic Press, 1995); Brian K. Blount, *Cultural Interpretation: Reorienting New Testament Criticism* (Minneapolis: Fortress Press, 1995); David M. Rhoads (ed.), *From Every People and Nation: The Book of Revelation in Intercultural Perspective* (Minneapolis: Fortress Press, 2005). For cultural studies, see Fernando F. Segovia, *Decolonizing Biblical Studies: A View from the Margins* (Maryknoll, NY: Orbis Books, 2000), pp. 3-35.

40. See Fernando F. Segovia and Mary Ann Tolbert (eds.), *Reading from This Place*. I. *Social Location and Biblical Interpretation in the United States*. II. *Social Location and Biblical Interpretation in Global Perspective* (Minneapolis: Fortress Press, 1995).

reasserting, and reinscribing identities, cultures, and traditions that colonial Christianity had marginalized, erased, suppressed, or pronounced 'idolatrous'.

How exactly is a contextual hermeneutic related to a postcolonial hermeneutic? The distance between the collection *Voices from the Margin* — an early landmark of contextual hermeneutics — and the subsequent collection *The Postcolonial Bible* — an early landmark of postcolonial biblical criticism, assembled by the same editor — is not considerable, but neither is it insignificant.[41] The multinational contributors to the former volume frequently attend to the lingering specter of colonialism, insufficiently exorcized even in the majority of former colonies that have officially achieved independence and undergone decolonization. Not surprisingly, the colonial and the postcolonial assume thematic centrality in a higher percentage of the essays in *The Postcolonial Bible*. Furthermore, and unlike *Voices from the Margin*, the field of extra-biblical postcolonial studies provides at least some of the contributors to *The Postcolonial Bible* with a fresh conceptual vocabulary and analytic apparatus with which to treat the themes of colonialism and imperialism in relation to biblical texts and their histories of interpretation and appropriation. Like most of the contributors to *Voices from the Margin*, however, most of the contributors to *The Postcolonial Bible* write explicitly out of their specific sociocultural locations, and this tactic, as much as the thematic focus on colonialism and its aftermath, might be said to be a defining trait of the latter collection.[42]

The still-small subfield of postcolonial biblical criticism would be a good deal smaller still were it not for the prodigious industry of R.S. Sugirtharajah.[43] Sugirtharajah's own relationship to liberation

---

41. R.S. Sugirtharajah (ed.), *Voices from the Margin: Interpreting the Bible in the Third World* (Maryknoll, NY: Orbis Books, 1991). The most recent edition of the collection (still in production as I write), which contains many essays not in the original edition, including Jeffrey Staley's '"Clothed and in her Right Mind": Mark 5.1-20 and Postcolonial Discourse', effectively blurs the line between contextual and postcolonial hermeneutics. In the interests of clarifying what that line might be, I will confine my comments to the first edition.

42. Further on *The Postcolonial Bible*, see the four reviews of the book (by Ralph Broadbent, Ivy George, David Jobling, and Luise Schottroff) in the *Journal for the Study of the New Testament* 74 (1999), pp. 113-21. Fernando Segovia, himself a contributor to *The Postcolonial Bible*, responds to the reviews in 'Notes toward Refining the Postcolonial Optic', *Journal for the Study of the New Testament* 75 (1999), pp. 103-14 (reprinted in Segovia, *Decolonizing Biblical Studies*, pp. 133-42).

43. A native of Sri Lanka, Sugirtharajah is currently Professor of Biblical Hermeneutics at the University of Birmingham, UK. By my count, he has to date

hermeneutics appears to be one of obvious debt and partial estrange-ment. Not the least significant feature of his work is his bold and extensive internal critique of the liberationist tradition from a 'post-colonial' perspective. Liberation hermeneutics, for Sugirtharajah, is largely prevented by its Christian presuppositions and investments from seeing the Bible as at once a source of emancipation and a source of oppression, and from respecting the truth claims of other religious traditions, even when those traditions are the characteristic religious expressions of the poor; while it conceives of oppression in turn in terms that are too exclusively economic, neglecting other forms of it based on gender, sexuality, or race/ethnicity.[44]

More straightforwardly rooted in liberation theology is *The Bible and Colonialism* by the Irish Roman Catholic priest Michael Prior, who two years earlier had published *Jesus the Liberator*.[45] When Prior declares near the end of *The Bible and Colonialism*, a study of the multiple ways in which biblical land traditions have been pressed into service for colonial ends in Latin America, South Africa, and Palestine/Israel, that he deems 'the...work to be an exploration into terrain virtually devoid of enquirers', he is not exaggerating.[46] His book was the first monograph on the title topic (Sugirtharajah's *Asian Biblical Hermeneutics and Postcolonialism*, which appeared the following year, was the second),[47] and it has not yet received the attention it deserves within postcolonial biblical criticism. Another significant (although widely read) work in this emergent field is Musa Dube's *Postcolonial Feminist Interpretation of the Bible*, which, unlike Prior's book, is also a thoroughgoing example of contextual hermeneutics.[48]

published five monographs and edited another five collections directly relevant to postcolonial biblical criticism (most of which are cited in this introduction and all of which are listed in the annotated bibliography at the end of this book).

44. See Sugirtharajah, *The Bible and the Third World*, pp. 203-75. An abridged and lightly rewritten version of the same material appears in R.S. Sugirtharajah, *Postcolonial Criticism and Biblical Interpretation* (Oxford: Oxford University Press, 2002), pp. 103-23.

45. Michael Prior, *The Bible and Colonialism: A Moral Critique* (The Biblical Seminar, 48; Sheffield: Sheffield Academic Press, 1997); Prior, *Jesus the Liberator: Nazareth Liberation Theology (Luke 4.16-30)* (The Biblical Seminar, 26; Sheffield: Sheffield Academic Press, 1995).

46. Prior, *The Bible and Colonialism*, p. 294.

47. R.S. Sugirtharajah, *Asian Biblical Hermeneutics and Postcolonialism: Contesting the Interpretations* (Maryknoll, NY: Orbis Books; Sheffield: Sheffield Academic Press, 1998).

48. Musa W. Dube, *Postcolonial Feminist Interpretation of the Bible* (St Louis: Chalice Press, 2000).

Writing explicitly out of a Botswanan, and, more generally, black African cultural context, Dube enacts a 'decolonizing' feminist reading of the exodus and conquest narratives in the Hebrew Bible, together with selected Matthean narratives, especially Jesus' enigmatic encounter with the 'Canaanite' woman; provides a devastating critique of previous readings of the latter pericope by white Euro-American interpreters, not least feminist interpreters; and champions non-academic readings of the pericope issuing from women members of the African Independent Churches.

A second cluster of works that fit less cozily under the umbrella of postcolonial biblical criticism stand out as a group in the first instance by the recurrence of the words 'empire' or 'imperial' in their titles, and they are located primarily on the New Testament side of the testamentary divide. The list includes *Jesus and Empire; Matthew and Empire; The Gospel of Matthew in its Roman Imperial Context; Paul and Empire; Paul and the Roman Imperial Order; Colossians Remixed: Subverting the Empire; Unveiling Empire: Reading Revelation Then and Now* (to which list the present book may now be added).[49] To this group belongs also, by reason of topic and/or the name of Richard Horsley (a name even more prominent in this second cluster than Sugirtharajah's was in the first), such works as *Matthew and the Margins; Hearing the Whole Story: The Politics of Plot in Mark's Gospel; Liberating Paul; Paul and Politics; The Message and the Kingdom: How Jesus and Paul*

---

49. Horsley, *Jesus and Empire*; Warren Carter, *Matthew and Empire: Initial Explorations* (Harrisburg, PA: Trinity Press International, 2001); John Riches and David Sim (eds.), *The Gospel of Matthew in its Roman Imperial* Context (Journal for the Study of the New Testament Supplement Series, 276; New York: T. & T. Clark International, 2005); Horsley (ed.), *Paul and Empire*; Horsley (ed.), *Paul and the Roman Imperial Order* (Harrisburg, PA: Trinity Press International, 2004); Brian J. Walsh and Sylvia C. Keesmaat, *Colossians Remixed: Subverting the Empire* (Downers Grove, IL: Intervarsity Press, 2004); Wes Howard-Brook and Anthony Gwyther, *Unveiling Empire: Reading Revelation Then and Now* (Bible & Liberation Series; Maryknoll, NY: Orbis Books, 1999). An important precursor of this current stream of 'empire' titles was the work of Richard J. Cassidy — see, for example, his *John's Gospel in New Perspective: Christology and the Realities of Roman Power* (Maryknoll, NY: Orbis Books, 1992; more recently he has published *Christians and Roman Rule in the New Testament: New Perspectives* [New York: Crossroad, 2001]) — as was the work of Ched Myers: see especially his *Binding the Strong Man: A Political Reading of Mark's Story of Jesus* (Maryknoll, NY: Orbis Books, 1988). Also significant was Loveday Alexander (ed.), *Images of Empire* (Journal for the Study of the Old Testament Supplement Series, 122; Sheffield: JSOT Press, 1991), a volume which included essays on Luke–Acts and Revelation.

Ignited a Revolution and Transformed the Ancient World; and *Rome in the Bible and the Early Church.*[50]

What all of the books in this entire cluster share in common is a sustained focus on the theme of empire as an exegetical lens through which to reframe and reread selected New Testament texts.[51] This, of course, is a lens that has always been employed by biblical scholars: to reconstruct the various 'backgrounds' against which the historical critic's Bible becomes visible is, in part at least, to conjure up a succession of ancient empires, as we noted earlier. But whereas the more traditional biblical scholar has tended to peer through that lens intermittently, the particular authors in the cluster we are considering tend to gaze through it unrelentingly. Despite a shared preoccupation with empire, however, members of this cluster also differ from each other in at least one significant respect. Whereas some of them seem solely interested in the ancient imperial contexts in which the biblical texts were generated (as is the case, for example, with Horsley's edited collection *Paul and Empire* or Carter's *Matthew and Empire*), others are intent on keeping the ancient imperial contexts in dialogue with the contemporary contexts in which the biblical texts are appropriated (so, for example, Howard-Brook and Gwyther's *Unveiling Empire* or Horsley's *Jesus and Empire*).

This preoccupation with reception is shared by certain authors in our first cluster as well—consider Prior or Dube, for instance, or, more especially, Sugirtharajah (whose predominant preoccupation throughout his many publications is with the history of biblical interpretation as a subset of the history of colonialism and of resistance to

50. Warren Carter, *Matthew and the Margins: A Sociopolitical and Religious Reading* (Bible & Liberation Series; Maryknoll, NY: Orbis Books, 2000); Horsley, *Hearing the Whole Story*; Neil Elliott, *Liberating Paul: The Justice of God and the Politics of the Apostle* (Maryknoll, NY: Orbis Books, 1994); Richard A. Horsley (ed.), *Paul and Politics: Ekklesia, Israel, Imperium, Interpretation. Essays in Honor of Krister Stendahl* (Harrisburg, PA: Trinity Press International, 2000); Richard A. Horsley and Neil Asher Silberman, *The Message and the Kingdom: How Jesus and Paul Ignited a Revolution and Transformed the Ancient World* (New York: Grossett/ Putnam, 1997); Peter Oakes (ed.), *Rome in the Bible and the Early Church* (Carlisle, UK: Paternoster Press; Grand Rapids, MI: Baker Book House, 2002).

51. Which is why I haven't included R.S. Sugirtharajah's *The Bible and Empire: Postcolonial Explorations* (Cambridge: Cambridge University Press, 2005) in the cluster: its primary focus is the 'history of biblical interpretation' in the distinctive mode, described below, that Sugirtharajah has made his own. The present book does belong in the cluster on thematic grounds, being at its core a set of essays on 'X and Empire'. Methodologically, however, it belongs in the third cluster outlined below, the one that is more fully engaged with extra-biblical postcolonial studies.

colonialism) — suggesting that the boundaries we are establishing here in this mapping of the field are, in the end, highly permeable. The mapping problem is further exacerbated by the fact that exceedingly few of the authors in the 'X and Empire' cluster evince any interest in affixing the label 'postcolonial' to their projects. 'Empire studies' may actually be a more accurate label for this cluster than 'postcolonial studies'. Symptomatically, one of the most explicit statements of location in relation to postcolonial studies in this burgeoning body of work to date, that of Sze-kar Wan introducing his contribution to *Paul and Politics*, is a cautious one, and should induce a corresponding caution in the cartographer: 'My reading here is not strictly postcolonial, but in some aspects it does coincide with the goals of postcolonial studies in which ethnic integrity, self-determination, anti-colonial and anti-imperial concerns are all inextricably intertwined'.[52] Since cartography has had largely unfortunate connotations in the history of colonialism, however, a map of postcolonial biblical criticism that disintegrates even as it is being drawn is not altogether inappropriate.

Pressing on, we note a third cluster of works, this one distinguished by heavy engagement with the field of extra-biblical postcolonial studies, in contrast to the light engagement characteristic of the first cluster and the non-engagement characteristic of the second (although there are exceptions in both camps).[53] There is, of course, no shortage of such work to engage, the past two decades having witnessed a modest stream of works on colonialism and imperialism, postcolonialism and neocolonialism swell into a torrent and eventually a

---

52. Sze-kar Wan, 'Collection for the Saints as Anticolonial Act: Implications of Paul's Ethnic Reconstruction', in Horsley (ed.), *Paul and Politics*, pp. 191-215 (192 n. 5). Compare Horsley himself, responding to Robert Gundry's critique of the 'postcolonial slant' of Horsley's *Hearing the Whole Story*: 'It is puzzling that Gundry takes the book as "a postcolonial critique of Mark's story". My combination of approaches in *Hearing* does not include (or even mention) postcolonial criticism.' Richard A. Horsley, 'A Response to Robert Gundry's Review of *Hearing the Whole Story*', *Journal for the Study of the New Testament* 26 (2003), pp. 151-69 (165), responding to Gundry's 'Richard A. Horsley's *Hearing the Whole Story*: A Critical Review of its Postcolonial Slant', pp. 131-49, in the same issue. Less reticent in his dealings with postcolonial studies is Philip F. Esler, who begins 'Rome in Apocalyptic and Rabbinic Literature', his contribution to Riches and Sim (eds.), *The Gospel of Matthew in its Roman Imperial Context*, with a section entitled 'Colonial and Post-colonial Perspectives'.

53. And there are also edited volumes whose contributors straddle both camps, such as Musa W. Dube and Jeffrey L. Staley (eds.), *John and Postcolonialism: Travel, Space and Power* (The Bible and Postcolonialism, 7; New York: Continuum, 2002).

flood, most notably in the field of literary studies. Leakage from this field, indeed, more than any other single factor, might be said to account for the origins of postcolonial biblical criticism. The first volume on the Bible and postcolonialism to make its appearance was *Postcolonial Literature and the Biblical Call for Justice*, edited by Susan VanZanten Gallagher, a Professor of English, although it seems to have had little or no impact on postcolonial biblical criticism.[54] More influential by far was the next such collection, *Postcolonialism and Scriptural Reading*, edited by Laura E. Donaldson, a Professor of English and Native American Studies.[55] It would be misleading, however, to relay the impression that all the essays in this eclectic collection—which range over topics as diverse as colonial Yehud under the Persian Empire; *El Evangelio de Lucas Gavilán*, a modern Mexican paraphrase of the Gospel of Luke; African-American spirituals; and the *faux* Australian Aboriginal novels of B. Wongar—are thoroughly rooted in extra-biblical postcolonial studies: some are, while others are not.

A book less obviously relevant to our third cluster is *A Materialist Reading of the Gospel of Mark* by Portuguese scholar Fernando Belo—not that the book engages with postcolonial theory, for there was as yet no postcolonial theory, in the strict sense of the term, in 1974 when Belo's book first appeared.[56] Indeed, if postcolonial theory can be defined, as it so often is, as the harnessing of structuralist/post-structuralist theory to analyze selected aspects of colonialism or postcolonialism, not least the literature issuing from either side of the colonizer/colonized divide, then Belo's work might even be said to precede Said's *Orientalism* as the first book to employ (post)structuralist theory to that end. For Belo makes extensive use of Roland Barthes' *S/Z* (the work that, more than any other, marked Barthes' transition from 'structuralist' to 'poststructuralist' modes of reading)

54. Susan VanZanten Gallagher, *Postcolonial Literature and the Biblical Call for Justice* (Jackson: University Press of Mississippi, 1994).

55. Laura E. Donaldson (ed.), *Postcolonialism and Scriptural Reading* (Semeia, 75; Atlanta: Scholars Press, 1996). Roland Boer's edited collection, *A Vanishing Mediator? The Presence/Absence of the Bible in Postcolonialism* (Semeia, 88; Atlanta: Society of Biblical Literature Publications, 2002), can be considered the obverse of the Donaldson collection: instead of a literary scholar assembling a team largely composed of biblical scholars to ponder the Bible's intersections with empire, we have a biblical scholar assembling a team largely composed of literary scholars for the same task.

56. It was originally published in French; see Fernando Belo, *Lecture matérialiste de l'évangile de Marc: récit-pratique-idéologie* (Paris: Cerf, 1974; ET: Matthew J. O'Connell; Maryknoll, NY: Orbis Books, 1981).

to argue that Mark is a politically subversive text that pits the poor and oppressed peasant masses, with Jesus as their champion and liberator, against both the Roman imperial authorities and their elite Judean puppets.[57]

Notable among more recent critics whose primary training was in biblical studies but who have achieved fluency in 'theory' as a kind of scholarly second language, not least postcolonial theory, are Erin Runions, whose *Changing Subjects* draws upon the analytic categories of Homi Bhabha, bringing them to bear (against all the odds) on the book of Micah; and Roland Boer, whose *Last Stop before Antarctica* ranges more eclectically across the theoretical landscape, and also ranges from the books of Exodus and Daniel to the journals of nineteenth-century European explorers of the Australian interior.[58] No less eclectic in inclination is Tat-siong Benny Liew, whose *Politics of Parousia*, discussed earlier, harnesses a broad assortment of theoretical resources to resituate Mark's story of Jesus in its multilayered imperial framework. Like Dube, but unlike any of the authors in our 'X and Empire' cluster, and also unlike classic liberation hermeneutics, Liew is sharply critical of the ideology of the biblical text he is considering, as we saw. In Liew's work, as in Dube's, postcolonial biblical criticism meshes seamlessly with (is, indeed, an instance of) that other relatively recent development in biblical studies known as 'ideological criticism'.[59]

The intensely interdisciplinary, theory-fluent mode of postcolonial biblical criticism has recently found further expression in Yong-Sung Ahn's *The Reign of God and Rome in Luke's Passion Narrative: An East Asian Global Perspective*[60] and in the collection *Postcolonial Biblical*

---

57. Roland Barthes, *S/Z* (trans. Richard Miller; New York: Hill & Wang, 1974). Admittedly, it is the structuralist side of *S/Z* that Belo primarily plugs into. Barthes is also a resource for Bhabha in certain of the essays collected in *The Location of Culture*. For a discussion of Belo's book that contrasts it to Ched Myers's *Binding the Strong Man*, see The Bible and Culture Collective, *The Postmodern Bible* (New Haven, CT: Yale University Press, 1995), pp. 297-300.

58. Erin Runions, *Changing Subjects: Gender, Nation and Future in Micah* (Playing the Texts, 7; Sheffield: Sheffield Academic Press, 2001); Roland Boer, *Last Stop before Antarctica: The Bible and Postcolonialism in Australia* (The Bible and Postcolonialism, 4; Sheffield: Sheffield Academic Press, 2001).

59. On ideological criticism, see David Jobling and Tina Pippin (eds.), *Ideological Criticism of Biblical Texts* (Semeia, 59; Atlanta: Scholars Press, 1992); The Bible and Culture Collective, *The Postmodern Bible*, pp. 272-308.

60. Biblical Interpretation Series, 80; Leiden: E.J. Brill, 2006. The book engages broadly with literary and cultural theory, including postcolonial theory, especially in its opening chapter. Ahn's extended analysis of Luke's relations to Rome

Criticism: Interdisciplinary Intersections, edited by Moore and Segovia, which had its origins in the inaugural session in 2000 of the Society of Biblical Literature program unit, New Testament Studies and Post-colonial Studies. Yet, if I had to bet on the future of postcolonial biblical criticism, I would hesitate put my money on the theory-friendly mode. There are forms of intellectual challenge that biblical scholars clearly relish—the Synoptic Problem, for example—and forms they just as clearly do not—poststructuralist theory, for exam-ple, of which postcolonial theory is an offshoot. My hunch is that the story of New Testament narrative criticism will be replayed in a dif-ferent register in postcolonial criticism of the New Testament, at least in the Anglophone world. Because narrative criticism represented the smoothest and least painful extension of redaction criticism, it has permeated gospel scholarship, especially in North America,[61] while poststructuralism (long the lingua franca of 'secular' literary studies in North America) has remained a fringe phenomenon within New Testament scholarship and biblical scholarship in general. Currently and analogously, the 'X and Empire' brand of postcolonial biblical criticism seems poised for widespread dissemination within biblical studies—certainly within New Testament studies—as the one that represents the smoothest, least taxing, and least threatening exten-sion of traditional historical criticism.[62]

In the Two-Thirds World, meanwhile (to continue to paint with an overly broad brush), it is not hard to imagine the liberationist variant of postcolonial biblical criticism continuing to ride in the slipstream

(and not only in the passion narrative) concludes: 'Luke is an excellent example of why imperialism works so well. Luke witnesses to the reasons Empire is so hard to overthrow, either because colonized people are brought in as collabora-tors or because colonized people who resist are required to speak and act with ambiguity and mimicry, not directly and boldly' (p. 223).

61. As a prime symptom of this permeation, fully underway by the 1990s, look no further than Joel B. Green's 928-page commentary on Luke for the venerable New International Commentary on the New Testament series (*The Gospel of Luke* [Grand Rapids, MI: Eerdmans, 1997]). The jacket blurb explains that the commentary understands 'the text of Luke as a wholistic, historical nar-rative', focuses 'primarily on how each episode functions within Luke's narrative development', examines 'Luke's literary art and Luke's narrative theology', and insists 'on the narrative unity of Luke–Acts'.

62. Some weeks after penning these words, a line in another blurb on another commentary caught my eye. Fortress Press's fall 2006 catalog description of Robert Jewett's forthcoming Hermeneia commentary on Romans claims that among its other achievements, it will be '[t]he first commentary to interpret Romans within the imperial context…'.

of contextual hermeneutics — and continuing to counter postcolonial biblical criticism's inherent inclination as an academic enterprise to coagulate into an esoteric discourse herme(neu)tically sealed off from the extra-academic world.[63]

63. The brush is overly broad, because exceptions will continue to abound. Horsley's *Jesus and Empire*, for example, produced within the corpulent belly of the American Empire, is written in a language and style that will make it accessible to many more non-academic readers than, say, Ahn's excellent but more esoteric *The Reign of God and Rome*, even though the latter is explicitly written out of a South Korean sociocultural location that the author characterizes as fundamentally disadvantaged, the product of 'a history of unequal relations in the East Asian global space' and of 'corporate globalization or Americanization' (p. 47).

2

'MY NAME IS LEGION, FOR WE ARE MANY': REPRESENTING EMPIRE IN MARK

Nation

They came to the other side of the lake, to the country of the Gerasenes. And when he had stepped out of the boat, immediately a man out of the tombs with an unclean spirit met him. He lived among the tombs; and no one could restrain him any more, even with a chain; for he had often been restrained with shackles and chains, but the chains he wrenched apart, and the shackles he broke in pieces; and no one had the strength to subdue him. Night and day among the tombs and on the mountains he was always howling and bruising himself with stones. When he saw Jesus from a distance, he ran and bowed down before him; and he shouted at the top of his voice, 'What have you to do with me, Jesus, Son of the Most High God? I adjure you by God, do not torment me'. For he had said to him, 'Come out of the man, you unclean spirit!' Then Jesus asked him, 'What is your name?' He replied, 'My name is Legion; for we are many' (Mk 5.1-9 NRSV).

What's in a name, not least a name that gestures simultaneously to demonic possession and colonial occupation—if, indeed, it does? 'Since the text explicitly associates Legion with numerousness', one leading Markan scholar has protested, 'we have no reason to think of a covert reference to the occupation of Palestine by Roman legions'.[1]

---

1.   Robert H. Gundry, *Mark: A Commentary on his Apology for the Cross* (Grand Rapids, MI: Eerdmans, 1993), p. 260. R.S. Sugirtharajah notes that the Gerasene demoniac pericope 'has been exegeted in at least three ways that take no account of the colonial context'. First, the episode has been used to legitimate the missionary enterprise, Jesus' 'outreach' to this territory east of the Sea of Galilee, predominantly inhabited by Gentiles, being understood as both foreshadowing and authorizing later missions to Africa, Asia, and the Americas. 'Another interpretation has the behaviour of the Demoniac explained in terms of social scientific categories and Western psychological theories', while '[i]n a third interpretation, African biblical interpreters have recently tried to vernacularize the incident by reading it in light of African belief-systems regarding demon possession, witchcraft, and the spirit world' (*Postcolonial Criticism and Biblical Interpretation*

No reason whatsoever, perhaps, unless our desire be for a Mark for whom the occupation of Palestine by Roman legions *is* a concern — or for *which* that occupation is a concern, 'Mark' now naming the text rather than the author; for even what cannot plausibly be ascribed to an author's intentions can always be ascribed to the text that invariably exceeds them. That, apparently, is the dual lesson of 'precritical' biblical exegesis and poststructuralist literary theory. Yet we need not break free of the current of mainstream biblical criticism in order to dredge up readings of Mark's Gerasene episode attuned to colonial issues. Even the improbably prolonged moment in Markan scholarship of which Gundry's monumental commentary is a consummate product — the 'historical-critical' moment, with its single-minded preoccupation with the Gospel's 'original' context, coupled with the evangelist's putative intentionality, and the corollary exclusion (necessarily incomplete) of contemporary contexts from the task of exegesis — yielded a small but significant trickle of assertions that Roman military occupation, no less than demonic possession, was indeed in view in this pericope. And in recent years, with the multiplication of 'political' readings of Mark and of early Christian texts and traditions more generally, that assertion has become almost commonplace.[2] With the emergence of a newly sharpened focus on

[Oxford: Oxford University Press, 2002], p. 92). Even if none of these three interpretive trajectories engage explicitly with the colonial context of the Markan pericope itself, however, it is probably safe to assert that the first and third, in particular, are implicitly engaged with modern colonial and postcolonial contexts, given the intimate interconnections between European missionary and colonial ventures, on the one hand, and 'vernacular' hermeneutics and anti- or post-colonial consciousness, on the other. I would add that the *principal* way in which the pericope has been exegeted with no regard for its colonial context is that epitomized by Gundry in the quotation above, who himself speaks for a legion of European and North American New Testament scholars who have managed to write on Mk 5.1-20 for a century or more without explicit reference to any colonial framework, whether ancient or modern (although there have been exceptions to the rule; see n. 2 below).

2.   Not that an unequivocal 'progression' from the 'historical-critical' to the 'political' is clearly discernible in this regard. Baird's and Derrett's articles listed below, for example, along with Winter's and Theissen's monographs, clearly belong to the older paradigm, but so does Marcus's recent commentary, while Crossan's magnum opus might be said to straddle older and newer. The following all read Mk 5.1-9, in whole or in part, as referring obliquely to the Roman military presence in the Jewish homeland: Mary M. Baird, 'The Gadarene Demoniac', *The Expository Times* 31 (1920), p. 189 (the earliest instance of this interpretation that I have been able to locate); Paul Winter, *On the Trial of Jesus* (Studia judaica: Forschungen zur Wissenschaft des Judentums, 1; Berlin: De Gruyter, 1961), pp. 180-81; J.D.M. Derrett, 'Contributions to the Study of the Gerasene

'empire' within New Testament studies, moreover, a focus enabled, on occasion at least, by the conceptual tools and critical vocabulary of extra-biblical postcolonial studies, as elaborated at length in the previous chapter, we do have, *pace* Gundry, compelling reasons for hearing in Mk 5.9 a dual reference to demonic possession *and* colonial occupation.

The fraught tale of the Gerasene demoniac, then, seems like a logical enough place from which to launch a 'postcolonial' reading of the Gospel of Mark, centered on the perennial and intractable issues of land, invasion, occupation, and liberation. If the demons are, by their own admission, to be identified analogically with the Roman 'army of occupation',[3] then the demoniac may be identified in turn as the land and people under occupation — which, it may be argued, is why the demons earnestly entreat the exorcist 'not to send them out of the land [*exō tēs chōras*]' (5.10).[4] And if the act of exorcism is to be accorded anti-colonial significance is *this* pericope, why should it not

Demoniac', *Journal for the Study of the New Testament* 3 (1979), pp. 2-17; Paul Hollenbach, 'Jesus, Demoniacs, and Public Authorities: A Socio-Historical Study', *Journal of the American Academy of Religion* 49 (1981), pp. 567-88; Gerd Theissen, *The Miracle Stories of the Early Christian Tradition* (trans. Francis McDonagh; Philadelphia: Fortress Press, 1983), pp. 255-56; Ched Myers, *Binding the Strong Man: A Political Reading of Mark's Story of Jesus* (Maryknoll, NY: Orbis Books, 1988), pp. 190-94; Herman C. Waetjen, *A Reordering of Power: A Socio-Political Reading of Mark's Gospel* (Minneapolis: Fortress Press, 1989), pp. 115-18; John Dominic Crossan, *The Historical Jesus: The Life of a Mediterranean Jewish Peasant* (San Francisco: HarperSanFrancisco, 1991), pp. 314-18; Joel Marcus, *Mark 1–8: A New Translation with Introduction and Commentary* (Anchor Bible, 27; New York: Doubleday, 1998), pp. 341-53 *passim*; Richard Dormandy, 'The Expulsion of Legion: A Political Reading of Mark 5.1-20', *The Expository Times* 111 (2000), pp. 335-37; Richard A. Horsley, *Hearing the Whole Story: The Politics of Plot in Mark's Gospel* (Louisville, KY: Westminster John Knox, 2001), pp. 140-41, 47; Horsley, *Jesus and Empire: The Kingdom of God and the New World Disorder* (Minneapolis: Fortress Press, 2003), pp. 100-108 *passim*; Sugirtharajah, *Postcolonial Criticism and Biblical Interpretation*, pp. 91-94; Michael Willett Newheart, *'My Name Is Legion': The Story and Soul of the Gerasene Demoniac* (Interfaces; Collegeville, MN: Liturgical Press, 2004), especially pp. 70-85; Jeffrey L. Staley, '"Clothed and in her Right Mind": Mark 5.1-20 and Postcolonial Discourse', in R.S. Sugirtharajah (ed.), *Voices from the Margin: Interpreting the Bible in the Third World* (enlarged edn; Maryknoll, NY: Orbis Books, forthcoming). This list, while representative, is by no means intended to be exhaustive.

3.   A token force, to be sure, stationed primarily at Caesarea — but able to call upon the Syrian legate and his legions whenever the scarcity of its numbers instilled hope of effective armed resistance in the native populace.

4.   'The translation ["out of the land"] attempts to capture two nuances of *chōra*: a region…and dry land as opposed to the sea…' (Marcus, *Mark 1–8*, p. 345).

be accorded similar significance in every other exorcistic episode in Mark, that most exorcistic of gospels (see 1.23-27, 32-34; 6.7, 13; 7.24-30; 9.14-29; cf. 3.11-12, 14-15, 22-30; 9.38)? Jesus' earlier boast that his plundering of the property of the 'strong man' portends the end of Satan's empire (3.23-27) could then be read as equally portending the end of Rome's empire, the latter being implicitly construed as but an instrumental extension of the former. To begin to read Mark in this way is tantamount to using 5.9 ('My name is Legion...') as a 'herme-neutical key' with which to unlock the Gospel as a whole.[5] Such keys generally break off in the lock, as the history of biblical scholarship never tires of telling us, and so I do not intend to overuse this one.[6] But it may at least open up a reading that will lead to an as yet unforeseeable destination.

To set foot, however tentatively, on this interpretive path is to begin to read the narrative of the Gerasene 'demoniac', and much else in the larger narrative in which it is embedded, as *allegory*, to read as the Markan Jesus himself has taught us to read (4.13-20) — a strategy that accrues added interest from the ongoing debate in literary studies concerning the extent to which so-called 'national allegories', in which literary representations of individual colonial subjects stand in allegorically for the histories and destinies of entire colonized peoples, may be seen as a defining characteristic of contemporary postcolonial literatures.[7] Allegory, in any case, once unleashed, cannot easily be contained — not unlike the Gerasene

5. Which, essentially, is what Myers, and especially Horsley, have done. See Myers, *Binding the Strong Man*, pp. 192-94; Horsley, *Hearing the Whole Story*, pp. 146-48, and *Jesus and Empire*, pp. 100-102, 107-108.

6. A determination reinforced by reading Laura Donaldson's 'Gospel Hauntings: The Postcolonial Demons of New Testament Criticism' (in Stephen D. Moore and Fernando F. Segovia [eds.], *Postcolonial Biblical Criticism: Interdisciplinary Intersections* [The Bible and Postcolonialism, 8; New York: T. & T. Clark International, 2005], pp. 97-113), which incisively elucidates the hazards of imposing a unitary meaning on the gospel exorcisms. Not least among these hazards is a certain gender blindness. While the Gerasene wails at the top of his lungs, notes Donaldson, the demon-possessed daughter of Mk 7.24-30 and pars. is mute; while he engages in frenzied activity, she lays immobile on her mattress; and while he vividly inhabits the main narrative, she is absent from it. Such stereotyping undercuts 'any attempt to yoke men and women indiscriminately together under the master term of "the colonized"' (p. 11).

7. For the beginnings of the debate, see Fredric Jameson, 'Third World Literature in the Era of Multinational Capitalism', *Social Text* 15 (1986), pp. 65-88; Aijaz Ahmad, 'Jameson's Rhetoric of Otherness and the "National Allegory"', *Social Text* 17 (1987), pp. 3-25; Stephen Slemon, 'Monuments of Empire: Allegory/Counter-Discourse/Post-Colonial Writing', *Kunapipi* 9 (1987), pp. 1-16.

demoniac himself whom no shackle or chain can restrain (5.4), and who thereby becomes an allegory of allegory itself. It would not be unduly difficult to track allegory's inexorable verse-by-verse rampage through this entire pericope, should strategy demand it. In the event, a few sample steps will suffice to relay a sense of the dance.

They came to…the country of the Gerasenes (5.1). The Hebrew root *grš* means 'banish', 'drive out', 'cast out', as more than one commentator has observed, and so, by extension, commonly signifies exorcism.[8] The exorcist has landed, but on what shore? Hardly 'the land of the exorcists'; 'the land in need of exorcism' better suits the context. The very name of the country in which he has just set foot 'hails' Jesus, then, and 'interpellates' him, as the Marxist Louis Althusser might have said — and by which he might have meant that the name, simultaneously a summons, reaches out subtly yet imperiously to mold and manipulate the one thus called.[9] Jesus has arrived among a people whose very appellation constitutes a preexisting appeal to (and hence a covert construction of) his (now) manifest destiny to drive out the powers that possess them.

[A] man out of the tombs in an unclean spirit [*en pneumati akathartō*] **met him** (5.2). The peculiar *en* should be allowed its full, engulfing force here.[10] It signifies that the possessed subject's identity has been utterly submerged in that which possesses him — as is indeed evident from that fact that, in the dialogue that ensues, *it* speaks in him, through him, and for him. One would be hard pressed to find a more apt image — or allegory — of the colonial subject's self-alienation when compelled to internalize the discourse of the colonizer.

[N]o one could restrain him any more, even with a chain; for he had often been restrained with shackles and chains, but the chains

---

8.   J.D.M. Derrett, 'Spirit-Possession and the Geresene Demoniac', *Man* NS 14 (1979), pp. 286-93 (287); Marcus, *Mark 1–8*, p. 342; cf. Gundry, *Mark*, p. 256. While 'appropriate symbolically', the name Geresa is 'difficult geographically', notes Marcus (p. 342), since the place was not on the shore of the lake, as the narrative would lead us to assume, but thirty-seven miles southeast of it. The possessed swine would thus have had an exhausting run, to say the least, before plunging (not without relief?) into the lake. But it is the very difficulty of the reading 'Gerasenes', together with its superior attestation in the manuscript tradition (cf. Bruce Metzger, *A Textual Commentary on the Greek New Testament* [London and New York: United Bible Societies, 1971], pp. 23-24, 840), that makes it preferable to 'Gadarenes' or 'Gergasenes'.

9.   Louis Althusser, 'Ideology and Ideological State Apparatuses (Notes towards an Investigation)', in his *Lenin and Philosophy and Other Essays* (trans. Ben Brewster; London: New Left Books, 1971), pp. 121-73.

10.   Cf. Marcus, *Mark 1-8*, pp. 187, 342, 348.

he wrenched apart, and the shackles he broke in pieces; and no one
had the strength to subdue him. Night and day...he was always
howling and bruising himself with stones (5.3-5). Possession is *mad-
dening*, eliciting spectacular acts of masochistic resistance. Here the
national allegory projects onto the parallel screen the disastrous and
increasingly desperate armed rebellion that culminated with the
Roman decimation of Jerusalem and its temple. When the occupying
power is too overwhelming, armed resistance can only effect self-
annihilation – which, however, is also self-immolation; and from the
ashes of martyrs rebellion is reborn.

And the unclean spirits came out and entered the swine; and the
herd...rushed down the steep bank into the sea... (5.13). The reason
for the pigs' lemming-like rush into the sea is unstated. The simplest
explanation would seem to be that the exorcist has compelled them to
do so, thereby cleansing the land of their polluting presence. Not to
put too delicate a point on it, the Romans are here shown up for the
filthy swine that they are, and triumphantly driven back into the sea
from whence they came – the dream of every Jewish peasant resister,
as one of our own sages has observed.[11] Cleansing the (com)promised
land of unclean occupants so that God's people can possess it more
completely is a theme thoroughly rooted in the Israelite myth of
origins.[12] But whereas in the Israelite conquest narratives the invaders
are charged with sweeping the land clean, now it is the invaders
themselves who must be swept into the sea. Genocide and nationalism share a certain fastidious tidiness – which, no doubt, is why the
former has at times sprung from the head of the latter.

And it is not just the invaders who must be swept away, but the
comprador class who have made the invaders' continuing control of
the land and its people possible. The first step in ridding the land of
the polluting Roman presence, it emerges (once we begin to survey
larger stretches of the narrative, employing Gerasa as our vantage
point), is to rid it of the collaborating local elites. In due course,
Mark's Messiah will embark on his single-minded march to Jerusalem (cf. 10.32-34). But to what end? Primarily, so that he may enact
the symbolic destruction of the Jerusalem temple, essential seat of
power of the indigenous elite: 'Then they came to Jerusalem. And he
entered the temple and began to drive out [*ekballein*] those who were

11. Crossan, *The Historical Jesus*, p. 314.
12. The companion theme of prior liberation from bondage is also discernible
in the pericope, the phantasmic destruction of the Romans in the sea serving to
evoke the mythic destruction of the Egyptians in the sea (cf. Horsley, *Jesus and
Empire*, p. 101).

selling and those who were buying in the temple...' (11.15). Again, we are faced with an exorcism of sorts: the spectacle is one of expulsion, cleansing, dispossession, and repossession. Thematically, at least, this pericope is intimately imbricated with that of the Gerasene demoniac. The 'cleansing' of God's house ('My house [*ho oikos mou*] shall be called a house of prayer...', 11.17) performed with such passion by Mark's Messiah, and seen as so threatening by the Jerusalem elites ('And when the chief priests and the scribes heard it, they kept looking for a way to kill him...', 11.18), is a symbolic prelude to the 'cleansing' of the entire land that properly belongs to the owner of the house (cf. 12.1ff.), a cleansing that the exorcism at Geresa anticipates.

The Messiah's symbolic destruction of the temple precipitates his own destruction, however, his public annihilation upon the colonial cross. But in engineering Jesus' own obliteration in retribution for the symbolic destruction of their temple (11.18; cf. 14.58; 15.29-30), the local elite unwittingly and catastrophically engineers the *actual* destruction of the temple, according to Mark, and as such their own inevitable eradication. Consider the positioning of the 'temple-cleansing' incident. It interrupts the two-part anecdote of Jesus cursing and thereby blasting an unproductive fig tree (11.12-14, 20-22). The 'temple-cleansing' material thus forms the filling in a narrative sandwich. It is, indeed, one of the more notable examples of Mark's celebrated 'sandwich technique' (the menu also includes 3.20-21 [22-30] 31-35; 5.21-24 [25-34] 35-43; 6.7-13 [14-29] 30-32; 14.53-65 [66-72] 15.1-5), and is generally regarded as one of the less enigmatic examples of the device, the material in the two outer layers of the sandwich imposing a relatively transparent meaning upon the material in the middle layer: the destruction of the unproductive fig tree portends the destruction of the 'unproductive' temple.[13] Mark thereby obliquely signals his conviction that the Roman annihilation of the temple and city that brought the Jewish rebellion of 66 CE to a catastrophic close was an act of divine retribution. The sandwich is followed almost immediately by the Parable of the Vineyard and the Tenants (12.1-12), which deftly reinforces the message: 'What then will the owner of the vineyard do? He will come and destroy the tenants.... [T]hey ["the chief priests, the scribes, and the elders"] realized that he had told this parable against them...' (12.9, 12).

---

13. The standard study detailing and advancing this interpretation is that of William R. Telford: *The Barren Temple and the Withered Tree* (Journal for the Study of the New Testament Supplement Series, 1; Sheffield: JSOT Press, 1980).

Of course, the Jerusalem temple's destruction is itself but the eschatological prelude to Jesus' parousia, as the ensuing apocalyptic discourse (13.1-37) makes plain. And what the parousia will signify, among other things, is the unceremonious cessation of the Roman Empire, as of every other human *basileia*. Jesus will bump Caesar off the throne. Is this the *telos*, then, toward which everything in the Markan narrative is tending? Yes and no, it seems to me. *Yes*, because a reading of Mark along these lines — a 'zealot' reading, if you will — is not only possible; in certain contexts — straitened contexts, especially, occasioned by overt state-sponsored oppression, akin to that experienced, or anticipated, by the Markan community itself — a reading of Mark as anti-imperial resistance literature, pure and simple, may be absolutely necessary. And *no*, because such a reading, in order to run smoothly, must aqua-glide over the intense ambivalence that, on an alternative reading, can be shown (and will be shown below) to characterize and complicate Mark's representations of empire. Practices of reading acutely attuned to such complexities are a signal feature of contemporary postcolonial theory, and not the least of its benefits for the biblical critic. Outside of biblical studies, postcolonial studies has tended to be infused and enabled by a generic poststructuralism, as noted in the previous chapter, itself intimately attuned to the inherent instabilities of discourse and representation. Postcolonial biblical criticism has, to date, been less shaped by poststructuralism, as we also saw, tending instead, in some of its most notable manifestations, to operate under the aegis of a hermeneutic of suspicion and in the mode of ideology critique. A defining feature of 'postcolonial' biblical exegesis, one might argue, as distinct from (although by no means in opposition to) 'liberationist' biblical exegesis is a willingness to press a biblical text at precisely those points at which its ideology falls prey to ambivalence, incoherence, and self-subversion — and not least where its message of emancipation subtly mutates into oppression.[14] We have seen, in miniature at least, how an unreserved reading of Mark as anti-imperial resistance literature might proceed.[15]

---

14. Cf. R.S. Sugirtharajah, *The Bible and the Third World: Precolonial, Colonial and Postcolonial Encounters* (Cambridge: Cambridge University Press, 2001), pp. 259-61.

15. One way, at least. Other strategies have been developed, and fleshed out much more fully, in such works as Fernando Belo, *A Materialist Reading of the Gospel of Mark* (trans. Matthew J. O'Connell; Maryknoll, NY: Orbis Books, 1981); Myers, *Binding the Strong Man*; Waetjen, *A Reordering of Power*; and Horsley, *Hearing the Whole Story*. All of these works read Mark as unequivocally anti-imperial.

It remains to inquire how else a reading of Mark attuned to issues of empire might unfold.

Empire

Let us begin again, then, this time by noting that Mark altogether lacks the snarling, fang-baring hostility toward the Roman state that possesses Mark's near-contemporary, and yet more apocalyptic, cousin, the book of Revelation,[16] a text that shares with Mark an intense preoccupation with the prospect of persecution, and likewise proffers an apocalyptic solution to that problem: 'the one who endures to the end will be saved', is Mark's summation of the solution (13.13), but it could just as easily be John's. The face of Rome comes into explicit focus in Mark only in 15.1-39, Jesus' trial before the Roman Prefect of Judea and his public execution at the hands of the Roman military. But the expression on that face is curiously difficult to decipher. How is the figure of Pontius Pilate in Mark to be construed? As a basically benign but morally feeble official, who would release the accused if he could, but is unable to out-maneuver, or is merely unwilling to override, the Sadduceean elite and the vociferous mob whose strings they control? Or rather as himself a consummate manipulator, who unblinkingly dispatches the peasant troublemaker, while skillfully contriving to make it seem as though he is simply acceding to the impassioned demands of the peasant's own countrymen?[17] The only other Roman official who makes an explicit appearance in Mark, albeit a cameo one, is, if anything, still more ambiguously delineated. What does the Roman centurion's celebrated pronouncement in 15.39 actually amount to? In declaring the bloody corpse dangling before him to have 'truly [been] a Son of God' (*Alēthēs houtos ho anthrōpos huios theou ēn*) is he, in good crypto-

---

16. And not only Revelation, of course. Three (other) Jewish apocalypses roughly contemporary with Revelation also predict the destruction of Rome: see *2 Baruch* 36.1–46.7; *4 Ezra* 11.1–12.39; *Apocalypse of Abraham* 27.3-5. All three, together with other relevant Jewish literature, are discussed in Philip F. Esler, 'Rome in Apocalyptic and Rabbinic Literature', in John Riches and David C. Sim (eds.), *The Gospel of Matthew in its Roman Imperial Context* (Journal for the Study of the New Testament Supplement Series, 276; New York: T. & T. Clark International, 2005), pp. 9-33.

17. It is Matthew's Pilate who, of late, has been the more notable recipient of the latter line of interpretation: see Warren Carter, *Matthew and Empire: Initial Explorations* (Harrisburg, PA: Trinity Press International, 2001), pp. 145-68. Much of Carter's analysis, however, might be applied *mutatis mutandis* to Mark's Pilate.

Christian fashion, succeeding spectacularly where Jesus' own disciples have so singularly failed, effortlessly coupling the concepts of divine sonship and dishonorable death where they could not, and thereby giving climactic and definitive expression to Mark's *theologia crucis*? Or is he merely engaging in grim gallows humor instead ('Some Son of God!'), only unwittingly giving expression thereby to a 'truth' that is not his but belongs to the evangelist/ventriloquist instead? Unaware that he is a dummy, is the centurion simply parroting the derision of everybody else in the vicinity of the cross (15.29-32), not least the local elites with whom his commander is in cahoots: 'Those who passed by derided him.... In the same way, the chief priest, along with the scribes, were also mocking him among themselves and saying, "...Let the Messiah, the King of Israel, come down from the cross now...." Those who were crucified with him also taunted him' (15.29-32)?[18] Jesus' sole explicit pronouncement on Rome in Mark — 'Give to Caesar the things that are Caesar's, and to God the things that are God's' (12.17) — is itself no less enveloped in ambiguity, as its history of reception amply attests. It can be, and has been, read to mean that since, in accordance with Israelite covenantal theology, everything belongs to God, nothing is due to Caesar;[19] far more frequently, however, it been read unabashedly as an affirmation of the imperial status quo.[20] In consequence of these assorted uncertainties, it seems to me, Mark's stance vis-à-vis Rome cannot plausibly be construed as one of unambiguous opposition. Turning now to less explicit or immediate representations of Rome in Mark, my working assumption instead is that Mark's attitude toward Rome is imbued with that simultaneous attraction and repulsion — in a word, ambivalence — to which Homi Bhabha, in particular, has taught us to be attuned when analyzing colonial or anti-colonial discourses.[21]

18. Cf. Horsley, *Hearing the Whole Story*, p. 252.

19. An interpretation championed by Horsley in particular: see his *Jesus and the Spiral of Violence* (San Francisco: Harper & Row, 1987; reprinted Minneapolis: Fortress Press, 1993), pp. 306-17, as well as his *Hearing the Whole Story*, pp. 36, 43, 112-13, and *Jesus and Empire*, pp. 98-99.

20. See, for example, the survey of late nineteenth and twentieth century British biblical commentaries undertaken by Ralph Broadbent, which finds the 'render to Caesar' logion, among others, almost invariably accommodated to the status quo ('Ideology, Culture, and British New Testament Studies: The Challenge of Cultural Studies', *Semeia* 82 [1998], pp. 33-62 [47-55]).

21. See Homi K. Bhabha, 'Of Mimicry and Man: The Ambivalence of Colonial Discourse', in his *The Location of Culture* (London and New York: Routledge, 1994), pp. 85-92; also see 'Articulating the Archaic: Cultural Difference and Colonial Nonsense' in the same volume, pp. 123-38, esp. pp. 129-38.

The clamor of Roman legionaries breaching the walls of Jerusalem and putting its inhabitants to the sword can dimly be heard in Mk 13.14-20, according to the dominant critical reading. Earlier in the apocalyptic discourse, Jesus' disciples are forewarned that they must stand before Roman governors or client kings, just as Jesus himself did, and possibly be executed for their testimony, just as he himself was (13.9-13). When the Son of Man returns 'in the clouds with great power and glory' (13.26), however, as he is soon destined to do, his behavior and demeanor will be markedly different from his Messianic counterpart in Revelation, who, on his own return through an 'opened heaven', will be riding at the head of the 'armies of heaven', 'to judge and make war', armed with the 'sharp sword' of his mouth 'with which to strike down the nations', which will result in a nightmarish mountain of rotting human flesh upon which 'all the birds that fly in midheaven' will be invited to gorge (Rev. 19.11-21). What of the parousia of the Markan Messiah? What preordained plan of action will he execute when he makes his own appearance on the clouds?

We are told only that 'he will send out the angels, and gather his elect from the four winds, from the ends of earth to the ends of heaven' (13.27). The Markan parousia is, in essence, a search-and-rescue mission, not a punitive strike, as in Revelation. Nowhere in Mark are Roman officials who have persecuted Christians, nor even Judean collaborators with Rome who, on Mark's view, have conspired to murder their Messiah, threatened explicitly with a post-parousia reckoning.[22] Whereas in Revelation, Rome's imminent destruction, and its eschatological consignment, in the guise of the Beast, to 'the lake of fire and sulfur' (20.10) is an immense and intense preoccupation, in Mark the only characters threatened with the Son of Man's displeasure upon his return and with the everlasting torments of hell are Jesus' own disciples (8.38; 9.42-49). In marked contrast to the Apocalypse of John, Mark's 'Little Apocalypse' (ch. 13) predicts not the destruction *of* Rome, but rather an act of destruction *by* Rome (the demolition of city and temple, that is, and the concomitant decimation of the Judean populace) — a particularly arresting symptom of the profound ambivalence that attends Mark's representation of the empire.

---

22. Although the latter are threatened implicitly with a pre-parousia reckoning, as we have seen, the destruction of their city and temple.

Mark's anti-imperial invective really only extends to the local elites.[23] Indeed, far from predicting divine punishment of Rome for the destruction of Jerusalem and its temple and the attendant massacre of its people, Mark appears to interpret this destruction and slaughter as divine punishment of the Judean elites for their exploitation of the common people (7.9-13; 11.12-21; 12.38-44), as we have already seen, coupled with their rejection of the Galilean Messiah (12.7-12). So whereas Rome in Revelation embodies and epitomizes intractable opposition to and alienation from the God of Israel and his salvific interventions in human history, Rome in Mark is merely God's instrument, his scourge, which he employs to punish the indigenous Judean elites. Rome therefore occupies roughly the same role in Mark's deuteronomistic theodicy as in that of his contemporary Josephus, as the latter's *Jewish War* 5.395 in particular suggests: 'Indeed, what can it be that has stirred up a Roman army against our nation? Is it not the impiety of the inhabitants?'

Mark thereby falls prey spectacularly to the divide-and-rule strategy entailed in the Roman policy of ceding administrative authority to indigenous elites in the provinces. As has been remarked with regard to the advantages to modern European empires of indirect rule in colonial Africa, 'popular resentments and hatreds could be deflected on to the local officials while the ultimate authority could remain remote, unseen and "above the battle"'[24] — at least until, as in the case of the Jewish revolt and its suppression many centuries earlier, the ultimate authority finds it necessary temporarily to relinquish its godlike remoteness and relative invisibility in order to intervene decisively and irresistibly in the corrupt affairs of its creatures, in an attempt to contain the chaos that its own administrative policies have created.

And yet, even if Mark lacks the explicitly hostile attitude toward Roman rule evident in Revelation, he also lacks the explicitly 'quietist' attitude toward Roman rule evident in at least two other first-century

---

23. Cf. Mary Ann Tolbert, 'When Resistance Becomes Repression: Mark 13.9-27 and the Poetics of Location', in Fernando F. Segovia and Mary Ann Tolbert (eds.), *Reading from This Place*. I. *Social Location and Biblical Interpretation in the United States* (Minneapolis: Fortress Press, 1995), pp. 331-46 (336).

24. Peter Worsley, *The Third World* (Nature of Human Societies Series; Chicago: University of Chicago Press, 2nd edn, 1970), p. 38. Cf. Richard A. Horsley, 'The Imperial Situation of Palestinian Jewish Society', in Norman K. Gottwald and Richard A. Horsley (eds.), *The Bible and Liberation: Political and Social Hermeneutics* (Maryknoll, NY: Orbis Books, 2nd edn, 1993), pp. 397-400, which also has recourse to Worsley.

Christian texts, namely, the letter to the Romans (cf. 13.1-7: 'Let every person be subject to the governing authorities; for there is no author-ity except from God, and those authorities that exist have been instituted by God. Therefore whoever resists authority resists what God has appointed, and those who resist will incur judgment…') and 1 Peter (cf. 2.13-17: 'For the Lord's sake accept the authority of every human institution, whether of the emperor as supreme, or of gover-nors, as sent by him to punish those who do wrong and praise those who do right…').[25]

Generally speaking (and putting it rather too mildly), Mark does not enjoin its audience to respect human authorities.[26] Every human authority in Mark, indeed, whether 'religious' or 'political' (a distinc-tion largely meaningless, however, in the context) is a persecutor, or potential persecutor, of John, Jesus, or the disciples of Jesus, aside from three incidental, but rule-proving, exceptions: the synagogue leader, Jairus (5.22ff.); the scribe commended by Jesus for not being 'far from the Empire of God' (12.28-34); and the Sanhedrin member, Joseph of Arimathea (15.42-46). In addition, Jesus is repeatedly repre-sented in Mark as urging his followers not to aspire to authority, glory, power or wealth (9.33-37; 10.17-31, 35-44; cf. 12.41-44), but to adopt for emulation instead such liminal role models as the child (*paidion*) and the servant (*diakonos*) or slave (*doulos*) (9.35-37; 10.13-16, 42-45; cf. 13.34). Mark's relentless narrative undermining of Jesus' own elite corps of disciples — namely, the Twelve (4.13, 40; 6.52; 7.18; 8.21, 32-33; 9.5-6, 33-34, 38-39; 10.35-45; 14.10-11, 32-46, 50, 66-72) —

---

25. William R. Telford, *The Theology of the Gospel of Mark* (New Testament Theology; Cambridge: Cambridge University Press, 1999), p. 206, groups Mark's 'Render to Caesar…' pericope (12.13-17) with these two texts, and not without reason, given the uses to which it has primarily been put down through the ages. As we have seen, however, the passage does admit of alternative readings, and far more readily than the Romans or 1 Peter passages. Two studies have recently appeared that usefully compare and contrast representations of Rome in various New Testament texts: Werner H. Kelber, 'Roman Imperialism and Early Christian Scribality', in Jonathan Draper (ed.), *Orality, Literacy, and Colonialism in Antiquity* (Semeia Studies, 47; Atlanta: Society of Biblical Literature Publications, 2004), pp. 135-53, reprinted in R.S. Sugirtharajah (ed.), *The Postcolonial Biblical Reader* (Oxford: Blackwell, 2006), pp. 96-111, which deals with Mark, Luke, and Revela-tion; and Peter Oakes, 'A State of Tension: Rome in the New Testament', in Riches and Sim (eds.), *Matthew in its Roman Imperial Context*, pp. 75-88, which deals with 1 Thessalonians, Romans, Mark, Acts, and Revelation.

26. Cf. Tolbert, 'When Resistance Becomes Repression', p. 335; Tat-siong Benny Liew, *Politics of Parousia: Reading Mark (Inter)contextually* (Biblical Inter-pretation Series, 42; Leiden: E.J. Brill, 1999), pp. 86-93 *passim*.

themselves the repositories of significant authority by the time the Gospel was written, may be regarded as a further component of this elaborate anti-authoritarian theme.

There *is*, however, one major human authority figure in Mark whose authority is not the object of repeated narrative erosion but rather of constant reassertion and reification, that figure being, of course, Jesus himself. The question then arises: in attributing absolute, unassailable authority to Jesus, is Mark merely mirroring Roman imperial ideology, deftly switching Jesus for Caesar[27] (to replay the ending of the 'zealot' reading performed earlier), but thereby undercutting the Gospel's anti-authoritarian thematics, and inaugurating an Empire of God that inevitably evinces many of the oppressive traits of the Roman Empire it displaces?[28] This question is best addressed within the framework afforded by another, more encompassing question: what does the Empire of God in Mark actually amount to?

Arguably, Mark's deployment of the term *basileia* ('empire')[29] may be deemed a stunning example of what the postcolonial theorist Gayatri Spivak has dubbed *catachresis*, originally a Greek rhetorical figure denoting 'misuse' or 'misapplication'. As employed by Spivak, the term denotes the process by which the colonized strategically appropriate and redeploy specific elements of colonial or imperial culture or ideology. As such, it is a practice of resistance through an act of usurpation.[30]

---

27. Cf. Tae Hun Kim, 'The Anarthous *huios theou* in Mark 15.39 and the Roman Imperial Cult', *Biblica* 79 (1998), pp. 221-41.

28. As Liew has, in effect, contended (*Politics of Parousia*, pp. 93-108). Pivotal to his argument is a reading of the Markan parousia (13.24-27), in tandem with the passage on Gehenna (9.43-48), as a show of ultimate force and authority that 'will right all wrongs with the annihilation of the "wicked"' (p. 107). As my earlier remarks indicate, however, I find Mark's parousia to be much milder and more muted affair.

29. In common with a still small but growing number of interpreters, I believe that *basileia* in Mark, as in other early Christian texts, is best rendered in English by the term 'empire' rather than by the more innocuous 'kingdom', a term whose political edge has been all but rubbed smooth by centuries of theological usage.

30. References to catachresis are scattered throughout Spivak's work; see, for example, Gayatri Chakravorty Spivak, 'Identity and Alterity: An Interview' (with Nikos Papastergiadis), *Arena* 97 (1991), pp. 65-76 (70); Spivak, 'More on Power/ Knowledge', in Donna Landry and Gerald Maclean (eds.), *The Spivak Reader: Selected Works of Gayatri Chakravorty Spivak* (London and New York: Routledge, 1996), pp. 143-54 *passim*. My definition of catachresis here, which I expand further in Chapter 5 (see p. 105-106), represents, to a degree, my own appropriation of Spivak's definition of it. For a similar elaboration of catachresis, see Bill

In any Roman province, the primary referent of *basileia* would have been the *imperium Romanum*.[31] Mark's practice of catachresis, as it pertains to *basileia*, can therefore be said to border on the parodic. 'The time is fulfilled, and the Empire of God has come near', Mark's ragtag peasant protagonist proclaims (1.15), marching through the remote rural reaches of southern Galilee, and drawing assorted other peasant nonentities in his wake, fellow builders-to-be of this latest and greatest of empires. The intrinsic, indeed surreal, unlikelihood of this Empire of empires begs elucidation, and as such is virtually the sole topic of Jesus' first extended public address in Mark (only one of two), namely, his parables discourse (4.1-33). (His other extended 'sermon', the apocalyptic discourse [ch. 13], also has the advent of God's Empire as its topic, although it is delivered from the other side of the eschatological curtain.) The parables of the Seed Growing in Secret (4.26-29) and the Mustard Seed (4.30-32) contrast the present concealment (cf. 4.11-12) and seeming inconsequentiality of the Empire of God with its impending and impressive public manifestation, as does the parable of the Sower (4.1-9, 14-20), albeit to a lesser degree.

Mark's next explicit mention of the Empire of God glosses its imminent public disclosure as the moment when the seemingly vanquished Son of Man will reappear in unequivocal majesty (8.38–9.1). But the next several occurrences of the term play again on the paradoxically inglorious character of the present as opposed to future Empire of God. Physical deformity will pose no obstacle to membership in the imperial ranks ('better for you to enter the Empire of God with one eye…' [9.45]), nor will childlikeness (which, on the contrary, will be a necessary qualification: 'whoever does not receive the Empire of God as a little child…' [10.15]). Social status, however, epitomized by wealth, *will* pose a near-insurmountable stumbling block to membership ('How hard it will be for those who have wealth

Ashcroft, Gareth Griffiths, and Helen Tiffin, *Post-Colonial Studies: The Key Concepts* (London and New York: Routledge, 2nd edn, 2001), p. 34. Spivak also employs the concept, however, to characterize aspects of colonizing and oppressive discourse, on which see Stephen Morton, *Gayatri Chakravorty Spivak* (London and New York: Routledge, 2003), pp. 33-35.

31.   Even in the Jewish homeland and Diaspora, presumably. Contrary to what the Synoptic Gospels and other early Christian writings might lead us to expect, the term *hē basileia tou theou* is highly infrequent in the extant Jewish literature of the period. According to Burton Mack (*A Myth of Innocence: Mark and Christian Origins* [Philadelphia: Fortress Press, 1988], p. 73 n. 16), it is found only in Philo, *On the Special Laws* 4.164; *The Sentences of Sextus* 311; and Wisdom 10.10.

to enter the Empire of God!' [10.23]), which is to say that those who have benefited most egregiously from participation in Caesar's empire will be least eligible for admittance to God's empire. The latter pronouncement occurs in the immediate context of others which, as we have already noted, proffer servanthood and slavery as the supreme models for Christian existence, in marked contrast to the practice of the 'Gentiles' (read: Romans) — a cluster of countercultural sayings and anecdotes (9.30–10.45 passim) that, in the absence of anything else approximating a Markan 'Sermon on the Mount', gives much-needed (if still insufficient) substance to its singularly unimperial concept of divine empire, as it translates into Christian practice.

The present Empire of God, then, dimly conjured up in Mark, seethes with countercultural valence. But is it effectively domesticated and defused by the coming Empire of God? Is the Markan Jesus' self-proclaimed ethic of self-giving and self-emptying ('the Son of Man came not to be served but to serve…'), culminating in his voluntary submission to torture and execution ('…and to give his life as a ransom for many' [10.45]), in the end but the means to an end, that end being (not to put too subtle a point on it) incomparable personal power and glory ('Then they will see the Son of Man coming in clouds with great power and glory' [13.26])?

And what of Jesus' disciples? Neither Matthew nor Luke hesitate to extend the eschatological 'no pain, no gain' formula to disciples: 'You are those who have stood by me in my trials, and I confer on you, just as my Father has conferred on me, an empire,…and you will sit on thrones judging the twelve tribes of Israel' (Lk. 22.28-30; cf. Mt. 19.28).[32] Mark, however, in intriguing contrast, seems reticent about unequivocally promising eschatological power and glory to disciples who successfully imitate Jesus' practice of embracing a self-abnegating way of life fraught with the permanent risk of violent death: Jesus readily promises the suffering ('The cup that I drink you will drink…'), but is noticeably evasive on the matter of the reward ('…but to sit at my right hand or at my left is not mine to grant' [10.39-40]).

32. Compare, too, Mk 14.25 and Mt. 26.29. If, with the majority, we assume Markan priority, then we see that Matthew has changed the Markan Jesus' declaration, 'Truly I tell you, I will never again drink of the fruit of the vine until that day when I drink it new in the kingdom of God', to 'I tell you, I will never again drink this fruit of the vine until that day when I drink it new *with you* [*meth' hymōn*] in my Father's kingdom'.

Mark's curious caution in this regard, whatever its motivation might have been, arguably lends its ethics a contemporaneity that Matthew's and Luke's lack. From within the enabling assumptions and convictions that have characterized many modern experiments in community (not least, socialist experiments), a teleology of other-wordly reward has tended to be seen as serving only to devalue a community ethic built on egalitarianism and mutual service. The tendency instead has been to regard the community thereby constructed as sufficient 'reward', in and of itself, for the sacrifices that subtend it. Mark comes closer than most early Christian writings to approximating this perspective. Mark 10.29-30 is particularly notable in this regard: 'Truly I tell you, there is no one who has left house or brothers or sisters or mother or father or children or fields, for my sake and for the sake of the good news, who will not receive a hundredfold now in this age — houses, brothers and sisters, mothers and children, and fields, with persecutions…' (cf. 3.31-35). The concluding clause — 'and in the age to come, eternal life' — is interestingly akin to an afterthought: in contrast to the painstakingly itemized rewards of the present age, it is devoid of detail or substantive content.[33] All of this, too, contrasts starkly, yet again, with Revelation, whose only real ethic is an ethic of endurance, and which so scrupulously itemizes the spectacular benefits due to those who, through their endurance, have earned admittance to the heavenly city (21.1–22.5).

Apocalypse

To the extent that Mark can be said to locate the primary rewards for the radical community experiment that it advocates in the liminal communities themselves that will come into being in consequence, must its Christology be said to stand in tension with its ethics? By insisting on returning 'with great power and glory' (13.26), does Mark's Jesus betray Mark's own latent desire for a top-heavy, authoritarian, universal Christian Empire, an über-Roman Empire, so to speak — the kind that will arrive all too soon, anyway, unbeknown to Mark, long before Jesus himself does, taking root in the fourth century and flourishing like Mark's parabolic mustard tree thereafter? By insisting on returning in imperial splendor (however muted, relative to Revelation and even the other Synoptics), does Mark's Jesus relativize and undercut the radical social values that he has

33. Horsley, *Hearing the Whole Story*, p. 123 remarks: 'oddly enough the restoration of houses and fields is to occur in "this age", not the next'.

died to exemplify and implement? Can radical apocalypticism, in other words, only ever stand in tension or outright contradiction with radical ethics? Or to put it yet another way, can radical apocalypticism only mirror imperial or colonial ideologies (and reflect them in a convex mirror, what is more, so that what was oppressively over-sized to begin with now towers above the heavens: 'And then they will see the Son of Man coming in clouds...'), or can it instead be consonant with a counter-imperial or counter-colonial ethic?

Yes and no, it would seem to me (yet again); it all depends on how apocalypticism is to be construed. A radical ethic that shatters every previously imaginable social structure (not that Mark's ethic goes quite that far) is, in its own way, also radically apocalyptic, portending the end of the world as we know it. Mark's apocalyptic discourse (13.1-37) does not, however, portend the end of the Roman imperial order but rather its apotheosis.[34] To discover a counter-imperial apocalypse in Mark we must look elsewhere. Conveniently, however, we will find what we need on the very threshold of Mark 13. The Markan anecdote traditionally labeled 'The Widow's Mites' (12.41-44) may be read as encapsulating, or at least adumbrating, a counter-imperial apocalyptic ethic.

Traditionally, the widow's donation 'out of her poverty' (*ek tēs hysterēseōs autēs*) of 'everything she had, all she had to live on' (12.44), has been construed as an exemplary action enthusiastically lauded by Jesus, the woman's absolute self-giving dramatically prefiguring his own self-emptying in death. In recent years, however, a sharp reaction to this hallowed typological interpretation has set in, not least because the interpretation, at its least palatable, has traditionally been presented to the poor as an enticement to donate beyond their means to the Church. In the revisionary recasting of the anecdote, the woman is read as epitomizing instead the oppressed peasantry mercilessly bled dry by the indigenous, Rome-allied elites.[35]

---

34. To this extent I am fully in agreement with Liew (see his *Politics of Parousia*, pp. 93-107).

35. See, for example, Addison G. Wright, 'The Widow's Mites: Praise or Lament? — A Matter of Context', *The Catholic Biblical Quarterly* 44 (1982), pp. 256-65; Donald H. Juel, *A Master of Surprise: Mark Interpreted* (Minneapolis: Fortress Press, 1994), pp. 81-82; Liew, *Politics of Parousia*, p. 73; Horsley, *Hearing the Whole Story*, pp. 216-17; cf. Elizabeth Struthers Malbon, *In the Company of Jesus: Characters in Mark's Gospel* (Louisville, KY: Westminster John Knox Press, 2000), pp. 166-88 *passim*. Sugirtharajah understands this interpretive shift as a movement from a liberationist to a postcolonial paradigm. Having summarized representative readings of the pericope issuing from liberation hermeneutics, he claims:

The latter reading, unlike the former, enables interpreters to posit a high degree of narrative continuity between the anecdote about the widow and the apocalyptic discourse that succeeds it: it is because of what has been done to the weakest of the weak in its name that the Jerusalem temple has been marked by God for demolition, as Jesus immediately goes on to imply: 'Do you see these great buildings? Not one stone will be left here upon another; all will be thrown down' (13.2). The congeniality of this line of interpretation to an emancipatory reading of Mark is, however, severely undercut, it seems to me, by Mark's neo-deuteronomistic theodicy, which, when pressed, promptly implodes in horrific absurdity: impoverished denizens of Jerusalem, such as this widow, would have been among the first to fall victim, if not by slaughter then by starvation,[36] to the Rome-administered divine retribution against the city and temple — a retribution that the Roman-Judean administration, though its exploitation of the common people, had (in accordance with the theodicy imputed to Mark) provoked in the first place. The divine response to the unjust suffering of the poor, on this reading, is to escalate that suffering beyond measure: 'For in those days there will be such tribulation [*thlipsis*] as has not been from the beginning of the creation which God created until now, and never will be' (Mk 13.19).

A third reading of the widow anecdote is, however, possible. This one piggy-backs on the traditional ecclesiastical reading (the first one summarized above), and similarly styles the woman as an exemplary figure — not because she anticipates and dimly adumbrates Jesus' own self-emptying, however, but rather because she exceeds it. The woman's voluntary self-divestment of 'everything she had, all she had to live on' — at once an absolute and a thankless gesture — may be read as an act of epiphanic extravagance whose immeasurable immoderation thrusts it outside every conventional circle of economic exchange. As Jacques Derrida has remarked, apropos of his own liminal concept of a gift beyond reciprocity,

'Ultimately, in the name of liberation, what is offered to the poor is an old-fashioned evangelical exhortation to faith in God and trust in God's faithfulness. What postcolonialism does is to read the gospel incident from the point of view of the widow, and see it not as an approval of her action but as an exposure of abuse by the temple treasury authorities. If one sees it from the widow's angle, Jesus was not applauding her action but making an assault upon an institution which generated poverty in Israel' (*Postcolonial Criticism and Biblical Interpretation*, p. 121; cf. Sugirtharajah, *The Bible and the Third World*, pp. 262-63).

36. Cf. Josephus, *Jewish War* 6.199-212.

the gift is precisely, and this is what is has in common with justice,
something that cannot be reappropriated. A gift is something which
never appears as such and is never equal to gratitude, to commerce, to
compensation, to reward. When a gift is given, first of all, no gratitude
can be proportionate to it. A gift is something you cannot be thankful
for. As soon as I say 'thank you' for a gift, I start canceling the gift, I
start destroying the gift, by proposing an equivalence, that is, a circle
which encircles the gift in a movement of reappropriation.[37]

Read from this angle, the widow's self-divestment, as expenditure
without reserve and absolute gift, would represent (with only a
minimum of hyperbolic torquing) the breaking through, or breaking
out, of 'something inconceivable, hardly possible, *the* impossible'
even.[38]

In common with other radically countercultural currents in Mark
that we have pondered — only more so — this gift beyond reciprocity
would hint at liminal experiments in community that apocalyptically
deconstruct the world as we know it. The anecdote of 'The Widow's
Mites', then (mighty mites, indeed!), would be the real site of apocalypse in Mark, not the so-called 'apocalyptic discourse' that follows,
rather lamely, on its heels, and for which it ostensibly prepares.
Having already surpassed that for which it prepares, the anecdote
renders the apocalyptic metanarrative superfluous and hence expend-
able. And the non-imperial apocalypse preemptively unveiled in the
anecdote, far from undercutting the radical ethic that informs much
of the preceding narrative, instead epitomizes it. What the widow's
action prefigures, if anything, is not so much Jesus' self-divesting
investment — the Markan cross, in the end, is merely a bold entre-
preneurial wager that yields an eschatological empire — but rather the
expenditure without reserve exemplified by yet another anonymous
women in the narrative, the one who 'wastes' on Jesus (*eis ti hē apōleia
hautē…gegonen?*) the 'alabaster flask of ointment of pure nard, very

37. Jacques Derrida, 'The Villanova Roundtable', in John D. Caputo (ed.),
Deconstruction in a Nutshell: A Conversation with Jacques Derrida (New York: Ford-
ham University Press, 1997), p. 18. Further on Derrida's conception of the gift,
see Herman Rapaport, *Later Derrida: Reading the Recent Work* (London and New
York: Routledge, 2003), pp. 50-53.

38. John D. Caputo, *The Prayers and Tears of Jacques Derrida: Religion without
Religion* (Bloomington: Indiana University Press, 1997), p. 177, his emphasis.
Here I have been expanding and embroidering some passing, but illuminating,
comments of Caputo on the widow's gift. Similar to Caputo's reflections, but
more attentive to issues of gender, is Marion Grau's elucidation of the poor
widow anecdote in her *Of Divine Economy: Refinancing Redemption* (New York:
T. & T. Clark International, 2004), pp. 94-98, 103-105.

costly' (14.3-4), and whose tale is told almost immediately *after* the (official) apocalyptic discourse.

Sandwiched between two women of whom he is apparently in awe, Mark's Jesus nonetheless fails to learn the lesson wrapped up in the absolute gift that he lauds, not once but twice, and cancel his planned parousia accordingly. In the end, then, Mark's Gospel refuses to relinquish its dreams of empire, even while deftly deconstructing the models of economic exchange that enable empires, even eschatological ones, to function.

3

'THE ROMANS WILL COME AND DESTROY OUR HOLY PLACE AND OUR NATION': REPRESENTING EMPIRE IN JOHN

Prologue

The true light that enlightens everyone was coming into the world.
—Jn 1.9

We penetrated deeper and deeper into the heart of darkness.... We were wanderers on prehistoric earth, on an earth that wore the aspect of an unknown planet. We could have fancied ourselves the first men taking possession of an accursed inheritance, to be subdued at the cost of profound anguish and of excessive toil.
—Joseph Conrad[1]

Here, sailing toward an alien land in uncharted waters, and yet it was as if he were coming home.
—Colin Falconer[2]

The Fourth Gospel numbers among its distant descendants the diverse travel narratives of modern European colonialism. For the Johannine Jesus, too, is as an envoy from a distant realm who claims the world through which he is journeying and all its inhabitants for the supreme power whom he purports to represent. This is the sensibility that Musa Dube incisively brings to the Fourth Gospel in her contribution to *The Postcolonial Bible*. For Dube, the Johannine Jesus is a precursor of the 'earth-swallowing' Mr Kurtz, a Conradian traveler journeying into *The Heart of Darkness* that is the unredeemed Johannine cosmos: 'The light shines in the darkness, and the darkness has not overcome it' (Jn 1.5).[3]

1. Joseph Conrad, *Heart of Darkness and Selections from The Congo Diary* (New York: The Modern Library, 1999 [1902]), p. 43.
2. Colin Falconer, *Feathered Serpent: A Novel of the Mexican Conquest* (New York: Three Rivers Press, 2002), p. 9.
3. Musa W. Dube, 'Savior of the World, But Not of This World: A Postcolonial Reading of Spatial Construction in John', in R.S. Sugirtharajah (ed.), *The*

A further illuminating intertext for the Fourth Gospel, it seems to me, is a rather more recent novel, Colin Falconer's *Feathered Serpent*, a vivid and wrenching narrative of the Spanish conquest of Mexico. The eponymous Feathered Serpent is the Aztec deity Quetzalcóatl. But in the fertile hermeneutic imagination of the novel's compelling female protagonist, Ce Malinali Tenepal — better known to posterity as La Malinche[4] — Feathered Serpent is also Hernán Cortés. More precisely, the arrival of the conquistador in her land is interpreted by Malinali as the long-awaited advent of Feathered Serpent. The physical aspect of Quetzalcóatl had been imprinted in her mind since childhood: almost human, he is tall, bearded and fair-skinned, the most beautiful of the gods.[5] When she is confronted with the unfathomable Other, then, in the persons of the ragtag Spanish landing party, the appearance of their leader trumpets forth his identity:

> Out there on the river is the great canoe they speak of, flying a banner with the red cross of Feathered Serpent.[6] There can be no doubt. The day has finally come.
>
> 'Look', I whisper to Rain Flower.
>
> 'I see it, Little Mother'.

Postcolonial Bible (The Bible and Postcolonialism, 1; Sheffield: Sheffield Academic Press, 1998), pp. 118-35, esp. pp. 122-24. Cf. Musa W. Dube and Jeffrey L. Staley, 'Descending from and Ascending into Heaven: A Postcolonial Analysis of Travel, Space and Power in John', in Dube and Staley (eds.), *John and Postcolonialism: Travel, Space and Power* (The Bible and Postcolonialism, 7; New York: Continuum, 2002), pp. 1-10 (1, 9). Dube quotes Conrad on Kurtz: 'I saw him open his mouth wide...as though he had wanted to swallow...all the earth' (Conrad, *Heart of Darkness*, p. 74, in Dube, 'Savior of the World', p. 122).

4.   La Malinche makes her first appearance in the historical record in Bernal Díaz del Castillo's 1568 eyewitness account of the Spanish conquest, *Historia verdadera de la conquista de la Nueva España*. Díaz, however, as a loyal son of Spain, does not brand her a traitor to her people. That infamous characterization of her comes of age in Félix Varela's 1826 novel *Jicoténcal* and the nineteenth century Mexican independence movement. See further Sandra Messinger Cypess, *La Malinche in Mexican Literature: From History to Myth* (Austin: University of Texas Press, 1991); Norma Alarcón, 'Traddutora, Traditora: A Paradigmatic Figure of Chicana Feminism', in Anne McClintock, Aamir Mufti, and Ella Shohat (eds.), *Dangerous Liaisons: Gender, Nation and Postcolonial Perspectives* (Minneapolis: University of Minnesota Press, 1997), pp. 278-97; Amanda Nolacea Harris, 'Imperial and Postcolonial Desires: *Sonata de Estío* and the Malinche Paradigm', *Discourse* 26 (2004), pp. 235-57. For an earlier attempt to bring La Malinche into dialogue with a biblical text, see Robert D. Maldonado, 'Reading Malinche Reading Ruth: Toward a Hermeneutic of Betrayal', *Semeia* 72 (1995), pp. 91-110.

5.   Falconer, *Feathered Serpent*, p. 23.

6.   The cross happens to be a symbol of fertility in her culture (Falconer, *Feathered Serpent*, p. 36).

'I told you! It has happened!'

But still I cannot see *him*. I know he is not the god with the corn silk hair and turquoise eyes or the fire-haired one…not any of these other bearded, pink-faced creatures, many of them with faces pitted like lava stone, others with…

There!

For a moment it is hard to breathe. He is just as I have imagined him, as I saw him on the pyramid at Cholula, as he has been depicted a thousand times on statues and carvings and reliefs in temple walls: a dark beard, black hair falling to his shoulders, his face framed by his helmet, which is itself decorated with a quetzal-green plume.[7] The gray eyes watch me intently, as if he, too, has experienced this same moment of recognition.

And now he approaches.[8]

I, for my part, meanwhile, find myself no less predisposed to identify this mesmerizing stranger with yet another divine being. Although he is not Quetzalcóatl, this other god's totem is also the serpent: 'And as Moses lifted up the serpent [*ton ophin*] in the wilderness, so must the Son of Man be lifted up, that whoever believes in him may have eternal life' (Jn 3.14-15; cf. 12.32-34). Of course, the Fourth Gospel declines to describe the physical appearance of its protagonist. But the blank silhouette thereby outlined afforded imperial Christianity the opportunity to imprint its own idealized features onto the conquering hero of the Johannine travel narrative. Appropriately enough, therefore, Falconer's Cortés in his physical aspect is a virtual twin of the Christ endlessly produced and reproduced by the early modern European imagination:

> Montecuhzoma took an agave thorn from the shrine and stabbed at his own flesh, repeatedly, until the blood ran down his arms. 'Did you see this stranger who claimed to be Quetzalcóatl?'
>
> 'Yes, my lord. His skin was white, like chalk, and he had a dark beard and a straight nose'.[9]

Like the denizens of Jerusalem who agonize over Jesus' identity (Jn 7.25-27, 31), the Mexica debate the identity of the incomprehensible stranger. 'The ancient prophecies are fulfilled!' Malinali assures them; 'Feathered Serpent has returned!' 'Is he truly a god?' one of them doubtfully inquires, to which Malinali replies, in effect, that his divinity is written all over his face: 'Look at his white face, his black beard.

7. Another of Quetzalcóatl's symbols, as is later made explicit (Falconer, *Feathered Serpent*, p. 60).

8. Falconer, *Feathered Serpent*, p. 35.

9. Falconer, *Feathered Serpent*, p. 60. These features are coupled with dark hair falling to his shoulders, as we saw earlier.

Do you not recognize him?'[10] Within the densely ironic weave of the narrative, Malinali has become the unwitting mouthpiece for the conquistadors' own self-representation as emissaries of Christ, conformed to his image and likeness. Like the Samaritan woman of Jn 4.1-42, Malinali is the female personification of her people — more accurately, the personification of her people as susceptible to seduction and eventual domination by the unfathomable stranger: 'Many Samaritans from that city believed in him because of the woman's testimony…. So when the Samaritans came to him, they asked him to stay with them…' (4.39-40).[11]

Cortés/Christ represents himself to the Mexica as harbinger of 'the good news of the one true religion'.[12] More ambitiously, he explains that he has been 'sent by his most Catholic majesty, Charles V, king of Spain…to show…the way to true religion',[13] impelling Malinali to muse: 'I wonder who this great god might be that Feathered Serpent serves in this way. He must surely be referring to Olintecle, the Father of All Gods'.[14] Her identification of Cortés's Lord as his heavenly Father later finds elegant expression in her explanation to a fellow native that 'The bearded god speaks Castilian, the language spoken in heaven'.[15] The immeasurable superiority of the 'Cloud Lands'[16] from whence Cortés/Christ has journeyed ('My kingdom is not of this world', Jn 18.36) confers upon him absolute authority over the patently inferior lands that he has condescended to visit. Shocked at the stranger's stunning arrogance, a representative of the local elite protests to Malinali 'He has only just arrived in our lands', to which she serenely responds, 'They are his lands, so he may do as he wishes'.[17]

10. Falconer, *Feathered Serpent*, p. 50.
11. Cf. Musa W. Dube, 'Reading for Decolonization (John 4.1-42)', in Dube and Staley (eds.), *John and Postcolonialism*, pp. 51-75 (57, 69, 71). Further on this recurrent trope whereby the seduction of a native woman by a foreign conqueror becomes 'a micro-colonization pregnant with allegorical implications', see Harris, 'Imperial and Postcolonial Desires', p. 244 (from whom this pithy quote comes), and also Peter Hulme, 'Polytropic Man: Tropes of Sexuality and Mobility in Early Colonial Discourse', in Francis Barker *et al.* (eds.), *Europe and its Others* (Colchester: University of Essex Press, 1985), pp. 17-32. As Harris notes, in the chronicles of the conquest of the Americas, the trope can be traced all the way back to Columbus's diary ('Imperial and Postcolonial Desires', p. 244).
12. Falconer, *Feathered Serpent*, p. 51.
13. Falconer, *Feathered Serpent*, p. 50.
14. Falconer, *Feathered Serpent*, p. 51.
15. Falconer, *Feathered Serpent*, p. 82.
16. Falconer, *Feathered Serpent*, p. 70.
17. Falconer, *Feathered Serpent*, p. 51.

In the far distance, meanwhile, the uncertain outline of the sword-less (cf. Jn 18.10-11) but world-conquering Johannine Jesus shimmers softly in the harsh Samaritan sun (cf. 4.6), and his hypnotic voice, only faintly distorted, carries over the centuries and the seas to his sword-wielding, world-conquering followers poised on the shores of yet another Samaria: 'I tell you, lift up your eyes, and see how the fields are already white for harvest.... For here the saying holds true, "One sows and another reaps." I sent you to reap that for which you did not labor; others have labored, and you have entered into their labor' (4.35-38).[18]

18. Further parallels between the plot of *Feathered Serpent* and that of the Fourth Gospel could be multiplied (although I would stop short, nonetheless, of suggesting that the novel's author consciously modeled it on the Fourth Gospel, or any gospel for that matter: read the book and you'll see what I mean). In the following scene, for instance, Cortés/Christ prepares to cleanse the temple. Malinali once again is the narrator:

> I cannot stop thinking about Feathered Serpent. During the meeting in the plaza, something angered him. Several times during that encounter, I saw his gaze return to the smoke rising from the pyramid, and I think I know what is troubling him.
> I feel the stirring of a god.
> The next morning I am summoned to the patio, along with...several of the Thunder Lords. Feathered Serpent's expression is stern. He is dressed in his suit of black velvet, he has his sword buckled to his hip, and he wears a silver medal around his neck bearing a picture of the goddess they call Virgin.
> 'Gentlemen, we are called to do God's work', he announces, and strides out of the gates and across the plaza, the rest hurrying after him, running to keep pace....
> The black-robed priests are watching from the shrine above us, clustered together like carrion crows. Feathered Serpent's face is terrible. I hear the rattle of steel as he draws his sword from its scabbard... (*Feathered Serpent*, pp. 92-93).

In another scene, Cortés reenacts Jesus' triumphant entry to Jerusalem:

> The Cempoalans had prepared a welcome for them. As they rode through the streets, they were feted like returning heroes. The Totonacs crowded in, throwing garlands of flowers about their necks....
> Cortés worked his mount carefully through the press of brown bodies and white mantles. The Totonacs parted for him, wary of the horses. He found Malinali on her litter....
> 'Ask her to what do we owe such a welcome', he shouted to Aguilar [his priest and interpreter].
> Malinali and Aguilar had to shout to make themselves heard over the noise of the crowd and the clamor of the drums and clay flutes.
> 'She says we are liberators, my lord!'
> 'Liberators?'

Of course, there are other voices also in the Fourth Gospel; there are even other incarnations of its protagonist. But are there also other paths out of Samaria that lead elsewhere than to Mexico by way of Rome? How best to characterize the political ideology of this gospel?

'I Find This Man to Be Politically Innocuous'

John is at once the most — and the least — political of the canonical gospels. It is the *most* political, because both popular support for, and official opposition to, Jesus' mission in this gospel are each accorded a rationale that is more explicitly political than in the Synoptic Gospels.[19] Consider Jn 6.15, on the one hand, in which the people are poised to 'take [Jesus] by force to make him king' (cf. 12.12), and 11.48, on the other hand, in which the religious authorities anxiously articulate the potentially catastrophic political consequences of this popular fervor: 'If we let him go on like this, every one will believe in him, and the Romans will come and destroy our holy place and our nation'. Consider, too, the unique prominence given to the theme of Jesus' kingship in the Johannine passion narrative. Apart from a single reference to him as 'Son of God' (19.7), 'King of the Jews' is the only title used of Jesus throughout that narrative. The term *basileus* ('king', 'emperor') occurs no fewer than eleven times, and the term *basileia* ('kingdom', 'kingship', 'empire') an additional three, in the relatively terse exchanges between Pilate and Jesus and Pilate and Jesus' accusers — which is to say that John represents the charges brought against Jesus as *political* charges with a consistency and single-mindedness that is altogether absent from the Synoptic tradition. Yet John is also the *least* political of the canonical gospels, it

> 'I do not understand all of it. She says something about the return of a serpent god. Somehow these people know that we have come to save them from barbarity and lead them to salvation!'
> A Totonac woman, braver than her fellows, ran toward Cortés and threw a garland of flowers at him, even had the temerity to touch his horse before she rushed away, giggling (*Feathered Serpent*, pp. 88-89).

19. Recognition of which fact began in earnest, apparently, with Heinrich Schlier, 'Jesus und Pilatus nach dem Johannesevangelium' (1941), in his *Die Zeit der Kirche* (Freiburg: Herder, 4th edn, 1966), pp. 56-74; cf. 'The State according to the New Testament', in his *The Relevance of the New Testament* (Freiburg and New York: Herder & Herder, 1967), esp. pp. 224-25. Notable among more recent readings of John as a deeply political text are David Rensberger, *Johannine Faith and Liberating Community* (Philadelphia: Westminster Press, 1988); and Richard J. Cassidy, *John's Gospel in a New Perspective: Christology and the Realities of Roman Power* (Maryknoll, NY: Orbis Books, 1992).

might equally be argued, because the same passion narrative seems to
place Jesus' kingship front and center only in order to depoliticize it.

Throughout the Roman trial and crucifixion narrative in John, Jesus
is — yet is not — 'King of the Jews'. His kingship is an object of incessant ambivalence in the narrative (18.33-40; 19.14-15, 19-22), and also
of mockery and mimicry (19.2-5).[20] And yet, like any other trial, John's
Roman trial disallows an ambivalent verdict. The reader encoded and
embedded in the text, constructed and called into being through
engagement with the text, is expected to take sides. Far from being
granted a godlike position above, behind, or beyond the text, the
reader is summoned to adopt one or other of the roles scripted in
advance by the text and, indeed, dramatized within it.[21] And Johannine commentators have tended traditionally and overwhelmingly to
assume Pilate's role, improvising on his lines, and siding with him
over against 'the Jews' on the issue of Jesus' kingship. Raymond
Brown speaks for most when he writes of the latter stages of the trial,
'Pilate now understands that Jesus claims no political kingship, for
he has found Jesus innocent'.[22] The implicit tone is one of approval:
Pilate is correct in his estimate. And the meaning of 'innocent' here
would appear to be 'politically unthreatening'.[23]

If Jesus' royal claim, however, is not to be construed as a threat
to Roman hegemony — imperial, colonial, political, military, or cultural — then the embarrassing question arises: Of what use is it then?

20. Alternatively, or simultaneously, depending on how we read, it is Jewish
nationalism that is the object of such treatment in the passion narrative. See
David Rensberger, 'The Politics of John: The Trial of Jesus in the Fourth Gospel',
Journal of Biblical Literature 103 (1984), pp. 395-411 (402-404), which is paralleled
in his *Johannine Faith and Liberating Community*, pp. 93-96.

21. For fuller elaboration of this deconstructive trope, see Stephen D. Moore,
Mark and Luke in Poststructuralist Perspectives: Jesus Begins to Write (New Haven,
CT: Yale University Press, 1992), pp. 28-38.

22. Raymond E. Brown, *The Gospel according to John XIII–XXI* (Anchor Bible,
29A; New York: Doubleday, 1970), p. 885.

23. Other scholars are more explicit and emphatic than Brown in this regard.
Hans Kvalbein, for instance, states that John 18.28–19.19 'shows a Jesus who is no
political challenge to the Roman Empire', and has no intention 'of undermining
the Roman authorities' ('The Kingdom of God and the Kingship of Christ in the
Fourth Gospel', in David E. Aune, Torrey Seland, and Jarl Henning Ulrichsen
[eds.], *Neotestamentica et Philonica: Studies in Honor of Peder Borgen* [Leiden: E.J.
Brill, 2003], pp. 215-32 [227-28]). Kvalbein is echoing approvingly the position
earlier taken by Martin Hengel in his 'Reich Christi, Reich Gottes und Weltreich
im Johannesevangelium', in Martin Hengel and Anna Maria Schwemer (eds.),
*Königsherrschaft Gottes und himmlischer Kult in Judentum, Urchristentum und in der
hellenistischen Welt* (Tübingen: Mohr Siebeck, 1991), pp. 163-84.

To anyone but the Romans, that it. If the Roman prefect's 'I find no crime in him [*egō oudemian heuriskō en autō aitian*]' (18.38) is to be construed — approvingly and unequivocally — as meaning that the Jewish Messiah's brand of kingship is not, in the end, a threat to the Roman Emperor's brand, then pro-Roman apologetics would here seem to be extending themselves to the limit and paving the royal road to the fourth century and an unproblematic fusion of Christianity and Rome.

In an irony not foreseen by this consummately ironic evangelist, the only characters in the drama proposing a more satisfactory interpretation of Jesus' kingship — one singularly at odds with Jesus' own interpretation, that of Pilate, and that of most Johannine commentators — are 'the Jews'. 'The Jews' expound a Christology that runs counter to Pilate's — and Jesus' own — apolitical Christology. 'The Jews' expound a Christology whose long-delayed fruit, it might even be said, is less fourth-century Constantinian Christianity than late twentieth-century liberation theology, prompting the following paraphrase of the dialogue:

> Pilate: 'Your accusations notwithstanding, I find this man to be politically innocuous'.
> 'The Jews': 'On the contrary, he deserves to be executed in the excruciating manner reserved for those who imperil the imperial status quo. He is actually more of an affront to the Emperor, and hence a more serious threat to you, even than that rabidly militant insurgent Barabbas'.

In that they were wrong, however, if history is to be the judge.

Hurrying to the Praetorium

More even than in Mark, the face of Rome in John is the blurred face of the Prefect of Judea, Pontius Pilate. This is not only because, unlike Mark, and Matthew and Luke following him, no centurion hovers at the foot of the cross in John as an ancillary personification in the passion narrative of Roman imperial authority. It is also because the figure of Pilate looms considerably larger in the Fourth Gospel in general than in the Synoptics, and for two reasons. First, the Johannine Pilate is simply accorded more lines than his Synoptic counterparts, and more memorable lines at that. The relative complexity of the Johannine Pilate as a character owes much to such enigmatic utterances as 'Am I a Jew?' (18.35); 'What is truth?' (18.38); 'Behold the man!' (19.5); and 'What I have written I have written' (19.22).[24]

---

24. For literary studies of the characterization of John's Pilate, see, for example, R. Alan Culpepper, *Anatomy of the Fourth Gospel: A Study in Literary Design*

Second, the Judean religious leadership is accorded a far more effaced role in the Johannine trial narrative than in the Synoptic trial narratives, which has the effect of casting the Roman leadership, almost wholly embodied in the person of Pilate, in still sharper relief—*almost wholly*, because there is, apparently, one further Roman of rank in John's passion narrative.[25]

On a literal reading of Jn 18.3, 12—one matter-of-factly embraced by quite a number of scholars[26]—a cohort (*speira*) of Roman troops under the command of a tribune (*chiliarchos*) is present at Jesus' arrest. The term *speira* ordinarily designates six hundred soldiers. John thus floods the garden with Roman troops, by implication, cramming them in shoulder-to-shoulder and cheek-to-jowl, so that they overwhelmingly outnumber the other named component of the arresting party, 'the attendants [*hypēretai*] of the chief priests and the Pharisees' (18.3; cf. 18.12). From the outset, then, and to a degree entirely unmatched by its Synoptic counterparts, the Johannine passion narrative represents its towering protagonist as engaged in a toe-to-toe contest with Roman imperial might—and with Rome hitting the canvas hard early in the first round: 'When he said to them *Egō eimi*, they drew back and fell to the ground' (18.6).

It is not that the Jewish leadership plays no role whatsoever in this championship bout, but only that its role is strictly secondary. The

(Foundations and Facets; Philadelphia: Fortress Press, 1983), pp. 142-43; Colleen M. Conway, *Men and Women in the Fourth Gospel: Gender and Johannine Characterization* (Society of Biblical Literature Dissertation Series, 167; Atlanta: Scholars Press, 1999), pp. 154-63.

25. The only other such Roman in the entire Fourth Gospel if we resist the temptation to conflate the *basilikos* ('courtier', 'royal official') of Jn 4.46, 49 with the *hekatontarchos* ('centurion') of Mt. 8.5, 8, 13, and Lk. 7.2, 6, in line with a commentarial tradition that, while by no means unanimous, has had a long history; for an early instance of it, see J.H. Bernard, *A Critical and Exegetical Commentary on the Gospel according to St John* (ed. A.H. McNeile; The International Critical Commentary, 29; Edinburgh: T. & T. Clark, 1928), I, p. 167.

26. Those who take 18.3, 12 at face value have included C.K. Barrett, *The Gospel according to St John: An Introduction with Commentary and Notes on the Greek Text* (Philadelphia: Westminster Press, 2nd edn, 1978), pp. 518, 524; Rensberger, 'The Politics of John', pp. 399-400, and *Johannine Faith and Liberating Community*, p. 90; Raymond E. Brown, *The Death of the Messiah: From Gethsemane to the Grave. A Commentary on the Passion Narratives in the Four Gospels* (New York: Doubleday, 1994), I, pp. 248-51; Gail R. O'Day, 'The Gospel of John: Introduction, Commentary, and Reflections', in Leander E. Keck (ed.), *The New Interpreter's Bible* (Nashville: Abingdon Press, 1995), IX, pp. 801-802; and, more tentatively, Rudolf Schnackenburg, *The Gospel according to St John* (trans. David Smith and G.A. Kon; New York: Crossroad, 1982), III, pp. 222-23.

Johannine narrator seems to want to march us briskly through Jesus' interrogations by Annas and Caiaphas in order to get us as expeditiously as possible to the interrogation by Pilate. In place of the energetic, crisis-inducing questioning of Jesus attributed to the high priest in Mark and Matthew, culminating in the high priest's dramatic rending of his robe and impassioned condemnation of the accused (Mk 14.53-65; Mt. 26.57-68; cf. Lk. 22.66-71), we find in John only the bland summary statement, 'The high priest [here referring to Annas, apparently] then questioned Jesus about his disciples and his teaching' (18.19). The interrogation does, to be sure, evoke a spirited response from the Johannine Jesus (18.20-21), but nothing nearly as momentous as the Markan Jesus' 'I am [the Christ, the Son of the Blessed One]' (14.62), his first and final public spilling of his 'messianic secret'.

Following his questioning by Annas, Jesus is passed on to Caiaphas. Presumably we are to imagine that Jesus is interrogated by Caiaphas as well, but the text does not say so explicitly, much less indicate the content of the questioning. Jesus is 'sent...bound to the house of Caiaphas the high priest' (18.24), only to be 'led...from the house of Caiaphas to the praetorium' and the Roman prefect (18.28). So heavily foregrounded in the Johannine passion narrative, then, is Jesus' confrontation with Rome, personified by the Prefect of Judea, as to relegate the confrontation with the local Judean elite to the periphery and all but evacuate it of content—a curiously anticlimactic twist to this climactic phase of the plot, given the plot-propelling antagonism that has characterized the protagonist's relations with 'the Jews' in so many of the scenes leading up to his arrest.

Viewed differently, however, this anticlimax is not altogether devoid of narrative logic. All of the outraged or incredulous questions or accusations put to Jesus by 'the Jews' that the narrator can devise have already been 'reported' in the body of the narrative, and responded to either by Jesus or the narrator, and hence do not need repeating at its climax—questions or charges such as:

> 'It has taken us forty-six years to build this temple, and will you raise it up in three days?' (2.20).

> 'Is not this Jesus, the son of Joseph, whose father and mother we know? How does he now say, "I have come down from heaven"?' (6.42).

> 'How can this man give us his flesh to eat?' (6.52).

> 'Who are you?' (8.25).

'Are we not right in saying that you are a Samaritan and have a demon?' (8.48; cf. 7.20).

'Are you greater than our father Abraham...? And the prophets...? Who do you claim to be?' (8.53).

'You are not yet fifty years old, and have you seen Abraham?' (8.57).

'Are we also blind?' (9.40).

'If you are the Christ, tell us plainly' (10.24).

'We stone you for no good work but for blasphemy; because you, being a man, make yourself God' (10.33).

This onslaught of questions and accusations distributed throughout the narrative has the effect of simultaneously preempting and delocalizing Jesus' official trial and conferring the character of a displaced trial on the narrative at large. Martin Kähler famously dubbed Mark's Gospel 'a passion narrative with an extended introduction'.[27] But the trial and hence the passion of Jesus looms still larger in John's Gospel. The Johannine plot (such as it is) unfolds in an outsized courtroom, with 'the world', epitomized in this instance by 'the Jews', as plaintiff, Jesus as defendant, and God as judge.[28] By the time we arrive at the official trial before the local Judean leadership, therefore, there is exceedingly little left to say — as Jesus himself reminds his interrogators: 'I have spoken openly to the world; I have always taught in synagogues and in the temple, where all Jews come together; I have said nothing secretly. Why do you ask me?' (18.20-21). There is considerably more to say to the Roman leadership, in contrast, an entirely fresh dialogue partner for the dialogue-loving protagonist.[29] And whereas the principal topic of Jesus' dialogues with 'the Jews' was his relationship to the God of Israel, the principal topic of his dialogue with the Roman prefect will be his relationship to that other, more proximate, god, the Roman Emperor.[30]

27. Martin Kähler, *The So-called Historical Jesus and the Historic, Biblical Christ* (trans. and ed. Carl E. Braaten; Philadelphia: Fortress Press, 1964 [German original 1896]), p. 80, n.11.

28. The widespread recognition that a trial motif permeates the Fourth Gospel (see, e.g., 3.19; 5.22, 30; 8.16, 26; 9.39; 16.8-11) owes much to Josef Blank's *Krisis: Untersuchungen zur johanneischen Christologie und Eschatologie* (Freiburg: Lambertus, 1964). For a recent study of the motif, see Andrew T. Lincoln, *Truth on Trial: The Lawsuit Motif in the Fourth Gospel* (Peabody, MA: Hendrickson, 2000).

29. Contrast Jesus' silence before Pilate in Mark, broken only by the taciturn 'You have said so [*su legeis*]' (15.2).

30. Granted, the emperor in question, Tiberius — like Caligula, Nero, and Domitian and unlike Augustus, Claudius, Vespasian, and Titus — was not deified

Pilate Picks Up the Lash

The face of Rome in the Fourth Gospel is the face of Pontius Pilate, as we already remarked, which is also to say that when Rome finally assumes a speaking role in this gospel[31] it is in the person of the Prefect of Judea. But it is not in his ordinary capacity as chief administrator and head bureaucrat that Pilate makes his entrance in John so much as in his extraordinary capacity as chief inquisitor and head torturer: Pilate's questioning of the accused is punctuated by Pilate's scourging of the accused.

Now, we are probably not to suppose that the Roman prefect applies the scourge to the peasant upstart with his own hands — or are we?[32] In the Markan account of the Roman trial we read that 'having flogged Jesus, [Pilate] handed him over to be crucified' (*kai paredōken ton Iēsoun phragellōsas hina staurōthē*, 15.15), while Matthew parrots Mark, only reshuffling Mark's syntax yet again (*ton de Iēsoun phragellōsas paredōken hina staurōthē*, 27.26).[33] More decisively even than the Markan formulation, however, the Johannine formulation seems to thrust the lash into the prefect's hand: 'Then Pilate took Jesus and scourged him' (*Tote oun elaben ho Pilatos ton Iēsoun kai emastigōsen*, 19.1). Why not simply take the statement at face value altogether, and understand it to be claiming that Pilate himself, quite literally,

at his demise because the Senate, out of antipathy, refused to vote him the honor. His provincial subjects, however, knew better. As Robert L. Mowery notes: 'Tiberius…is identified as *theou Sebastou huios* ["son of the divine Augustus"] by various inscriptions and coins, and he is called *theou huios* ["Son of God"] by inscriptions located in such widely-scattered regions as Egypt, Achaia, Asia, Cilicia, and even the northern shore of the Black Sea. Tiberius is called a god by various Greek inscriptions and coins, and he is hailed as both "god" and "son of god Sebastos" by a few Greek sources. Early Christians who heard about these imperial honors may not have known that Tiberius was never officially declared a *divus* by the Roman Senate' ('Son of God in Roman Imperial Titles and Matthew', *Biblica* 83 [2002], pp. 100-110 [102]).

31. Beyond the one-line role accorded to it in 18.5, 7, that is: 'Jesus…said to them, "Whom do you seek?" They answered him, "Jesus of Nazareth"… Again he asked them, "Whom do you seek?" And they said, "Jesus of Nazareth."'

32. The reflections that follow have been stimulated in part by conversations with Jennifer Glancy and Rob Seesengood, although I alone bear responsibility for their present form.

33. Luke, for his part, discreetly omits any description of the scourging in his passion narrative, even though he has Jesus (18.33), and even Pilate (23.16), predict it. Two different verbs are used, *mastigoō*, 'scourge', in 18.33 (which is also the verb that John uses, as we will see), and *paideuō*, 'chastise', in 23.16, both in contrast to Mark and Matthew's *phragelloō*, 'flog'.

scourged Jesus?[34] Or would this be an overly literal interpretation of the Greek construction? After all, recourse to the eminently flexible and resourceful aorist tense was koine Greek's standard way of saying that X had Y flogged, or scourged, or crucified, or subjected to any other action entailing indirect agency, as example after example indicates.[35] But the ambiguity inherent in the Greek construction, taken in and of itself, does leave open the possibility Pilate himself is the direct agent of the scourging.

Of course, a possibility is not always a plausibility, for it is never merely a matter of grammar. And so it will be objected that the spectacle of Pilate himself scourging the accused would have been beneath his dignity as a Roman official.[36] But perhaps the Johannine author is not unduly concerned with the dignity of Roman officials, or even with verisimilitude (and it is with the twists of his narrative rather than the turns of the history that putatively underlies it that I myself am concerned with here). Is the image of the prefect personally laying into the peasant troublemaker with a flagrum[37] intrinsically

34. Note how the agency ascribed to Pilate in 19.1 parallels that ascribed to his soldiers in 19.2: 'Then Pilate took Jesus and scourged him. And the soldiers plaited a crown of thorns, and put it on his head, and arrayed him in a purple robe...'

35. See Plutarch, *Caesar* 29.2, for instance: 'Marcellus, while he was consul, beat with rods [*ēkisto rabdois*] a senator of Novum Comum who had come to Rome, telling him besides that he put these marks upon him to prove that he was not a Roman, and bade him go back and show them to Caesar' (LCL translation). Or Josephus, *Jewish War* 2.14.9: 'they [the Roman troops] also arrested and brought before [Gessius] Florus [Prefect of Judea] many of the peaceful citizens, whom he first scourged and then crucified [*hous mastixin proaikisamenos anestaurōsen*]... For Florus ventured that day to do what none had ever done before, namely, to scourge before his tribunal and nail to the cross [*mastigōsai te pro tou bēmatos kai staurō proselōsai*] men of equestrian rank...' (LCL translation, modified). Such examples could be multiplied from accounts of flagellation and crucifixion alone in the relevant Greek literature.

36. Cf. William Fitzgerald, *Slavery and the Roman Literary Imagination* (Cambridge: Cambridge University Press, 2000), p. 35: 'The man of intellect distinguishes himself from the man of the body and the passions by having an intermediary act out his anger for him...' Fitzgerald cites the scene in Seneca's *On Anger* (3.12) where Plato is said to freeze, hand in the air, having almost succumbed to the temptation to strike a slave. Pilate, however, is no Plato.

37. Or flagellum, either instrument being a short leather whip with multiple thongs (fewer thongs in the case of the flagellum, when the term is not simply interchangeable with flagrum), each thong being weighed with fragments of bone, metal balls, and/or metal spikes. Roman practices of scourging, flogging, and beating are exhaustively detailed in Henri Leclercq, 'Flagellation (Supplice de la)', in Fernand Cabrol and Henri Leclercq (eds.), *Dictionnaire d'archéologie chrétienne et de liturgie* (Paris: Letouzey et Ané, 1907–1953), V, pp. 1638-43; and

less verisimilar than the image of a full Roman cohort being dis-
patched to arrest this unarmed peasant — and falling prostrate before
him in the process (18.3-6) — or of the prefect responding with fear to
the peasant's claims to divine sonship (19.8)?[38]

So far as I have been able to ascertain, however, even the most
encyclopedic Johannine commentaries, for all their exhaustive industry, fail to register Pilate's directly agency in the scourging as even an
easily dismissible interpretation. Personal scourging of a prisoner
would certainly be out of character for the mild-mannered Pilate of
Christian tradition, although not for the cruel and brutal Pilate of
Philo and Josephus arguably,[39] nor even, perhaps, for the Pilate of
certain contemporary interpreters, such as David Rensberger, who
argues persuasively that the Johannine Pilate, far from being 'a man
of just intentions but weak character', is instead 'callous and relentless, indifferent to Jesus and to truth, and contemptuous of the hope
of Israel that Jesus fulfills and transcends'.[40]

In the end, however, whether or not the prefect administers the
scourging in person is a moot, if not uninteresting, point given the
Johannine wording of the event: 'Then Pilate took Jesus and scourged
him'. The agency of the underlings who, in accordance with the traditional assumption, actually administer the punishment is entirely
erased in this formulation: they are every bit as much instruments in
the hands of the prefect as are the scourges gripped in their own
hands — and are made so by this standard grammatical construction

Josef Blinzler, *The Trial of Jesus: The Jewish and Roman Proceedings against Jesus
Christ Described and Assessed from the Oldest Accounts* (trans. Isabel McHugh and
Florence McHugh; Westminster, MD: Newman, 1959), pp. 222-35.

38. Cf. John Dominic Crossan, *The Historical Jesus: The Life of a Mediterranean
Jewish Peasant* (San Francisco: HarperSanFrancisco, 1991), p. xii: 'it is now impossible for us to imagine the offhand brutality, anonymity, and indifference with
which a peasant nobody like Jesus would have been disposed of'.

39. See Philo, *The Embassy to Caligula* 299-305; Josephus, *Jewish Antiquities*
18.55-59; *Jewish War* 2.169-74. Philo's and Josephus's portraits of Pilate are analyzed in Helen Bond, *Pontius Pilate in History and Interpretation* (Society for New
Testament Studies Monograph Series, 100; Cambridge: Cambridge University
Press, 1999), Chapters 2 and 3 respectively.

40. Rensberger, 'The Politics of John', p. 406; cf. Rensberger, *Johannine Faith
and Liberating Community*, pp. 92-95. This is a fate that has recently befallen the
Matthean Pilate as well; see Warren Carter, *Matthew and Empire: Initial Explorations* (Harrisburg, PA: Trinity Press International, 2001), pp. 145-68. Some of the
savagery of Philo's Pilate is, in effect, ascribed to John's Pilate by Rensberger,
who notes that while the latter 'at first declines any involvement' with Jesus'
case, 'he is at once willing to proceed with the hearing when he learns that a
crucifixion is in the offing' (*Johannine Faith and Liberating Community*, pp. 92-93).

that unsettlingly deconstructs the distinction between direct and indirect agency. Language itself, then, thrusts the lash into the prefect's hand. Moreover, as we are about to see, it represents Rome as always already wielding the whip.

The successive episodes of the Roman trial narrative unfold in accordance with an inflexible numerical logic, familiar to readers of the Fourth Gospel, reaching a climax with the first drawing of the victim's blood. For as has often been remarked, John structures the Roman trial in seven chiastic episodes (a number with which he is, of course, much taken), and it is in the middle episode of the chiasm that the scourging occurs[41] — which is to say, on the topmost level of the narrative pedestal. Imperial Rome, in the person of Pontius Pilate, confronts Jesus atop that pedestal, flagrum in hand (symbolically at least, if not actually), the inquisitor now become torturer.

Commentators regularly note the apparent oddity of the Johannine placement of the scourging — not immediately preceding the crucifixion, as in Mark and Matthew, but in the middle of the Roman trial. Brown, in common with many, distinguishes three functions for Roman floggings: a punishment for lesser crimes (and probably what Pilate has in mind in Lk. 23.16); 'a chastisement bordering on inquisitional torture to extract information from the prisoner or get him to confess'; or a prelude to crucifixion intended both to increase the condemned's suffering and shorten his sojourn on the cross.[42] But Brown

---

41. Brown (*Death of the Messiah*, I, p. 758), building on the proposal of Janssens de Varbeke and modifying those of Rudolf Bultmann and Ernst Haenchen, plausibly suggest the following chiastic structure for the Roman trial narrative:

1.	*Outside* (18.28-32) Jews demand death	=	7.	*Outside* (19.12-16a) Jews obtain death
2.	*Inside* (18.33-38a) Pilate and Jesus on kingship	=	6.	*Inside* (19.9-11) Pilate and Jesus on power
3.	*Outside* (18.38b-40) Pilate finds no guilt; choice of Barabbas	=	5.	*Outside* (19.4-8) Pilate finds no guilt; 'Behold the man'

4.   *Inside* (19.1-3)
Soldiers scourge Jesus

Scene #4, however, would be better titled 'Pilate scourges Jesus', following John's own formulation of the event — and rendering unnecessary Brown's caveat: 'Pilate appears as a major actor in every episode of [the Roman trial narrative] except...the middle episode containing the scourging and mockery of Jesus' (*Death of the Messiah*, I, p. 758; cf. I, p. 827).

42. Brown, *Death of the Messiah*, I, pp. 851-52. The third function listed by Brown is attested in Mk 15.20; Mt. 27.26; *Gospel of Peter* 3.9; and in Josephus,

is unable to fit the Johannine scourging into this tripartite schema: 'Harder to classify is the scourging of Jesus in Jn 19.1; Pilate's motive seems to be to make Jesus look wretched so that "the Jews" will be satisfied and accept his release'.[43] Brown's (implicit) disqualification of the second option, that the Johannine Jesus' scourging is 'a chastisement bordering on inquisitional torture', typifies that of the commentarial tradition generally, as does his inability to account satisfactorily for the placement of the scourging in the middle rather than at the end of the Roman trial.

This tendency in the tradition provides Jennifer Glancy with her cue to argue compellingly that the Johannine scourging is best construed as an instance of Roman judicial torture.[44] The stark definition of torture proffered in the *Digest of Justinian* encapsulates the Roman stance on judicial torture: 'By torture we mean the infliction of anguish and agony on the body to elicit the truth' (48.10.15.41; cf. 48.19.28.2).[45] Sources attesting to this practice are numerous, ranging from Acts 22.24, the only unequivocal instance of judicial torture in the New Testament, in which a Roman tribune orders Paul 'to be examined with scourges [*mastixin anetazesthai auton*] that he might fully know what crime [the mob] were clamoring he had committed',[46] to a letter of Pliny, governor of Bithynia, to the emperor Trajan, which contains the statement: 'I deemed it that much more necessary to extract the real truth, by means of torture (*per tormenta*), from two female slaves, who were styled deacons'.[47]

To read the Johannine scourging through a Markan or Matthean lens is to view it as a prelude to crucifixion, whereas to read it through

Jewish War 2.14.9; 5.11.1; 7.6.4; Seneca, *To Marcia on Consolation* 20.3; and Livy, *History* 33.36.3.

43. Brown, *Death of the Messiah*, I, p. 852.

44. A suggestion formerly made in passing by C.H. Dodd, and independently by Edward Peters, as Glancy acknowledges. See Jennifer A. Glancy, 'Torture: Flesh, Truth, and the Fourth Gospel', *Biblical Interpretation* 13 (2005), pp. 107-36; C.H. Dodd, *Historical Tradition in the Fourth Gospel* (Cambridge: Cambridge University Press, 1963), pp. 102-103; Edward Peters, *Torture* (New York: Blackwell, 1985), p. 27. Craig S. Keener, *The Gospel of John: A Commentary* (Peabody, MA: Hendrickson, 2003), II, p. 1120 n. 463, lists further scholars who have ventured the suggestion, although Glancy develops it much more fully.

45. Quoted in Glancy, 'Torture', p. 118. For the ancient Greek practice and philosophy of judicial torture, which profoundly influenced the Roman, see Page duBois's classic study, *Torture and Truth* (New York: Routledge, 1991).

46. My translation.

47. Pliny the Younger, *Letters* 10.96, my translation. This letter, generally dated to around 112 CE, was part of a prolific correspondence between the governor and the emperor.

a Lukan lens is to view it as a lesser punishment that, Pilate hopes, may stave off the necessity of execution. Reading it on its own terms, however, with particular attention to its unique placement in the middle of the Roman trial, invites the conclusion that it is here represented as judicial torture. This is not to say that all the mystery is thereby sieved out of the Johannine scourging. For even if we are dealing with an instance of judicial torture here, the account of it is extraordinarily condensed. The problem is not so much the lack of graphic detail on the manner in which the accused is scourged or the severity of the scourging[48] as the lack of questions directed to him to motivate and accompany the ordeal. In much the same way in which the Jewish trial in John is evacuated of content in its telling, as we have seen, most of the charges and questions that should have constituted it having already been disseminated through the preceding narrative, so too are the questions that should punctuate the scourging dissociated from it and displaced around it:

'Are you the King of the Jews?' (18.33).

'So you are a king?' (18.37).

'Where are you from?' (19.9).

'Do you refuse to speak to me? Do you not know that I have power to release you, and power to crucify you?' (19.10).

Torture, it goes without saying, is not the preserve of empire. Yet, as history has persistently taught us (most recently at Abu Ghraib and Guantanamo Bay), empire and torture tend to be inextricably intertwined. The Roman Empire, as is commonly noted, had as its fundamental enabling condition the institution of slavery.[49] But what in turn was the fundamental condition of slavery? Not to have one's own physical person at one's disposal would seem to be the obvious answer. And the permanent possibility, not to say outright probability, of rape, flogging, or other forms of physical abuse or torture— including judicial torture—can be said to have epitomized the slave's lack of autonomy over his or her body. Put another way, if the slave ensured the efficient operation of the empire, the permanent possibility

48. In contrast to certain other contemporary accounts of scourging, such as Josephus, *Jewish War* 2.21.5; 6.5.3; Josephus, *Life* 30.147; or 4 *Maccabees* 6.3-7.

49. See, for example, Fitzgerald, *Slavery and the Roman Literary Imagination*, p. 2; Jennifer A. Glancy, *Slavery in Early Christianity* (Oxford: Oxford University Press, 2002), p. 5. For more detailed discussion, see Keith Bradley, *Slavery and Society at Rome* (Cambridge: Cambridge University Press, 1994), pp. 31-81; F.H. Thompson, *The Archaeology of Greek and Roman Slavery* (London: Duckworth, 2003), pp. 1-34.

of physical punishment, epitomized by torture, was what ensured the efficient operation of the slave. And what was true of the slave was also true, albeit to a lesser degree, of non-citizens generally, not least in backwater territories of the empire such as the province of Judea. The relationship between empire and torture, therefore, while ordinarily oblique, was nonetheless symbiotic, even fundamental and central, in the Roman imperial order.

And it is that relationship that comes to veiled but succinct expression in the Johannine Roman trial narrative. So far as I can discover, nobody has yet managed to explain satisfactorily in relation to Johannine theology — or ideology, for that matter — why 19.1-3, Jesus' brutal torture within the Roman praetorium by scourging, crowning with thorns, blows to the body and/or face, and psychological abuse should be the central term in the seven-term chiasm that structures the Roman trial narrative, and hence the term that is singled out for special emphasis.[50] What I would suggest, however, is that this emphasis makes excellent sense when set in relation to Roman imperial ideology — or, rather, the implicit Johannine critique of such ideology. The central term in the chiasm, namely, torture, is none other than the central mechanism designed to keep every Roman subject — slave, peasant, every other non-citizen, and, in certain cases, even citizens themselves — firmly in their respective, and respectful, places in relation to Roman imperial authority, and never more so than when torture is the prelude to death.[51] Whether or not the Fourth Evangelist may plausibly be said to have intended it,[52] therefore, his placement of the torture scene as the foregrounded feature of the

50. On the significance of chiastic central terms, see, for example, John W. Welch, *Chiasmus in Antiquity: Structures, Analysis, Exegesis* (Hildesheim: Gerstenberg Verlag, 1981), p. 10; John Breck, *The Shape of Biblical Language: Chiasmus in the Scriptures and Beyond* (Crestwood, NY: St Vladimir's Seminary Press, 1994), pp. 330-50, esp. 335.

51. This mechanism preceded the Roman Empire, needless to say, and survived its demise, even down to the modern period, when 'societies of the spectacle' finally gave way in western Europe to 'societies of surveillance' and 'the birth of the prison', as famously, and controversially, chronicled by Michel Foucault in *Discipline and Punish: The Birth of the Prison* (trans. Alan Sheridan; New York: Vintage Books, 1977).

52. What the evangelist probably intended was to highlight the soldiers' ironic acclamation of Jesus as 'King of the Jews' (19.2-3), as Conway insightfully suggests (*Men and Women in the Fourth Gospel*, p. 158 n. 267). But the mock coronation occurs in the context of Jesus' torture — is itself, indeed, an intrinsic feature of the torture that permeates and unifies this scene. Narratively, then, the torture is the more basic element whose chiastic centering needs explaining, and should not be swept too swiftly under the Christological rug.

chiasm that structures his account of Roman judicial procedure admits—indeed invites—interpretation as a singularly scathing indictment of the Roman imperial order in general and of Roman justice in particular.

Johannine Atonement: Propitiating Caesar

Searing indictment of Roman imperialism is ordinarily thought by New Testament scholars to be a feature not of the Fourth Gospel so much as the book of Revelation. Undeterred by stylistic or theological dissimilarities, early Christian tradition cast the two texts as siblings, progeny of a single apostolic author.[53] But how do they compare in their respective representations of Rome?

In Revelation as in the Fourth Gospel, Rome is, by implication at least, an agent of torture and death: 'And I saw that the woman was drunk with the blood of the saints and the blood of the witnesses to Jesus' (17.6; cf. 2.13; 6.9-11; 7.14; 18.24; 19.2b). Far more conspicuously and spectacularly, however, is Rome the *object* of torture in Revelation. Revelation's imagistic code does not always permit us to distinguish cleanly between the Roman Empire, the city of Rome, and the Roman Emperor; but all three are unequivocally consigned to torture in the following catena (which is not, however, intended to be exhaustive). If the scourge and the cross are the preferred means of torture in the Fourth Gospel, in Revelation the preferred means is fire:

> 'Anyone who worships the beast and its image...will...be tortured [*basanisthēsetai*] with fire and sulfur before the holy angels and before the Lamb. And the smoke of their torture [*tou basanismou autōn*] ascends forever and ever' (14.9-11).

> 'And the ten horns that you saw and the beast, they will hate the whore, and they will violate her and strip her naked [*kai ērēmōmenēn poiēsousin autēn kai gymnēn*], and they will devour her flesh and burn her with fire' (17.16).

> '[T]herefore her plagues will come in a single day...and she will be burned with fire...' (18.8).

> '[H]e has judged the great whore...and he has avenged on her the blood of his slaves.... Her smoke ascends forever and ever' (19.2-3).

> 'And the beast was seized, and with it the false prophet.... Both of them were thrown, while still alive, into the lake of fire that burns with sulfur' (19.20).

53. Dionysius of Alexandria providing the exception that proved the rule (as reported in Eusebius, *Ecclesiastical History* 7.25).

'And the devil...was thrown into the lake of fire and sulfur, where the beast and the false prophet also were, and they will be tortured [_basanisthēsontai_] day and night forever and ever' (20.10).[54]

In Revelation, then, relative to the Fourth Gospel, the tables are dramatically turned in the Jesus-Rome confrontation. It is as though Jesus had abruptly leaped on Pilate, overpowering him and tying him to the flogging post and viciously laying into him with the lash—not unlike Rambo in the eponymous Reagan-era Vietnam rewrite, a one-man army (like the Jesus of Revelation), who, having been bound in a crucified posture and cruelly tortured with electricity, suddenly turns the tables on his tormentor, throwing him back against the torture device and jamming the voltage up to the maximum setting. The cheers of the patriotic audience in the movie auditorium mingle with the cheers of the celestial audience in the heavenly throne room while the stench of charred flesh fills the air.

Revelation's tortured torturer motif also finds a parallel, however, in a work somewhat closer to it in time, the Fourth Book of Maccabees. The last and youngest of the seven Jewish brothers put to the death-torture by Antiochus Epiphanes echoes and outdoes his brothers in predicting a still more terrible fate for the tyrant: 'You profane tyrant, most impious of all the wicked, since you have received good things and also your kingdom from God, were you not ashamed to murder his servants and torture on the wheel those who practice religion? Because of this, justice has laid up for you intense and eternal fire and tortures [_pyknoterō kai aiōniō pyri kai basanois_], and these throughout all time will never let you go' (12.11-12, echoing 9.8-9 and 10.10-11; cf. 11.3, 23; 12.18; 18.5, 22).[55]

In John's Gospel, in stark contrast, the tyrannical empire is never represented as the _object_ of divine punishment, whether realized or merely anticipated. Rome is only ever the _agent_ of punishment in John. More even than in Mark, it is the Judean elite—the Judean comprador class, so to speak, and the primary referent, arguably, of the Johannine epithet 'the Jews' (_hoi Ioudaioi_)[56]—who are the object of

54. My translations.

55. NRSV translation. 4 _Maccabees_ is probably best dated to the early second century CE. Elsewhere I have discussed Revelation's relations to 4 _Maccabees_ at greater length; see my _God's Beauty Parlor: And Other Queer Spaces in and around the Bible_ (Contraversions: Jews and Other Differences; Stanford, CA: Stanford University Press, 2001), pp. 191-99.

56. 'The term is mostly, although...not always, used for the authorities headquartered in Jerusalem' (Keener, _The Gospel of John_, I, p. 221), a position particularly associated with Urban C. von Wahlde; see his 'The Johannine "Jews": A

unrelenting, scathing criticism, both explicit and implicit, while their Roman overlords are — ostensibly, at least — let off the hook. In Mark's Gospel, arguably, the actions of the indigenous Judean elite vis-à-vis the misunderstood protagonist are interpreted as precipitating the annihilation of Jerusalem and its temple.[57] John's treatment of Jesus' relationship to the (about-to-be) destroyed temple and city is far more oblique, as 11.47-52 in particular suggests:

> So the chief priests and the Pharisees assembled the council [*synedrion*] and said, 'What are we to do, because this man is performing many signs? If we let him go on like this, everyone will believe in him, and the Romans will come and destroy our holy place[58] and our nation' [*kai eleusontai hoi Rōmanoi kai arousin hēmōn ton topon kai to ethnos*]. But one of them, Caiaphas, being high priest that year, said to them, 'You know absolutely nothing, nor do you understand that it more expedient for you that one man die for the people than that the entire nation perish'. Now he did not say this of his own accord, but being high priest that year he prophesied that Jesus was about to die for the nation, and not for the nation only, but to gather into one the scattered children of God (11.47-52).[59]

This unique passage assigns political motivation to the indigenous Judean leadership with a degree of explicitness that is entirely lacking in the Synoptic tradition. In the Synoptics, or so it has frequently been argued, it is Jesus' symbolic action in the temple that, more than anything else, consolidates the Judean elite's opposition to him and precipitates his arrest (cf. Mk 11.18; 14.57-58; Mt. 26.59-61; Lk. 19.45-47; Acts 6.12-14).[60] The temple incident cannot, of course, assume this

Critical Survey', *New Testament Studies* 28 (1981–82), pp. 33-60, and 'The Gospel of John and the Presentation of Jews and Judaism', in David P. Efroymson *et al.* (eds.), *Within Context: Essay on Jews and Judaism in the New Testament* (Collegeville, MN: Liturgical Press, 1983), pp. 67-84. For further discussion of this complex issue, see Stephen Motyer, *Your Father the Devil? A New Approach to John and 'the Jews'* (Carlisle: Paternoster Press, 1997), pp. 54-56; and Adele Reinhartz, *Befriending the Beloved Disciple: A Jewish Reading of the Gospel of John* (New York: Continuum, 2001), pp. 72-75.

57. See pp. 30, 35 above.

58. With the majority, I take *hēmōn...ton topon* (literally, 'our...place') to refer to the Jerusalem temple rather than the city itself; cf. Jn 4.20 (also Acts 6.13-14; 7.7) in which *ho topos* unambiguously denotes the former. For this understanding of *topos* in Jn 11.48, see, *inter alios*, Brown, *The Gospel according to John I–XII*, p. 439; Ernst Haenchen, *Das Johannesevangelium: Ein Kommentar* (ed. Ulrich Busse; Tübingen: J.C.B. Mohr, 1980), p. 422; Keener, *The Gospel of John*, II, p. 855.

59. My translation.

60. See, for example, Joseph A. Fitzmyer, *The Gospel according to Luke X–XXIV* (Anchor Bible, 28A; New York: Doubleday, 1985), pp. 1260-67.

catalytic role in the Fourth Gospel, occurring as it does at the outset of Jesus' public activity (2.13-22). On the face of it, too, John would seem to have passed up on the other major incident that might have provided a neat logical segue into the Judean elite's expressed concern about a calamitous Roman backlash—namely, the festival crowd's explicit and enthusiastic acclamation of the Galilean upstart as 'King of Israel' upon his entrance to Jerusalem.[61] Instead, what would appear to be a more politically neutral event—the raising of Lazarus from the dead—is assigned the role of bringing the Judean leadership's anxieties about a Roman military intervention to a head.

On closer examination, however, it appears that their fears are not misplaced. On the contrary, their analysis of the situation proves extremely shrewd. For while the raising of Lazarus might at first glance seem an extremely unlikely pretext for concerns about a Roman retaliation, certain details in the ensuing narrative (see 12.9-11, 17-19)[62] make the rationale plain. 'Everyone' is starting to 'believe in him', and what they are believing, apparently, and not just believing but openly proclaiming, is that he is the long-awaited King of Israel (12.12-13; cf. 1.49; 6.15), certainly a provocation, if not an open invitation, to the Romans to 'come and destroy' the nation and the temple that, more than any other single symbol, publicly epitomizes its identity. 'Everyone', then, is believing that Jesus is what he does—and does not—claim to be, namely, the King of Israel. If they 'let him go on like this', 'everyone will believe' that he is the divinely appointed deliverer destined to wrest the nation back from the Romans, and the Romans will indeed clamp down. But even if the indigenous Judean elite succeed in stopping Jesus by engineering a shameful execution for him, entirely incompatible with claimed messianic status, 'the Romans will come' anyway. The Romans will still come and destroy the temple and the nation—but not as divinely orchestrated punishment for Israel's perceived rejection of its Messiah, as in Mark. It is

61. The other event in the narrative that has the effect of causing the crowds to acclaim Jesus king is yet another one of the 'many signs' 'this man is performing' (11.47), the multiplication of the loaves and fish (6.1-15).

62. 12.9-11 reads: 'When, therefore, the great crowd of the Jews knew that he was there, they came, not only because of Jesus but also to see Lazarus whom he had raised from the dead. So the chief priests determined to put Lazarus to death also, because on account of him many of the Jews went and believed in Jesus'; while 12.17-18 reads: 'The crowd that had been with him when he summoned Lazarus out of the tomb and raised him from the dead thus bore witness. The reason why the crowd went to meet him was that they heard he had performed this sign. The Pharisees therefore said to each other, "Look how it does you no good; see how the world has gone after him!"' (my translations).

supersessionism, not theodicy, that is the primary theological engine wheeled out by John to make sense of the temple's destruction — or so it seems at first. As we are about to discover, the latter engine is secretly housed within the former.

For John, the Jerusalem temple must be destroyed because it is destined to be replaced by the temple of Jesus' body (2.19-22). Jesus himself will be the new temple and thus the new international center for 'the scattered children of God'. But he will also be the sacrificial lamb (cf. 1.29, 36) who by '[dying] for the nation' will render the new temple cult efficacious. The grip of Johannine irony on the unwitting Judean elite is thus a veritable stranglehold in the passage we are considering. If they permit the popular acclaim of the Galilean peasant as Messianic King of Israel to continue unchecked, the Romans will descend with irresistible force to annihilate their holy place and their nation. But if they intervene decisively to squelch that popular acclaim by engineering the Galilean's crucifixion — the Romans will *still* descend with irresistible force, etc., as the gospel's post-war audience is only too well aware, the destruction of the temple being but the consummation of the crucifixion. Either way, responsibility for the temple's obliteration is laid squarely (and unfairly) at their feet. 'Destroy this temple...', Jesus challenges 'the Jews' in 2.19. 'He was speaking of the temple of his body [*tou naou tou sōmatos autou*]', the narrator is quick to add (2.21). But within the starkly simplifying universe of Johannine supersessionism, the injunction 'Destroy this temple...', addressed to 'the Jews', applies to the literal temple as much as to the spiritual temple, and implicitly identifies 'the Jews' as the real agents of that destruction, who bear ultimate responsibility for it. Theodicy is the underside of supersessionism in John.

Johannine irony runs riot, as we have seen, around the theme of the temple. Consequently, the high priest's 'prophecy' in 11.47-52 is anything but straightforward; it is in fact riddled with peculiarities. The ostensible logic of the utterance is plain enough. The Galilean firebrand must be consigned to destruction by the Romans so that the 'nation' (*to ethnos*)[63] may be spared destruction by the Romans. The narrator's labeling of the utterance as prophecy (*eprophēteusen hoti emellen Iēsous apothnēskein...*, 11.51) is designed to signal its truth. But the 'nation', epitomized by its sacred city and 'holy place', *was* eventually destroyed by the Romans, notwithstanding the consignment of Jesus to the Romans by the local Judean leadership. Therefore the prophecy misses its mark.

---

63. Which term I take to refer primarily to the Judean temple-state.

Of course, to construe the prophecy thus is to give it a literal read-ing, whereas the narrator apparently intends it to be taken spiritually: '...he prophesied that Jesus was about to die for the nation, and not for the nation only, but to gather into one the scattered [*dieskorpis-mena*] children of God' (11.51-52). But the antecedent narrative has piled up too much literal freight to admit of instant transformation by a cursory wave of the spiritualizing wand: the chief priests' and Pharisees' warning, 'the Romans will come and destroy our nation', followed by the high priest's counsel, 'it is more expedient for you that one man die for the people than that the entire nation perish', reinforced by the narrator's own 'he prophesied that Jesus was about to die for the nation', leaves only the afterthought-like clause 'and not for the nation only but to gather into one the scattered children of God' to suggest that the high priest might have been saying more than he knew—and to suggest it insufficiently, since the image of dispersal so readily summons up as its primary or literal referent the Jewish Diaspora, Israel without borders, and only secondarily sum-mons up Jewish and/or Gentile Christianity.[64]

This is not to imply, however, that Caiaphas's statement is utterly devoid of theological resonance. Jesus must be punished, must be executed, must be sacrificed so that the populace at large may be spared. The logic is homologous with that of the 'doctrine of atone-ment'. Jesus must die a substitutionary death, according to the high priest. But to propitiate what? *Rome* is Caiaphas's implicit answer, or, if the 'what' be personified as a 'whom', *Caesar*. Substitution, propi-tiation, atonement is here elaborated in a register that is ineluctably physical, not metaphysical. Moreover, this statement is actually the most explicit, and as such the primary, interpretation in the Fourth Gospel of Jesus' death as substitution. The mechanism of substitu-tion, propitiation, atonement that comes to explicit expression in this passage is the same mechanism that implicitly drives Jn 1.29, 'Behold the Lamb of God who takes away the sin of the world!' (cf. 1.36), as well as the yet more subtle allusions to the substitutionary nature of Jesus' death in 19.14, 29, 36.[65]

---

64. As Keener notes (*The Gospel of John*, II, p. 857 n. 204), many commentators hold that Gentile Christians only are in view here, while others argue that both Jewish and Gentile Christians are envisioned.

65. For a recent discussion of Jesus' substitutionary death in John, see Herman C. Waetjen, *The Gospel of the Beloved Disciple: A Work in Two Editions* (New York: T. & T. Clark International, 2005), pp. 284-85.

Yet even if the basic mechanism is the same, it may be objected that the entity being placated is different in each instance: God on the one hand, Caesar on the other. What the high priest's prophecy reveals, however (so that he does after all say more than he knows), is a complicating factor within the doctrine of atonement, at least in its relatively undeveloped Johannine form, that ordinarily goes unremarked. It is only by appeasing Caesar that God can be appeased; or to put it another way, the propitiation of Caesar is the necessary precondition for the propitiation of God in the Fourth Gospel — which is simply to say in turn that the torture and execution of Jesus are performed in the symbolic presence of Caesar in the first instance, as even a cursory reading of the Johannine passion narrative reveals (see especially 19.12, 15).

But the degree of emphasis put on Caesar's placation throughout the trial narrative (in which the only real question at issue is whether or not Jesus is to be considered a threat to Caesar's authority) is such as to thrust the corresponding theme of God's placation exclusively into the realm of subtle allusion — or, to switch to a different discursive register, into the realm of the repressed. Crushed under the ponderous weight accorded to the theme of being in a right relationship to Caesar vs. not being in a right relationship to him, the theme of divine propitiation only finds expression through oblique means throughout the Roman trial and execution narrative. Essentially this dynamic is the familiar psychoanalytic one. Unconscious truth — here equivalent to Johannine theological truth — can only come to displaced expression in the seams and secret pockets of conscious discourse and action — here the arrest, trial, torture, and execution of the protagonist. And the role of the unconscious material in this narrative is, as we might expect, subversive in relation to the conscious or manifest material. In the Johannine passion narrative, the implicit, concealed, or unconscious material subverts the explicit, ostensive, or conscious material by suggesting that the propitiation of Caesar is only the *apparent* issue in Jesus' trial, torture, and execution. The 'real' issue is the propitiation of that other deity, the Jewish one — a theme that carries us even deeper into psychoanalytic territory, since the God–Jesus relationship in the Fourth Gospel is relentlessly framed as a Father–Son relationship.[66]

Implicit, too, in this conscious–unconscious dynamic is the subversion of one empire by another empire — so that Pilate's concern on behalf of Caesar is not, after all, misplaced. In the cracks and fissures

66. But that will have to await another essay.

of the Roman imperial order, the Fourth Gospel tells us, the Empire of God takes root. To be sure, God's Empire (*hē basileia tou theou*) is far less an explicit theme in the Fourth Gospel than in the Synoptic Gospels; but that does not mean that it is any less present or potent. For, ultimately, the Johannine resistance to Roman colonization might be said to be an alternative program of colonization yet more ambitious than the Roman: the annexation of the world by non-military means.

The conquest, however, begins at home. For it is in this gospel, more than any other, that Jesus is routinely represented as usurping and absorbing Jewish identity markers and sacred spaces.[67] Jesus' incessant march up and down the Holy Land in the Fourth Gospel is, in effect, a reconquest of the Holy Land (etymologically, after all, Jesus is Joshua). Roman expulsion of the Jewish populace from its sacred city, following the Bar Kochba revolt (132–35 CE), coupled with the Roman renaming of the city as Aelia Capitolina, all anticipated by Rome's earlier destruction of temple and city (70 CE), might be said to be the material corollaries of Jesus' systematic spiritual dispossession of Judaism in the Fourth Gospel. When Christianity eventually *becomes* Rome in the fourth century, the circle of dispossession is completed, both spiritually and materially. Before long, Rome and Jerusalem have become the twin spiritual, centers of imperial Christianity, while the displaced Jews, branded with the mark of Cain, continue to wander the earth homeless.

The Romans Will Come…on the Clouds of Heaven

The Son of Man will come (*erchomai*) in clouds, says Mark (13.26; 14.62; cf. 8.38). The Romans will come (*erchomai*), says John (11.48). How are these two comings related? The defining characteristic of both ancient Jewish and early Christian apocalyptic eschatology, arguably, is the concept of an imminent, public, unambiguous, and climactic divine irruption on the stage of human history. The Fourth Gospel, however, in contrast to the Synoptic Gospels, famously lacks an explicit parousia scenario, the central element of the Christian apocalyptic drama.[68] But this absence has profound implications for

67. Cf. Adele Reinhartz, 'The Colonizer as Colonized: Intertextual Dialogue Between the Gospel of John and Canadian Identity', in Dube and Staley (eds.), *John and Postcolonialism*, pp. 170-92 (182).

68. At the most, Jn 5.28-29, together with 6.39-40, 44, 54 and 12.48, might be read as implicit anticipations of an undramatized parousia. For discussion of the issue, see, for example, Herman N. Ridderbos, *The Gospel according to John: A Theological Commentary* (trans. John Vriend; Grand Rapids, MI: Eerdmans, 1997),

the presence of Rome in the Fourth Gospel. In the absence of a dramatized parousia, Rome can be said to assume apocalyptic agency in this gospel, lending uncanny veracity to the climactic confession of 'the Jews' in the Roman trial scene, 'We have no king/emperor but Caesar [*ouk echomen basilea ei mē Kaisara*]' (19.15). It is Caesar rather than God — or, rather, Caesar *as* God — whose potential (and potentially catastrophic) intervention assumes apocalyptic proportions in the Fourth Gospel: 'the Romans will come and destroy both our holy place and our nation' (11.48).

The Johannine Jesus himself is in denial of this uncomfortable fact, as is the implied author, his ventriloquist. 'You would have no power over me unless it had been given you from above', Jesus tells Pilate, gesturing heavenward; 'therefore the one who handed me over to you is guilty of a greater sin' (19.11). This assertion falls prey, however, to its own inherent ambiguity: the prefect would also have no power over the accused if it had not been bestowed on him by the emperor. And the statement is further fractured by a second instability: its first clause implicitly ascribes to the divine Judge responsibility for the death-torture of his Son, while the second clause explicitly — and awkwardly — attempts to displace that responsibility onto others (Judas or the Judean religious leadership, depending on how one reads).[69] The result is a curiously weak assertion.

Thomas's celebrated acclamation of the risen Jesus similarly accords covert homage to the Roman Emperor. Luminous artistic depictions of the risen Lord, from the ancient Church all the way down to the closing moments of *The Passion of the Christ*, have no basis in the Fourth Gospel, which ascribes only three traits to his resurrected body: it can be mistaken for that of a person on the lower rungs of the social ladder, a slave or common laborer ('Supposing him to be the gardener [*ho kēpouros*]...', 20.14-15; cf. 21.4); incongruent with the first trait, it can also pass through locked doors (20.26); and entirely congruent with the first trait, it bears the scars of brutal physical maltreatment ('Unless I...place my finger in the mark of the nails, and place my hand in his side...', 20.25; cf. 20.20, 27).

Of this eternally scarred body, Jennifer Glancy has remarked: 'Thomas's exclamation, "My Lord and my God!", ascribes authority

---

p. 199; Raymond E. Brown and Francis J. Moloney, *An Introduction to the Gospel of John* (New York: Doubleday, 2003), p. 241.

69. Early Brown attempts to grapple with the 'difficult logic' of the second clause (*The Gospel according to John XIII–XXI* [Anchor Bible, 29A; New York: Doubleday, 1970], p. 879, his expression), but most subsequent commentators — including later Brown (*Death of the Messiah*, I, p. 842) — gloss over it.

and sovereignty not to the one who imposes the mark but to the marked man'.[70] I both agree and disagree with this statement. John has cunningly, and catachrestically, adopted and adapted an acclamation employed in Roman imperial court ceremonial, reapplying it to the risen Jesus.[71] The acclamation thus glistens with freshly applied meaning, but the original meaning still seeps through the palimpsest. Thomas's exclamation pays awed homage to the ambiguous figure standing before him whose divine character has enabled him to transcend the ritual degradation of his body. But it simultaneously pays homage to the absent, yet present, figure of the Roman Emperor whose own divine authority, reaching effortlessly across the Mediterranean, has caused his peasant subject's body to be inscribed eternally, and hence indelibly, with the marks of a slave. Once again the Johannine text concedes inadvertently through subtle ambiguities in its narrative argumentation that Caesar's immeasurable bulk, center and anchor of the world out of which the text emerges, cannot simply be wafted away with a casual wave of the theological wand. In its furtive acknowledgement of this fundamental, unyielding reality, Johannine theology shows itself to be surreptitiously intermeshed with Roman imperial ideology, specifically that of the imperial cult, that overt acknowledgment of what the Fourth Gospel covertly concedes, namely, the irreducible fact of Caesar's omnipotence[72] — all of which brings us back to the lack of apocalyptic eschatology in the Fourth Gospel and the manner in which Rome automatically rushes

70. Glancy, 'Torture', p. 134.

71. As argued in particular by Cassidy, *John's Gospel in New Perspective*, pp. 13-16, 55, with reference to the *Dominus et Deus Noster* ('Our Lord and God') title applied to Domitian, according to Suetonius, *Domitian* 15.2; Martial *Epigrams* 5.8; 7.34; 8.2; 9.66; 10.72; Dio Chrysostom, *Discourses* 45.1; and Dio Cassius, *Roman History* 67.4.7; 67.13.4. (Pliny the Younger, *Panegyric on Trajan* 2.33.4; 78.2; and Aurelius Victor, *On the Caesars* 11.2 might also be added to Cassidy's list of sources.) Brian W. Jones, for his part, argues compellingly that while it is unlikely that Domitian himself demanded the title, as Suetonius in particular claims he did ('With...arrogance he began as follows in issuing a circular letter in the name of his procurators, "Our Lord and God bids that this be done"'), it was employed nonetheless by sycophants in his court (*The Emperor Domitian* [New York: Routledge, 1992], pp. 108-109). Craig R. Koester identifies 'savior of the world' (*ho sōtēr tou kosmou*) in Jn 4.42 as a further title used of the Roman Emperor, and ponders its implications for the larger narrative: '"The Savior of the World" (John 4.42)', *Journal of Biblical Literature* 109 (1990), pp. 665-80. Cassidy touches more briefly on 4.42 in *John's Gospel in New Perspective*, pp. 34-35. Dube memorably remarks on this verse, 'The Johannine Jesus now emerges fully clothed in the emperor's titles' ('Reading for Decolonization', p. 66).

72. Further on the significance of the imperial cult, see pp. 101-105 below.

in to fill the theological vacuum engendered by that lack. For it is not only nature that abhors a vacuum, seemingly; the supernatural abhors it as well.

In the Fourth Gospel, no end to Caesar's reign is prophesied or threatened, whether explicitly as in Revelation or implicitly as in the Synoptic apocalypses. Unlike those texts, the Fourth Gospel does not depict the Roman Empire as destined to be destroyed or replaced by the new Christian Empire from without, commencing with the public manifestation of the glorified Son of Man to friend and foe alike ('Behold, he is coming with the clouds, and every eye will see him...' –Rev. 1.7). Instead, by implication, the Fourth Gospel depicts the Roman Empire as destined to be transformed by Christianity from within. This assertion depends on a certain assumption, namely, that Rome can reasonably be construed as a major, if unspecified, component of 'the world' (*ho kosmos*) to which the gospel incessantly refers: if 'the world' does not contain Rome — is not, indeed, permeated by Roman power, and for all intents and purposes coextensive with it — then what weight, freight, or purchase could the term possibly have in John's own world?[73] If 'the world' is primarily the Roman world,[74] then the negative depiction of 'the world' in the Fourth Gospel — as plunged in darkness (8.12; 9.5; cf. 12.35; 1.5), given over to evil works (7.7), ignorant of the only true God (17.25; cf. 14.17; 17.3), ruled by Satan (12.31; 14.30; 16.11), hostile to Jesus and those who believe in him (7.7; 15.18-25; 17.14; cf. 16.20) — functions as a veiled or implicit denunciation of the Roman Empire.

At the same time, however, 'the world' is also explicitly represented in the Fourth Gospel as the object of God's extravagant love (3.16), Jesus' salvific self-sacrifice (1.29; 3.17; 12.47), and the disciples' future witness and mission (14.31; 16.8; 17.21, 23; cf. 4.35-42), issuing, incrementally but inexorably, in the annexation and transformation of 'the world' — its 'un-worlding', if you will. 'And I, when I am lifted up from the earth', the gospel's paradoxical protagonist declares, anticipating his imperial enthronement on the colonial cross, 'will draw all people to myself [*pantas helkusō pros hemauton*]' (12.32) — given enough time, that is. But no other gospel writer (not even Luke)

73. I thus find Adele Reinhartz's otherwise excellent analysis of John's relations to Rome too tentative on this point. She writes: 'More elusive is the question of whether the "world" as used in this Gospel includes a reference to the Roman empire' ('The Colonizer as Colonized', p. 179).

74. The Jewish, and, most importantly, Judean world being the major subset of that Roman world in the narrative world of this gospel (see, for example, 7.3-4; 12.19; 18.20).

allows Jesus' followers quite as much time to un-world 'the world', to appropriate and colonize it,[75] because no other Jesus is in less of a hurry to return.

What Revelation gets stunningly wrong, therefore, John gets uncannily right. What Revelation is entirely incapable of imagining or foreseeing is that Rome will eventually become Christianity and Christianity will eventually become Rome. But that is precisely what the Fourth Gospel seems to intuit, against all the odds. In tacitly allowing Rome to survive and thrive into the indefinite future, the Fourth Gospel shows itself to be the charter document of Constantinian Christianity not just in terms of its Christology, which is how it is normally seen, but also in terms of its political theology.

Yet again, however, this theology is neither stable nor self-consistent. For it is also the product of a narrative that contains, embedded within in, the most trenchant critique of Roman imperialism of any of the canonical gospels, not only in its implicit inclusion of Rome in a 'world' denounced in uncompromising terms, but also in its placement of its protagonist's judicial torture as the central term in the chiastic structure of its Roman trial narrative, discussed earlier, and the searing critique of the fundamental machinations of the *imperium Romanum* that that placement entails. Simultaneously and contradictorily, meanwhile, John's rejection of a death-sentence verdict for Rome—a sentence that would ordinarily be carried out through the parousia scenario integral both to the Synoptic tradition and ancient Christian apocalyptic more generally—makes it the gospel of the imperial status quo. The assessment with which this chapter began will thus serve also to end it: John is at once the most—and the least—political of the canonical gospels.

75. As such, this un-worlding is also a 'worlding'—Gayatri Spivak's term for the process whereby a colonizing agent assimilates a subject people and territory to his own worldview through systemic acts of epistemic violence: renaming, remapping, etc. (see, e.g., Spivak, *The Post-Colonial Critic: Interviews, Strategies, Dialogues* [ed. Sarah Harasym; New York and London: Routledge, 1990], pp. 1, 129; Spivak, *A Critique of Postcolonial Reason: Toward a History of the Vanishing Present* [Cambridge, MA: Harvard University Press, 1999], pp. 211-13). The all-encompassing Johannine conceptual vocabulary likewise performs a worlding of non-Johannine reality—or 'the world', to give it its Johannine appellation.

PART II

4

'AND THE GOSPEL MUST FIRST BE PUBLISHED AMONG ALL NATIONS': THE POSTCOLONIAL, THE POSTMODERN, AND THE EVANGELICAL

Positioning Postcolonialism

Driven by the subaltern history of the margins of modernity — rather than by the failures of logocentrism — I have tried, in some small measure, to revise the known, to rename the postmodern from the position of the postcolonial.

— Homi Bhabha[1]

Postcolonialism and postmodernism: one would be hard pressed by now to intone two more overdetermined, and overinflated, critical terms.[2] Is the 'post' in postcolonialism the same as the 'post' in

---

1.   Homi K. Bhabha, 'The Postcolonial and the Postmodern: The Question of Agency', in his *The Location of Culture* (London and New York: Routledge, 1994), pp. 171-97 (175).

2.   The term 'postcolonialism', for instance, 'designates too many things, all at once', as Aijaz Ahmad complains. 'It is said to refer, first, to conditions that are said to prevail in the former colonies, such as India. But the same term is also made to refer to a *global* condition of the relations between the West and the Rest... — so that "postcoloniality" becomes a "post" not only of colonialism but also of an indeterminate larger thing. At the same time, the term "postcolonial" also comes to us as the name of a *discourse* about the condition of "postcoloniality,"' and a discourse that presumes a 'prior consent to theoretical postmodernity', what is more. 'Between postcoloniality as it exists in a former colony like India, and postcoloniality as the condition of discourse practised by such critics as Homi Bhabha', he concludes sardonically, 'there would appear to be a very considerable gap' (Aijaz Ahmad, 'The Politics of Literary Postcoloniality', in Padmini Mongia [ed.], *Postcolonial Theory: A Reader* [London: Arnold, 1996], pp. 276-93 [283, his emphasis]). Postcolonialism's other discontents include Robert Young, who, although poles apart from Ahmad in other ways, proposes jettisoning the term 'postcolonialism' altogether and replacing it with 'tricontinentalism' (*Postcolonialism: An Historical Introduction* [Oxford: Blackwell, 2001], p. 57).

postmodernism,[3] so that the two terms are merely alternative names for the same phenomenon? At first glance, perhaps, it might appear that a case could be made for this position, particularly if 'postmodernism', or, better for our purposes, 'postmodernity', is understood as that which has replaced or displaced 'modernity' (to resort for the moment to a rather crude chrono-logic), the latter being understood in turn as the combined and cumulative product of the European Reformation, scientific revolution, and Enlightenment — together with the corollary colonization of the non-European world. Colonial exploitation, not least the slave trade, has often been said to have enabled the economies of early (and not so early) modern Europe in the material realm; while in the psychic realm, the non-European world, conceived as quintessentially 'superstitious' and 'primitive', served conveniently as the constitutive Other for Europe's dominant image of itself as quintessentially 'rational' and 'civilized'.[4] But if modernity is to be regarded as in no small part an effect of European colonialism, might not postmodernity and postcolonialism be regarded in consequence, not only as natural allies, but even as virtual synonyms?

To argue thus, however, would be to indulge in an over-benign reduction of the concept of postmodernity, or, to revert to the more

3.   Cf. Kwame Anthony Appiah, 'Is the Post- in Postmodernism the Post- in Postcolonialism?', *Critical Inquiry* 17 (1991), pp. 336-57. Appiah's voice is but one in a cacophonous chorus that has addressed this perplexing relationship — and arrived at a range of incommensurate conclusions. See, in addition, Helen Tiffin, 'Post-Colonialism, Post-Modernism and the Rehabilitation of Post-Colonial History', *Journal of Commonwealth Literature* 23 (1988), pp. 169-81; Ian Adam and Helen Tiffin (eds.), *Past the Last Post: Theorizing Post-Colonialism and Post-Modernism* (Hemel Hampstead: Harvester Wheatsheaf, 1989); Aron P. Mukherjee, 'Whose Post-Colonialism and Whose Postmodernism?', *World Literature Writers in English* 30.2 (1991), pp. 1-9; Bill Ashcroft, Gareth Griffiths and Helen Tiffin, *The Post-Colonial Studies Reader* (London and New York: Routledge, 1995), Part IV ('Postmodernism and Postcolonialism'); Bhabha, 'The Postcolonial and the Postmodern'; Bhabha, 'Postmodernism/Postcolonialism', in Robert S. Nelson and Richard Shiff (eds.), *Critical Terms for Art History* (Chicago: University of Chicago Press, 1996), pp. 307-22; Bart Moore-Gilbert, *Postcolonial Theory: Contexts, Practices, Politics* (London: Verso, 1997), pp. 121-30; Ming Xie, 'The Postmodern as the Postcolonial: Recognizing Chinese Modernity', *Ariel* 28 (1997), pp. 11-32; Ato Quayson, 'Postcolonialism and Postmodernism', in Henry Schwarz and Sangeeta Ray (eds.), *A Companion to Postcolonial Studies* (Blackwell Companions in Cultural Studies; Oxford: Blackwell, 2000), pp. 87-111. Also pertinent is David Chioni Moore, 'Is the Post- in Postcolonial the Post- in Post-Soviet? Toward a Global Postcolonial Critique', in Gaurav Desai and Supriya Nair (eds.), *Postcolonialisms: An Anthology of Cultural Theory and Criticism* (New Brunswick, NJ: Rutgers University Press, 2005), pp. 514-38.

4.   Cf. Moore-Gilbert, *Postcolonial Theory*, p. 123.

common term, postmodernism.[5] As the latter term is now frequently used, it names much more than an anti-hegemonic reaction to or repudiation of the world-annexing impulses of European modernity. In its more bloated forms, indeed, postmodernism is a code word for the cultural logic of late capitalism,[6] whose signal features include mass culture, mass media, multinational corporations, and information technology — although, seen from the 'underside', as it were, this same set of features appear as the dissolution of traditional societies, asymmetrical systems of economic exchange, crippling national debt, limited access to technology, and so on.

Postmodernism, thus distended, however, is, if anything, a synonym not for *post*colonialism so much as for *neo*colonialism. The latter term, which is less evocative, perhaps, of a state 'beyond' colonialism than of the West's continued domination of the Rest,[7] better names the socio-economic and socio-political constraints within which the majority of the world's population conducts its daily affairs. I am reminded of a now misplaced magazine article that tells of a certain African village's recent attempts to honor the parousia of the CEO of Microsoft Corporation, a visitation preceded by a gift to the village of a state-of-the-art PC. Bill Gates arrived with his entourage to discover that the computer had been hooked up to the sole electrical outlet in the village, thereby becoming a shrine to the *deus absconditus* of neo-colonialism, and a poignant symbol of the village's simultaneous inclusion in and exclusion from the benefits of global capitalism — or of 'postmodernism', in the distended sense. Far from being a synonym for 'postcolonialism', indeed, 'postmodernism', as neocolonialism, might instead be the primary phenomenon presently in need of postcolonial critique.

And yet there can be no clean subject-object separation of postcolonialism and postmodernism either, if for no other reason than that a third term regularly mediates between them in such a way as to muddy any clear distinction between them. That term is 'poststructuralism'.[8] In the minds of most who ponder such matters,

5.   Not that these two terms are invariably synonymous either (see Stephen D. Moore, 'The "Post"-age Stamp: Does It Stick? Biblical Studies and the Postmodernism Debate', *Journal of the American Academy of Religion* 57 [1989], pp. 543-59, esp. pp. 544-51), but it will not be necessary to tease them apart again here.

6.   Cf. Fredric Jameson, *Postmodernism, or, the Cultural Logic of Late Capitalism* (Durham, NC: Duke University Press, 1991).

7.   Cf. Kwame Nkrumah, *Neo-Colonialism: The Last Stage of Imperialism* (London: Heinemann, 1965); Young, *Postcolonialism*, pp. 44-56.

8.   A term that readily evokes a congeries of interrelated topoi: the systematic dismantling of 'metaphysical' concepts (origin, essence, identity, transcendence,

poststructuralism (epitomized by, although by no means confined to, Derridean deconstruction) is quintessential academic postmodernism – postmodernism *as* academic discourse. And postcolonial theory – the most visible manifestation of contemporary postcolonial studies, itself epitomized by the names of Edward Said, Gayatri Chakravorty Spivak, and Homi Bhabha, as noted in Chapter 1 – is, for the most part, poststructuralist through and through. Said's *Orientalism*, for instance, generally regarded as the charter document of postcolonial theory, makes strategic use of the analytic categories of Michel Foucault (but also those of Antonio Gramsci) to excavate the West's multi-discursive construction of the 'Orient'[9] – although Said's dealings with Foucault, never entirely uncritical, were subsequently marked with increasing caution. Spivak's embrace of poststructuralist thought, primarily that of Jacques Derrida, has been less equivocal (the epithet 'feminist Marxist deconstructivist' memorably bestowed upon her by Colin McCabe in the foreword to *In Other Worlds* seems apt,[10] despite her own caginess about being labeled), and the same is true of Bhabha, who is also heavily indebted to Derrida, as we shall see, but also to Jacques Lacan, and, to a lesser degree, to Foucault, Roland Barthes, Julia Kristeva, and even Louis Althusser (to add a 'structuralist' name to the familiar 'poststructuralist' litany), as well as to Mikhail Bakhtin.[11]

etc.) and hierarchical oppositions (presence/absence, primary/secondary, central/marginal, white/non-white, masculine/feminine, heterosexual/homosexual, etc.); the meticulous analysis of the ways in which literary, critical, and philosophical arguments are invariably destabilized by the figures and tropes that they necessarily employ; the exposure of the exclusions, omissions, and systemic blind-spots that enable texts, and societies, to function; the unearthing of the constructedness of the most solid-seeming features of our cultural landscapes ('man', the body, insanity, gender, sexuality, race/ethnicity, etc.); the investigation of the ineluctable place of power in the fabric(ation) of truth and knowledge; the exploration of the radical internal heteronomy allegedly fissuring every human subject; the examination of the ways in which every text, independently of the conscious intentionality of any author, traverses countless other texts, ceaselessly recycling and rewriting them; and so on. See further Stephen D. Moore, *Poststructuralism and the New Testament: Derrida and Foucault at the Foot of the Cross* (Minneapolis: Fortress Press, 1994).

9.   Edward W. Said, *Orientalism* (New York: Vintage Books, 1978).

10.   Gayatri Chakravorty Spivak, *In Other Worlds: Essays in Cultural Politics* (London and New York: Methuen, 1987), p. ix.

11.   Excellent (if exacting) individual chapters on Said, Spivak, and Bhabha can be found in Robert J.C. Young, *White Mythologies: Writing History and the West* (London and New York: Routledge, 1990); Peter Childs and Patrick Williams, *An Introduction to Post-Colonial Theory* (London and New York: Prentice Hall/

Postcolonial theory (or colonial discourse analysis, to restore its original name to it) has comfortably assumed its appointed place (all *too* comfortably, some would argue — more on this below) within the Anglo-American academy alongside New Historicism, third-wave feminism, queer theory, cultural studies, and other theory-savvy

Harvester Wheatsheaf, 1997); and Moore-Gilbert, *Postcolonial Theory*. Shorter introductions to all three can be found in John C. Hawley, *Encyclopedia of Postcolonial Studies* (Westport, CT: Greenwood Press, 2001). Moore-Gilbert has subsequently had a second shot at Spivak and Bhabha ('Spivak and Bhabha', in Schwarz and Ray [eds.], *A Companion to Postcolonial Studies*, pp. 451-66), while Young has returned to Said (*Postcolonialism*, pp. 383-94). Full length books on Said, Spivak, or Bhabha include Bill Ashcroft, *Edward Said* (Routledge Critical Thinkers; London and New York: Routledge, 2001); Abdirahman A. Hussein, *Edward Said: Criticism and Society* (London: Verso, 2002); Mustapha Marrouchi, *Edward Said at the Limits* (Albany: State University of New York Press, 2004); Stephen Morton, *Gayatri Chakravorty Spivak* (Routledge Critical Thinkers; London and New York: Routledge, 2002); Mark Sanders, *Gayatri Chakravorty Spivak: Live Theory* (New York: Continuum, 2006); and David Huddart, *Homi K. Bhabha* (Routledge Critical Thinkers Series; London and New York: Routledge, 2006). Said has been an important interlocutor for a handful of biblical scholars, notably R.S. Sugirtharajah, *Asian Biblical Hermeneutics and Postcolonialism: Contesting the Interpretations* (Maryknoll, NY: Orbis Books; Sheffield: Sheffield Academic Press, 1998); Steven J. Friesen, *Imperial Cults and the Apocalypse of John: Reading Revelation in the Ruins* (Oxford: Oxford University Press, 2001); Christopher A. Frilingos, *Spectacles of Empire: Monsters, Martyrs, and the Book of Revelation* (Divinations: Rereading Late Ancient Religion; Philadelphia: University of Pennsylvania Press, 2004); and Yong-Sung Ahn, *The Reign of God and Rome in Luke's Passion Narrative: An East Asian Global Perspective* (Biblical Interpretation Series, 80; Leiden: Brill, 2006). For attempts at biblical exegesis in a Bhabhan mode, see Erin Runions, *Changing Subjects: Gender, Nation and Future in Micah* (Playing the Texts, 7; Sheffield: Sheffield Academic Press, 2002); Eric Thurman, 'Looking for a Few Good Men: Mark and Masculinity', in Stephen D. Moore and Janice Capel Anderson (eds.), *New Testament Masculinities* (Semeia Studies, 45; Atlanta, Ga.: Society of Biblical Literature, 2003), pp. 137-62. See also Jin Hee Han, 'Homi Bhabha and the Mixed Blessing of Hybridity in Biblical Hermeneutics', *The Bible and Critical Theory* 1.4 (2005), http://publications.epress.monash.edu/loi/bc. Bhabha plays a more effaced, although by no means insignificant, role in Mark G. Brett, *Genesis: Procreation and the Politics of Identity* (London and New York: Routledge, 2000); Tat-siong Benny Liew, *Politics of Parousia: Reading Mark Inter(con)textually* (Biblical Interpretation Series, 42; Leiden: Brill, 1999); Simon Samuel, 'The Beginning of Mark: A Colonial/Postcolonial Conundrum', *Biblical Interpretation* 10 (2002), pp. 405-19; and Ahn, *The Reign of God and Rome*. I know of only one sustained biblical-critical engagement with Spivak's work, namely, Laura E. Donaldson's 'Gospel Hauntings: The Postcolonial Demons of New Testament Criticism', in Stephen D. Moore and Fernando F. Segovia (eds.), *Postcolonial Biblical Criticism: Interdisciplinary Intersections* (The Bible and Postcolonialism, 8; New York: T. & T. Clark International, 2005), pp. 97-114.

critical movements that all, to a greater or lesser degree, bring critical sensibilities forged in the crucible of an often generic poststructuralism to bear upon assorted 'material' domains (history, not least the colonial variety; gender; sex and sexuality; popular culture), frequently in explicit reaction to the first, neo-formalist, putatively apolitical phase of French poststructuralism's appropriation in the Anglophone academy. Said's *Orientalism*, in particular, can be regarded as a crucial catalyst in the politicization, not just of Anglo-American poststructuralism, but of the Anglo-American literary academy more generally,[12] a transformation that began in earnest in the early 1980s and has been unrelenting ever since.

Not surprisingly, perhaps, the spectacle of poststructuralism's systematic politicization, especially within the US academy, has itself elicited political critique, none more scathing, perhaps, than that of Aijaz Ahmad,[13] whose primary target happens to be postcolonial theory, the bull's-eye on the target being Edward Said. According to Ahmad (and the summary of his extended arguments that follows is a partial and rather freely paraphrastic one), postcolonial theory replicates troublingly within the Western academy the international division of labor characteristic of global capitalism, whereby raw materials generated in the Third World (in this case, the archival products of colonialism: administrative records, missionary tracts, traces of indigenous voices, and so on) are exported to the First World, where they are turned into refined or luxury products by a privileged intelligentsia (themselves thoroughly insulated from the harsh material realities of Third World existence) for consumption by a metropolitan elite of fellow-scholars and graduate students, which in fact constitutes their primary audience, all direct engagement with the extra-academic world, least of all the working class or underclass, even within the US itself, being foreclosed almost as a matter of course.

Symptomatic of the complicity of postcolonial theory with late capitalist ideology, presumably (to echo Ahmad further, but also to extrapolate from him), would be the fact that some of the wealthiest Western universities, ornate pillars of the social and political establishment, reserve some of their most coveted and most lucrative

12. Also worth noting in this regard is Said's once influential article, 'The Problem of Textuality: Two Exemplary Positions', *Critical Inquiry* 4 (1978), pp. 673-714 (reprinted in revised form in Said's *The World, the Text, and the Critic* [Cambridge, MA: Harvard University Press, 1983], pp. 178-225), which pitted a rhetorically politicized Foucault against a depoliticized Derrida.

13. Aijaz Ahmad, *In Theory: Classes, Nations, Literatures* (London: Verso, 1992).

positions for 'politicized' theorist-critics, not least leading postcolonial theorist-critics: Spivak holds a prestigious chair at Columbia, as
did Said until his recent death, while Bhabha holds a no less prestigious one at Harvard (having ascended there in incremental stages by
way of the University of Sussex and the University of Chicago, his
stock, like that of Spivak, formerly of the University of Pittsburgh,
inexorably rising with that of postcolonial studies). Such allegations,
while crude, can have a deep impact nonetheless. A few semesters
ago, to recite a personal example, an Argentinian student in one of my
courses read aloud, and in shocked tones, an excerpt from Ahmad's
blistering broadside at the outset of a class discussion of postcolonial
theory, after which many members of the class seemed to find it all
but impossible to take the topic seriously.

Rajeswari Sunder Rajan, writing in *Critical Inquiry*, has attempted
to respond on behalf of the accused (although the accusations he is
countering are not those of Ahmad per se so much as the related ones
of Arif Dirlik).[14] 'The operation of global capitalism as cause', note
Rajan, 'is so pervasive that it is only too easy to establish that intellectuals in particular (and of every persuasion) are co-opted within
its system'.[15] He goes on to suggest that what would be of significantly more interest would be 'the identification of criticism or critics
who could be considered exempt from the embrace of capitalism's
reward system'.[16] Rajan doesn't altogether succeed, however, in
deflecting Dirlik's (or Ahmad's) accusations; for there are rewards
and rewards, and the rewards attaching to an endowed chair at Harvard or Columbia are one thing, while those attaching to, say, a position at an inner-city community college are another altogether (to
remain for now within the US, although the renumeration for such a
position, even at entry level, would far exceed, even in real terms, that
for a senior position at, say, the University of Havana, to cull but one
example from a great many possible ones). But the argument now
threatens to undercut itself, for faculty at community colleges and
other institutions at the base of the US pyramid of higher learning
typically lack the institutional motivation and support to engage in
research and publication, so that the only First World postcolonial
intellectuals whose theoretical positions would, in accordance with

14. Arif Dirlik, 'The Postcolonial Aura: Third World Criticism in an Age of
Global Capitalism', *Critical Inquiry* 20 (1994), pp. 328-56.

15. Rajeswari Sunder Rajan, 'The Third World Academic in Other Places; or,
the Postcolonial Intellectual Revisited', *Critical Inquiry* 23 (1997), pp. 596-616
(597).

16. Rajan, 'The Third World Academic', p. 597.

the implicit canons advanced by Ahmad and Dirlik, be fully 'authen-
ticated' by their institutional locations would be those whose voices
would be altogether absent from published academic debate – unlike
those of Ahmad and Dirlik themselves.

What *is* highly instructive, nonetheless (and both Ahmad and
Dirlik serve to remind us forcibly of it), is how the US can brazenly
lavish its most exalted academic honors upon the very intellectual
class that tends to be most critical both of its domestic arrangements
and international operations, seemingly in the sure and certain
knowledge that the pronouncements of such intellectuals, once they
exit the academic sphere, will plummet silently into a bottomless well
of public indifference (unlike those of the Dixie Chicks, say, whose
moderate interrogation of Operation Iraqi Freedom raised a storm of
public reaction).[17] 'I always counsel people against the decision to go

17. The successful Texas country group's lead singer Natalie Maines
announced in a concert in London in March 2003 that she was 'ashamed the
president of the United States is from Texas', after which country stations across
the US, in response to calls from irate listeners, began to pull the Dixie Chicks'
songs from their playlists. Postcolonial theory, for its part, did succeed the same
year in making at least one splash in the extra-academic sphere in a hearing on
Capitol Hill that bizarrely turned into a seminar on postcolonial theory. As
Gaurav Desai and Supriya Nair tell it, '[o]n June 10, 2003…a U.S. Congressional
Subcommittee on Select Education met to discuss "International Programs in
Higher Education and Questions of Bias." Ostensibly a routine evaluation con-
ducted before the reauthorization of the next cycle of funding of Title VI in the
Higher Education Act, the proceedings were marked by the testimony of Stanley
Kurtz, a research fellow at the Hoover Institution and contributing editor of the
National Review Online. Kurtz…alleged that area studies programs funded by
Title VI monies were fundamentally anti-American in orientation and critical of
American foreign policy. This was, he asserted, in no small part a result of the
dominance of postcolonial scholarship in the academy. "The ruling intellectual
paradigm in academic area studies", Kurtz testified, "is called 'post-colonial
theory'. Post-colonial theory was founded by Edward Said. Said is famous for
equating professors who support American foreign policy with the 19th-century
European intellectuals who propped up racist colonial empires. The core premise
of post-colonial theory is that it is immoral for a scholar to put his knowledge of
foreign languages and cultures at the service of American power"' ('Introduction', in Desai and Nair [eds.], *Postcolonialisms*, p. 7). The ensuing debate included
the following statement from Congressman Timothy Ryan: 'I think that the fact
that our federal money is going to teach…post-colonial theory, I think [*sic*],
speaks volumes about what kind of country we live in and what we stand for,
that that would even be an option' ('Introduction', p. 9, quoting throughout from
a congressional document accessible at http://edworkforce.house.gov/hearings
/108th/sed/sedhearings.htm). Desai and Nair conclude: 'The rather muddled
formulation [of Congressman Ryan] rests on the by now numbingly familiar
apotheosis of democratic debate in this country but perhaps more complacently

into the academy because they hope to be effective beyond it', literary theorist Stanley Fish announced at a much publicized moratorium on 'theory' staged at the University of Chicago in April 2003.[18] For Aijaz Ahmad, as we noted earlier, Edward Said epitomizes theory's scandalous shortcomings. Yet it is precisely Said who might be said to constitute the outstanding contemporary exception to Fish's cynical rule: Until his premature death in 2003 from leukemia, Said was a leading US academic intellectual whose outspoken (and theory-honed) views on Israeli–Palestinian relations in particular, expressed in numerous newspaper and magazine articles and radio and television interviews, and anchored in years of active service on the Palestinian National Council, made him a familiar and formidable name to an indeterminate but surely sizeable international public, many or most of whom had never heard of postcolonial studies.

And what of Homi Bhabha — interestingly enough, the only one of the more than two dozen academic luminaries assembled around the table at the Chicago colloquium on theory's alleged bankruptcy to venture a defense of theory's political efficacy?[19] What I myself have encountered repeatedly in recent years, as have several of my immediate colleagues in neighboring theological disciplines, is that a striking number of students coming into our classes, international students in particular, with intense commitments to social justice, vernacular hermeneutics, liberative praxis, and activist politics, feel themselves personally addressed by Homi Bhabha, and discover in critical categories such as colonial ambivalence, mimicry, and hybridity analytic tools that enable them to reconceptualize their own relationships to their frequently complex socio-cultural locations in ways that they experience as transforming and even empowering — as do I myself.

In the cultural crucible in which I spent my own formative years, that of postcolonial, hyper-Catholic, southern Ireland of the 1950s and 1960s, the Bible was an English book — *the* English book, indeed — so much so that when in due course I went in search of a college degree program in biblical studies, the only avenues open to me in the Irish republic were the degrees offered at the University of Dublin, Trinity College, that enduring monument to British colonial rule

---

depends on the arguable irrelevance of critiques to state dominance. And yet the gnat must have some sting to warrant even momentary congressional energy' ('Introduction', pp. 9-10).

18. Emily Eakin, 'The Latest Theory is That Theory Doesn't Matter', *The New York Times* (April 19, 2003), p. D9.

19. Eakin, 'The Latest Theory', p. D9.

in Ireland, founded by Elizabeth I in 1592 to educate the sons of the Protestant Anglo-Irish aristocracy, and effectively closed to Catholics until the 1960s. My training in biblical studies at Trinity was simultaneously an induction in postcolonial studies, although I was insufficiently aware of it at the time. In any case (although I would not want to make too much of it), it is my own (necessarily eroded) identity as a member of that most unlikely of postcolonial peoples — a nation of white west-Europeans whose formative history includes some 800 years of colonial intervention (and not as agent, but as object)[20] — that equips me now with a keen appetite for pondering the complexities that characterize the often tortuous exchanges between colonizer and colonized during colonial occupation and after official decolonization (and not just in Ireland, of course), relations of domination and submission, coercion and co-option, attraction and revulsion (the very relations that most preoccupy Bhabha, as we shall see, and are the objects of his most incisive analyses) — and with tracing the Bible's ever-shifting place in this intricate web of exchanges.

Bhabha and Bible

And the holiest of books — the Bible — bearing both the standard of the cross and the standard of empire finds itself strangely dismembered
— Homi Bhabha.[21]

To begin again, but differently: postcolonial studies, poststructuralism, biblical interpretation — at least one notable interfacing of these three reading practices has already occurred, and occurred not in a corner but in a text that, arguably, ranks alongside Said's *Orientalism* as, simultaneously, the most celebrated and most contested product of contemporary postcolonial studies. I speak of Bhabha's 1994 collection of essays, *The Location of Culture*, and specifically of 'Signs

---

20. In applying the adjective 'colonial' in blanket fashion to this entire 800-year span, I am putting a simple spin on a complex issue. For an elaborately nuanced discussion of the ways in which the labels 'colonial' and 'postcolonial' may or may not be applied to Irish history, see Stephen Howe, *Ireland and Empire: Colonial Legacies in Irish History and Culture* (Oxford: Oxford University Press, 2000), pp. 7-20. Further primers on Ireland and postcoloniality include David Lloyd, *Anomalous States: Irish Writing and the Postcolonial Moment* (Durham, NC: Duke University Press, 1993); Declan Kiberd, *Inventing Ireland* (London: Jonathan Cape, 1995); and Clare Carroll and Patricia King (eds.), *Ireland and Postcolonial Theory* (Notre Dame, IN: University of Notre Dame Press, 2003).

21. Homi K. Bhabha, 'Of Mimicry and Man: The Ambivalence of Colonial Discourse', in his *The Location of Culture*, pp. 85-92.

Taken for Wonders: Questions of Ambivalence and Authority under a Tree Outside Delhi, May 1817', which was originally published in 1985, is the sixth of the book's eleven essays, and as such is a center-piece of sorts. Not unlike other essays of eighties vintage engaged in heady fusions of poststructuralism and historiography—New Historicist essays in particular—this one too opens with an historical anecdote.[22]

The date: May 1817. The place: a grove of trees 'just outside Delhi'.[23] An Indian catechist, Anund Messeh, has just arrived at the scene, having journeyed hurriedly and excitedly from his mission in Meerut, apparently in response to a report that a throng of some five-hundred souls, men, women and children, are seated in the shade of the trees and engaged in scriptural reading and debate. The following exchange, attributed to Anund and an elderly member of the assembly by the *Missionary Register* of January 1818, whence Bhabha exhumed it, ensues:

> 'Pray who are all these people? and whence come they?' 'We are poor and lowly, and we read and love this book'. — 'What is that book?' — 'The book of God!' — 'Let me look at it, if you please'. Anund, on opening the book, perceived it to be the Gospel of our Lord, translated into the Hindoostanee Tongue, many copies of which seemed to be in the possession of the party: some were PRINTED, others WRITTEN by themselves from the printed ones. Anund pointed to the name of Jesus, and asked, 'Who is that?' — 'That is God! He gave us this book'. — 'Where did you obtain it?' — 'An Angel from heaven gave it us, at Hurdwar fair'. — 'An Angel?' — 'Yes, to us he was God's Angel: but he was a man, a learned Pundit'. (Doubtless these translated Gospels must have been the books distributed, five or six years ago, at

22. For the strategic role of the anecdote in New Historicism, see Susan Lochrie Graham and Stephen D. Moore, 'The Quest of the New Historicist Jesus', *Biblical Interpretation* 5 (1997), pp. 438-64 (439-45). In brief, the classic New Historicist anecdote is assigned to blow a hole in the teleological (and frequently theological) metanarratives of traditional historiography, by infecting these over-plotted histories with elements of the contingent and the unassimilable. I would hesitate to ascribe an elaborate theory of the anecdote to 'Signs Taken for Wonders' (even within New Historicism, such a theory only comes to 'mature' expression in Joel Fineman, 'The History of the Anecdote: Fiction and Fiction', in H. Aram Vesser [ed.], *The New Historicism* [London and New York: Routledge, 1989], pp. 49-76; see further Catherine Gallagher and Stephen Greenblatt, *Practicing New Historicism* [Chicago: University of Chicago Press, 2000], pp. 20-74), but Bhabha does attempt to blow some sizeable holes in the metanarrative fabric of nineteenth-century colonial discourse by means of his own anecdote, as we shall see.

23. Bhabha, 'Signs Taken for Wonders', p. 102.

Hurdwar by the missionary.)... 'These books', said Anund, 'teach the
religion of the European Sahibs. It is THEIR book; and they printed it
in our language, for our use'.[24]

In the space of some half-a-dozen sentences, the supplier of this
divine book undergoes a rapid series of renamings that cascade in a
dizzying descent. First, God himself is said to have provided the
book out his bounty, then his Angel, then a mere mortal, albeit a
'learned Pundit' and missionary, and finally the 'European Sahibs'.
The transcendent Word has again become flesh — first brown flesh
and then white flesh. Shimmering undecidably at the juncture of two
incommensurate cultures, it belongs to both and neither at once.

The anecdote has barely begun to unfold, however; I shall return to
it a little later. Its intense attraction for Bhabha is hardly surprising.
Bhabha's intellectual idiom is a generic poststructuralism, as we
noted earlier, Derridean primarily, though Lacan also looms large on
the Bhabhan mindscape, as does Foucault on occasion, and assorted
other Parisian *penseurs*. Sizeable swathes of Bhabha's text approxi-
mate the near illegible density of early Derrida. Without the Derridean decoder ring, indeed, Bhabha simply cannot be deciphered. And
many of the early Derridean mana-words — not least *writing, inscrip-
tion, doubling, repetition, the book, the text* — are also Bhabhan obses-
sions, not to say fetishes (fetishism itself being another Bhabhan
obsession) — hence the allure of this anecdote for Bhabha, which he
reads as an epiphanic scene insistently repeated, 'played out in the
wild and wordless wastes of colonial India, Africa, the Caribbean',
namely, 'the sudden, fortuitous discovery of the English book'[25] — in
this case the quintessential English book, the one that is at once the
book of mission and the book of empire. What fascinates Bhabha is
the way in which this found book, redolent with originary meaning
and authority, universal and immutable, is inevitably and inexorably
dislocated and evacuated, hallowed and hollowed at one and the
same time, as it is subjected to linguistic and cultural reformulation
and deformation — to reiteration, repetition, reinscription, doubling,
dissemination, and displacement (to recite a deconstructive litany
that is as familiar to the reader of Bhabha as to the reader of Derrida).

Bhabha is not without his own conceptual and terminological
apparatus, however, drawn largely from Freud via Lacan — although,
in hyper-eclectic fashion, also from a range of other theorist-critics

---

24. Bhabha, 'Signs Taken for Wonders', pp. 102-103.
25. Bhabha, 'Signs Taken for Wonders', p. 102.

as diverse as Fanon and Bakhtin—and given a highly distinctive inflection: *ambivalence, mimicry,* and *hybridity* are merely some of its better known categories (the Bhabhan mana-words, indeed).[26] Nor does he hesitate to declare his distance from Derrida on occasion, most notably seven pages into the essay under discussion, when he announces his 'departure from Derrida's objectives in "The Double Session"', the Derridean text he has been milking, and a strategic redirection of attention from 'the vicissitudes of interpretation' in the act of reading 'to the question of the effects of power' in the colonial arena.[27] In the event, Bhabha doesn't stray very far from Derrida; we are immediately told that the announced 'departure' will actually constitute a 'return' to some underdeveloped themes in Derrida's essay. The question I wish to ponder here, however—hardly a novel question, I realize, although one that, so far as I am aware, has not yet been the subject of protracted reflection in the context of biblical studies—is whether or to what extent strategies of reading whittled in the laps of some of the master texts of the European philosophical tradition—for that is what Derrida's texts have by now become—or in the laps of some of the master texts of the European psychoanalytic tradition, in the case of Lacan, are adequate to the task of analyzing European colonialism and its effects, including the mobilization and counter-mobilization of biblical texts in colonial arenas.

What Bhabha's deployment of poststructuralist, largely Derridean, thought does enable, arguably, is a more adequate appreciation of the *complexity* of the cultural space occupied by the Bible in British India. While Bhabha readily acknowledges that Said's *Orientalism* was seminal for his own project,[28] he just as readily takes Said to task for his (largely implicit) characterization of colonial discourse, epitomized by Orientalist discourse, as self-confident and self-consistent, monolithic and monologic, animated by a single unifying intention (the will to power), as well as for his corollary assumption that colonization itself is characterized by a one-sided possession of power on the part of the colonizer.[29] Aided and abetted by Freud, as refracted

---

26. Detailed definition of these analytic categories is deferred to my final chapter, which 'applies' them to the book of Revelation.

27. Bhabha, 'Signs Taken for Wonders', p. 108; cf. Jacques Derrida, 'The Double Session', in his *Dissemination* (trans. Barbara Johnson; Chicago: University of Chicago Press, 1981), pp. 173-286.

28. Bhabha, *The Location of Culture*, p. ix.

29. In *Culture and Imperialism*, Said sets out to complicate his earlier characterization of the colonizer–colonized relationship, as he admits in a 1997 interview. See Edward W. Said, *Culture and Imperialism* (New York: Vintage Books,

through Lacan, but also through Fanon, Bhabha calls each of these assumptions acutely into question.[30] For Bhabha, colonial discourse is characterized above all by *ambivalence*. It is riddled with contradictions and incoherences, traversed by anxieties and insecurities, and hollowed out by originary lack and internal heterogeneity. For Bhabha, moreover, the locus of colonial power, far from being unambiguously on the side of the colonizer, inheres instead in a shifting, unstable, potentially subversive, 'in-between' or 'third' space between colonizer and colonized, which is characterized by *mimicry*, on the one hand, in which the colonized heeds the colonizer's peremptory injunction to imitation, but in a manner that constantly threatens to teeter over into mockery; and by *hybridity*, on the other hand, another insidious product of the colonial encounter that further threatens to fracture the colonizer's identity and authority.

What Bhabha doesn't address, directly at least, is what all this might mean for the colonizer's book — which is, of course, to say the 'European' book par excellence, the Bible — but it requires but little reflection to see that it means the book's *deconstruction*. (Could Bhabha's essential Derrideanism lead us to expect anything else?) If Said's conception of colonial discourse and colonial power admits, in principle at least, of a Bible that can function more or less straightforwardly as an effective instrument of the colonizer's will to subjugate the colonized, Bhabha's conception of colonial discourse and colonial power conjures up a rather different Bible, a far more mercurial Bible, which, as it permeates the cultural space of the colonized, effortlessly adapts to its contours, is rewritten in the process of being reread, and thereby subverts the colonizer's claims on its behalf of univocity and universality.

In the face of the subtle hermeneutical spectacle with which Bhabha implicitly presents us, however, all sorts of uncomfortable questions arise, many of which have already been posed in one form or another by Bhabha's critics.[31] Several touch on ostensibly universalizing

1993); Said, 'In Conversation with Neeladri Bhattacharya, Suvir Kaul, and Ania Loomba', in David Theo Goldberg and Ato Quayson (eds.), *Relocating Postcolonialism* (Oxford: Blackwell, 2002), pp. 1-14 (4-5).

30. Bhabha's relationship to Fanon is itself somewhat complex, because he also takes Fanon to task (specifically, the Fanon of *The Wretched of the Earth*) for his 'Manichaean' locating of power too asymmetrically on the side of the colonizer ('Interrogating Identity: Franz Fanon and the Postcolonial Prerogative', in *The Location of Culture*, pp. 40-65 [61-63]).

31. Huddart, *Homi K. Bhabha*, pp. 149-69, usefully surveys a wide range of critical reactions to Bhabha's work

moves in Bhabha's own text, most notably his exportation, lock, stock and barrel, to the colonies of European psychoanalytic theory in the Freudian-Lacanian mode.[32] This colonial export business is merely one aspect of a problem that is much larger than Bhabha, however, that of the blanket application of 'First World' theory more generally to 'Third World' cultures. (In biblical studies, the analogue has been a kind of methodological imperialism in which only methods and theories manufactured in Europe or North America have been deemed adequate to the task of exegesis — and not only by the manufacturers themselves, resulting in an incessant stream of students from Africa, Latin America, and especially Asia to study in European and North American universities and seminaries.) And yet, in the case of Bhabha, what is most problematic, perhaps, is not his *use* of psychoanalytic theory per se, but his failure to acknowledge its cultural specificity. In this regard, he has been compared unfavorably to Fanon, who also makes use of Freudian and even Lacanian categories, as we noted earlier, especially in *Black Skin, White Masks*, but never uncritically or unselfconsciously.

Still more problematic in Bhabha's writings is the thorny issue of *agency*[33] — although the limitations of his work in this regard are paradoxically bound up with its moments of greatest insight. Bhabha's basic approach to colonialism and its aftermath, it might be said, provides an exemplary, if incomplete, analytic model. To state it (all too) simply, critical approaches that concentrate exclusively on the 'outward' appurtenances of colonialism and its counter-effects, such as military interventions, administrative infrastructures, nationalist movements, civil disobedience, or armed insurrections — not to deny for a moment the importance of analyzing such fundamental phenomena — cannot account adequately for the immensely complex relations of collusion and resistance, desire and disavowal, dependence and independence that can characterize the exchanges between colonizer and colonized during colonial occupation *and* after official decolonization. Isolating and unraveling these often tortuous relations, tensions, and affiliations accounts for Bhabha's most impressive

32. See, for example, Young, *White Mythologies*, p. 144; Moore-Gilbert, *Postcolonial Theory*, pp. 140-51. For Bhabha's attempt to respond to this charge, see Homi Bhabha and John Comaroff, 'Speaking of Postcoloniality, in the Continuous Present: A Conversation', in Goldberg and Quayson (eds.), *Relocating Postcolonialism*, pp. 15-46 (29-32).

33. See, for example, Benita Parry, *Postcolonial Studies: A Materialist Critique* (London and New York: Routledge, 2004), pp. 13-36, 55-74 *passim*.

achievements, and his indispensable tools to this end have been those forged in the fires of poststructuralist thought.[34] As he himself has put it:

> My growing conviction has been that the encounters and negotiations of differential meanings and values within 'colonial' textuality, its governmental discourses and cultural practices, have enacted, *avant la lettre*, many of the problematics of signification and judgment that have become current in contemporary theory – aporia, ambivalence, indeterminacy, the question of discursive closure, the threat to agency, the status of intentionality, the challenge to 'totalizing' concepts, to name but a few.[35]

Bhabha's psychoanalytic and poststructuralist version of postcolonial criticism is most in its element, one might say, when applied to 'normal' colonial relations, as opposed to overtly coercive colonial relations when the use of armed force is paramount. That is when Bhabhan concepts such as mimicry and hybridity come into their own. Both implicitly and explicitly, Bhabha ascribes considerable

34. *European* poststructuralist thought (to resurrect the earlier issue)? Yes, on the face of it, although Robert Young, for one, has made a spirited case against seeing poststructuralism as simply or straightforwardly European, Euro-American, or Western. 'In fact, the "high European theory" of structuralism and post-structuralism is of broadly non-European origin: structuralism was developed by the Prague school as an anti-western strategy, directed against the hierarchical cultural and racial assumptions of imperialist European thought. Many of those who developed the theoretical positions known collectively as poststructuralism came from Algeria and the Maghreb. Though structuralism and poststructuralism were taken up and developed in Europe, both were indeed alien, and fundamentally anti-western in strategy' (*Postcolonialism*, pp. 67-68; Young's chapter on Derrida, in particular, 'Subjectivity and History: Derrida in Algeria', pp. 411-26, pushes this line of argument to the limit – and possibly over).

35. Homi K. Bhabha, 'Postcolonial Criticism', in Stephen Greenblatt and Giles Gunn (eds.), *Redrawing the Boundaries: The Transformation of English and American Literary Studies* (New York: The Modern Language Association of America, 1992), pp. 437-65 (439). Elsewhere, in an interview, Bhabha recalls that while working as a graduate student on the novels of V.S. Naipaul he was reminded of the fact that, 'in literature at least, no colonized subject had the illusion of speaking from a place of plenitude or fullness. The colonial subject was a kind of split subject and "knew" it both phenomenologically and historically. Whereas I was being taught that such splitting of the subject was the general condition of the psyche (Lacan)…there was a much more specific or "local" historical and affective apprehension of this which was part of the personhood of the postcolonial subject. The "decentering of the self" was the very condition of agency and imagination in these colonial or postcolonial conditions, and it becomes more than a theoretical axiom; it becomes a protean, everyday practice, a way of living with oneself and other…' ('Speaking of Postcoloniality', p. 21).

subversive potential to such phenomena. Yet where is this subversion, this sabotage, this resistance to colonial domination actually occurring? In the consciousness of the individual colonized subject? Or in his or her subconscious? Or unconscious? Or is its real locus instead in the tide of discourse that ebbs and flows between colonizer and colonized, causing the colonizer's identity and authority to be surreptitiously eroded in and through his discursive impositions on the colonized? Is the colonizer, then, the ultimate agent of his own discursive undoing? Characteristically, Bhabha never tackles such questions head on.[36]

'Signs Taken for Wonders', however, is one essay in which Bhabha is more than usually emphatic that the colonized are engaged in active subversion of the colonizer's discourse, in this case the colonizer's Scripture. Ostensibly, the encounter of the catechist Anund Messeh with the throng of five hundred outside Delhi in May 1817 is enacted amid *ruins*. As Bhabha reports, a letter from a representative of the Indian Church Missionary Society sent to London that same month expressed the desire that the Indian 'heathens', suitably catechized, themselves 'be made the instruments of pulling down their own religion, and of erecting in its ruins the standards of the Cross'.[37] Bhabha's countervailing desire, understandably enough, is that of interpreting these ruins, or runes, differently, by reading *with* the natives assembled under the tree outside Delhi, and *against* the narrator of the *Missionary Register* anecdote, for whom these natives, seemingly, are a gormless, guileless, and generally ignorant lot.

To take up the anecdote where we earlier left off: '"These [gospel] books", said Anund, "teach the religion of the European Sahibs. It is THEIR book; and they printed it in our language, for our use." "Ah! no", replied [his interlocutor], "that cannot be, for they eat flesh"'.[38] Bhabha remarks (and here I am both paraphrasing and amplifying his comment) that this 'canny' observation effectively challenges the assumption that the authority of the 'English book' is universal and self-evident by underscoring the cultural specificity and relativity of its provenance. Bhabha's exegesis of this canny rejoinder, and of the natives' subsequent declaration that they are willing to be baptized, but 'will never take the Sacrament [of the Eucharist]…because the Europeans eat cow's flesh, and this will never do for us'[39] — statements

36. Even in the essay in *The Location of Culture* entitled 'The Postcolonial and the Postmodern' whose subtitle is 'The Question of Agency'.
37. Bhabha, 'Signs Taken for Wonders', p. 106.
38. Bhabha, 'Signs Taken for Wonders', p. 103.
39. Bhabha, 'Signs Taken for Wonders', p. 104.

he characterizes as 'insurgent interrogations in the interstices' of colonial authority[40] — occupies a further five pages of dense meditation.

What is being accomplished under the tree outside Delhi, however,
at least on Bhabha's reading, is nothing less than the hybridization of
the 'English book'. The colonizers' missionary strategy of distributing
Hindi Bibles to the native populace, Bibles calculated to function as
timebombs that will eventually decimate the native's indigenous
religious culture from within, has exploded in the colonizers' faces.
'After our experience of the native interrogation', claims Bhabha, 'it is
difficult to agree entirely with Fanon that the psychic choice is to
"turn white or disappear". There is the more ambivalent, third choice:
camouflage, mimicry, black skins/white masks', he adds, reading
Fanon against Fanon, and quoting Lacan: 'It is not a question of har-
monizing with the background but, against a mottled background, of
being mottled — exactly like the technique of camouflage practised in
human warfare'.[41] And it is as a 'masque of mimicry' that Bhabha
ultimately construes the anecdote of the encounter under the tree
outside Delhi, a moment of 'civil disobedience' enacted openly under
the eye of colonial power by means of the subtle strategy that he
terms 'sly civility'.[42]

And it is surely in 'civil' colonial encounters such as this one — and
most of all in 'textual' encounters — that Bhabhan theory is at its
most persuasive, if it is ever to be persuasive at all. For if it is to be
objected — as indeed it has been[43] — that, in the larger scheme of things,
any amount of colonial ambivalence, mimicry, or hybridity did not,
in the end, effectively hamper British administration and exploitation
of India, it is no less evident that the colonizers at least failed to
impose their religious ideology uniformly upon the Indian populace.

In the end, however, Bhabha does not seem to know quite what to
do with the Bible. 'And what is the significance of the Bible?', 'Signs
Taken for Wonders' eventually inquires, only to answer lazily 'Who
knows?',[44] a shrug of the shoulders all the more surprising for the fact
that the essay has already implicitly provided an answer. The significance of the Bible in the Indian colonial situation, it has suggested,

40. Bhabha, 'Signs Taken for Wonders', p. 105.

41. Bhabha, 'Signs Taken for Wonders', pp. 120-21, quoting Jacques Lacan, *The
Four Fundamental Concepts of Psychoanalysis* (trans. Alan Sheridan; New York:
Norton, 1978), p. 99.

42. Bhabha, 'Signs Taken for Wonders', p. 121; cf. 'Sly Civility', in *The Location
of Culture*, pp. 93-101.

43. See, for example, Moore-Gilbert, *Postcolonial Theory*, pp. 134-35.

44. Bhabha, 'Signs Taken for Wonders', p. 121.

was that it was an especially fraught site of simultaneous compliance and resistance (the Indian Bible thus turns out, not altogether unexpectedly, to be a Bhabhan Bible). That it could, and did, function as a colonialist instrument of coercion and co-option hardly needs belaboring.

But the extent to which it could simultaneously function as an instrument of native resistance in that situation is further suggested by a final excerpt from the *Missionary Register* of May 1817, which Bhabha quotes, although without comment, thereby ending his essay. The author of this excerpt is yet another missionary to the Indians (this one British, unlike Anund Messeh), who can hardly contain his frustration:

> Still [every Indian] would gladly receive a Bible. And why? That he may store it up as a curiosity; sell it for a few pice; or use it for waste paper.... [A]n indiscriminate distribution of the scriptures, to everyone who may say he wants a Bible, can be little less than a waste of time, a waste of money and a waste of expectation. For while the public are hearing of so many Bibles distributed, they expect to hear soon of a corresponding number of conversions.[45]

In the colonial context, the practice of eagerly acquiring the European Book of books only to barter it without first having read it, or especially to employ it as waste paper,[46] might well be construed as the epitome of a *materialist* reading of the colonial Bible, a singularly sly and canny affirmation of the ineluctable materiality of this Sign of signs, and hence its cultural specificity and relativity. Simultaneously and consequently, however, these casual yet highly charged gestures might also be construed as the epitome of a *resistant* reading of the colonial Bible, one that resists precisely by refusing to read. More precisely still even, these gestures might be said to resist by resolutely remaining at the level of the material signifier, the papery substance itself—miraculously thin, almost transparent, yet wholly tangible nonetheless—refusing its translation, its sublation, into a transcendental, transcontextual, transcultural signified. Arguably, such a mode of reading would also be an entirely apt, if altogether paradoxical, model for a biblical critical practice that would aspire to be

45. Bhabha, 'Signs Taken for Wonders', p. 122.
46. Or worse? South African liberation theologian Itumeleng Mosala, on a visit to Drew Theological School in February 2000, began his public lecture with an eyebrow-raising anecdote of two opponents of apartheid held in a single, bleak prison cell, one bereft of toilet tissue and every other creature comfort, but thoughtfully furnished with twin Bibles; of the difficult decision facing each prisoner in consequence; and of the symbolic stakes in each course of action.

'postcolonial' and 'poststructuralist' at once — or to put it another way (a still more simplistic way), 'political' and 'postmodern' at once. And such a critical practice might, among other things, entail gingerly picking up the tangled thread that Homi Bhabha so abruptly drops at the end of 'Signs Taken for Wonders' and patiently picking at it until some of the denser knots that bind the biblical texts to diverse colonial contexts — knots themselves constituted by elaborate acts of reading — begin to unravel.

5

'THE WORLD EMPIRE HAS BECOME THE EMPIRE OF OUR LORD AND HIS MESSIAH': REPRESENTING EMPIRE IN REVELATION

[T]he Emperor himself invited and feasted with those ministers of God whom he had reconciled, and thus offered as it were through them a suitable sacrifice to God. Not one of the bishops was wanting at the imperial banquet, the circumstances of which were splendid beyond description. Detachments of the bodyguard and other troops surrounded the entrance of the palace with drawn swords, and through the midst of these the men of God proceeded without fear into the innermost of the imperial apartments, in which some of the Emperor's own companions were at table, while others reclined on couches arranged on either side. One might have thought that a picture of Christ's kingdom was thus shadowed forth, a dream rather than a reality (Eusebius, *Life of Constantine* 3.15, LCL).

To ponder the book of Revelation's relations to empire, as this final chapter proposes to do, is hardly a novel gesture. Critical scholars of Revelation have customarily read it as the most uncompromising attack on the Roman Empire, and on Christian collusion with the empire, to issue from early Christianity. Historical-critical reflection on Revelation and Rome crystallized in such studies as Leonard L. Thompson's *The Book of Revelation: Apocalypse and Empire*.[1] More recently, Wes Howard-Brook and Anthony Gwyther's *Unveiling Empire: Reading Revelation Then and Now*[2] has intensified such reflection, and also surpassed it, in the extent to which the authors place the phenomenon of empire fully at the center of their reading of Revelation, coupled with their intent to read the book as a critique of contemporary as well as ancient empire.[3] In the latter regard, they

1. Oxford: Oxford University Press, 1990.
2. The Bible and Liberation Series; Maryknoll, NY: Orbis Books, 1999.
3. Harry O. Maier's *Apocalypse Recalled: The Book of Revelation after Christendom* (Minneapolis: Fortress Press, 2002) likewise attempts a political reading of Revelation in a dual context.

have been anticipated by (other) liberationist readings of Revelation, notably Allan Boesak's *Comfort and Protest: The Apocalypse from South African Perspective*[4] and Pablo Richard's *Apocalypse: A People's Commentary on the Book of Revelation*.[5] None of the aforementioned works engage with, or even allude to, postcolonial theory or criticism as they situate Revelation in relation to empire. In noting this, I am not naming a failing so much as gesturing to a supplementary space, not yet a crowded one,[6] in which the present essay seeks to situate itself. Before launching into the main business of the chapter, however—a reading of Revelation impelled by the colonial discourse analysis of Homi Bhabha—a preliminary fleshing out of Revelation's sociopolitical context will be in order.

Imperium Romanum

The concept and practice of colonialism are by no means irrelevant to Revelation's historical provenance, as we shall see. The scope of postcolonial studies, however, is not limited to the phenomenon of colonialism; it also encompasses imperialism (and much else besides, as we observed in Chapter 1, not least decolonization, neocolonialism, and globalization). 'Imperialism' here denotes the multifarious, mutually constitutive ideologies (political, economic, racial/ethnic, religious, etc.) that impel a metropolitan center to annex more-or-less distant territories, and that determine its subsequent dealings with

4.   Philadelphia: Westminster Press, 1987.

5.   The Bible and Liberation Series; Maryknoll, NY: Orbis Books, 1995.

6.   It contains Jean K. Kim, '"Uncovering her Wickedness": An Inter(con)textual Reading of Revelation 17 from a Postcolonial Feminist Perspective', *Journal for the Study of the New Testament* 73 (1999), pp. 83-112; Kim, *Woman and Nation: An Intercontextual Reading of the Gospel of John* (Biblical Interpretation Series, 69; Leiden: Brill, 2004), which is also informed by postcolonial studies. Steven J. Friesen, *Imperial Cults and the Apocalypse of John: Reading Revelation in the Ruins* (Oxford: Oxford University Press, 2001), and Christopher A. Frilingos, *Spectacles of Empire: Monsters, Martyrs, and the Book of Revelation* (Divinations: Rereading Late Ancient Religion; Philadelphia: University of Pennsylvania Press, 2004), each have explicit recourse in their respective introductions (even if not in their remaining chapters) to the postcolonial theory of Edward Said. Catherine Keller, in her *God and Power: Counter-Apocalyptic Journeys* (Minneapolis: Fortress Press, 2005), subjects Revelation and contemporary US imperialism to feminist and postcolonial analysis; see Part 2, 'Of Beasts and Whores: Examining Our Political Unconscious'. Also pertinent is Vitor Westhelle, 'Revelation 13: Between the Colonial and the Postcolonial, a Reading from Brazil', in David Rhoads (ed.), *From Every People and Nation: The Book of Revelation in Intercultural Perspective* (Minneapolis: Fortress Press, 2005), pp. 183-99.

them.[7] Although the English word 'imperialism' did not emerge, apparently, until the late nineteenth century, being first used in connection with European expansionism and the ideologies that under-girded it, its etymological and conceptual roots lie in the Latin word *imperium*,[8] which under the Roman republic designated the authority vested in consuls, magistrates, and other select officials to exercise command and exact obedience, and in the post-Augustan era was deemed to reside supremely in the person of the emperor. The latter's *imperium*, voted to him by the Roman senate at his accession, extended in principle to all peoples and territories under Rome's dominion.[9]

At first or even second glance, Revelation would appear to be an anti-imperial(istic) text that, in effect, announces the transfer of world-wide *imperium* from the Roman Emperor to the heavenly Emperor and his Son and co-regent, the 'King of kings and Lord of lords' (19.16; cf. 17.14). As Revelation itself memorably phrases this transfer, 'The world empire [*hē basileia tou kosmou*] has become the empire of our Lord and his Messiah' (11.15; cf. 14.6-8).[10] The paramount question the present essay will raise, however (one engendered by the particular body of postcolonial theory it will be tapping), is whether or to what extent Revelation merely reinscribes, rather than effectively resists, Roman imperial ideology.

Coloniae Romanum

Revelation is explicitly addressed to seven urban churches in the Roman province of Asia (1.4, 11), the westernmost province of the larger geographical region known (somewhat confusingly) as Asia Minor, which extended from the Aegean to the western Euphrates, thus corresponding roughly to modern Turkey. The history of colonization in Asia Minor[11] extended back to the Hellenizing campaigns of

7.   Cf. Edward W. Said, *Culture and Imperialism* (New York: Vintage Press, 1993), p. 9.

8.   Cf. Dennis C. Duling, 'Empire: Theories, Methods, Models', in John Riches and David C. Sim (eds.), *The Gospel of Matthew in its Roman Imperial Context* (Journal for the Study of the New Testament Supplement Series, 276; New York: T. & T. Clark International, 2005), pp. 49-74 (51).

9.   Cf. Andrew Lintott, *Imperium Romanum: Politics and Administration* (London and New York: Routledge, 1993), pp. 22, 41-42, 115-22 *passim*.

10.   With Howard-Brook and Gwyther (*Unveiling Empire*, p. 115 n. 77; cf. pp. 224-25), I prefer 'empire' to 'kingdom' as a less anodyne translation of *basileia* in Revelation.

11.   On which see Barbara Levick, *Roman Colonies in Southern Asia Minor* (Oxford: Clarendon Press, 1967), in particular.

Alexander the Great and his successors, who sowed Greek cities (*poleis*) throughout the region — although several of Revelation's seven cities, notably Ephesus and Smyrna, were Greek colonies well before the advent of Alexander. The extent, indeed, to which the multilayered Hellenization of the region effected a cultural colonization that expedited its eventual absorption by the consummately Hellenized Romans can scarcely be exaggerated.

The English term 'colony' derives from the Latin *colonia* (the equivalent Greek term would be *apoikia*), but it would misleading to conceive of Roman *coloniae* purely on the model of the European colonies of the early modern period and its aftermath. The classic Roman *colonia* was a civic foundation, which is to say a city or town. Essentially, *coloniae* were civic communities of Roman citizens settled outside Italy and composed mainly of military veterans. The *colonia* was one of the three principal types of Roman provincial community, all of them urban; the others were the *municipia* (confined mainly to the Latin west, and of lesser status than the *colonia*), and the city or town that was neither an official *colonia* nor *municipia*, and as such less 'Romanized' than either. The classic unit of Roman colonization, then (in the contemporary sense of the term) was urban, and it was through an infrastructure of self-governing cities that Roman provinces were administered.

What of the province of Asia? Julius Caesar and especially Augustus had each engaged in the settlement of military veterans in various pockets of Asia Minor generally, which is to say that they 'seeded' the region with *coloniae*, but the systematic introduction of new settlers became rare in the post-Augustan period — which begs the question of the precise nature of Roman rule in Asia under the Principate.

Contemporary postcolonial discourse frequently distinguishes between *settler colonies*, on the one hand, and *colonies of occupation*, on the other (while acknowledging that many colonies fit neatly into neither category but straddle both at once).[12] Settler colonies (also known as settler-invader colonies) are those in which the indigenous population is decimated and uprooted, eventually becoming a minority in relation to the majority settler-invader population; modern examples of such colonies would include Australia, Canada, and the United States. In contrast, colonies of occupation are those in which the indigenous population remains in the majority numerically, but is

---

12. See Anna Johnston and Alan Lawson, 'Settler Colonies', in Henry Schwarz and Sangeeta Ray (eds.), *A Companion to Postcolonial Studies* (Oxford: Blackwell, 2000), pp. 360-76.

subjugated and governed by a foreign power; modern examples would include pre-independence India and Ireland.

Which of these two modes of colonization best approximates the situation of Roman Asia? As has already been implied, Asia could in no wise be regarded as a settler-invader colony (using the term colony now in its modern sense); it better fits the colony of occupation model instead. Roman culture was concentrated in the (mainly coastal) cities of the province in contrast to the rural Anatolian interior, which managed to preserve its indigenous character, conspicuous especially in its native languages and religious cults, more or less intact until the third century CE. Even in the cities, however, the Roman presence would have been relatively slight. In general, the number of elite Roman officials allotted to any one Rome province was minuscule relative to the amount of territory to be administered. Asia was one of the 'ungarrisoned' provinces of the empire, moreover, meaning that no full legion was stationed there; and what military presence there was tended to be concentrated in the interior. What, then, were the mechanisms that enabled continuous Roman control of Asia?

Hegemony

At this point, another concept commonly invoked in contemporary postcolonial studies may usefully be introduced, that of *hegemony*, in the special sense accorded to the term many decades ago by the Italian Marxist intellectual Antonio Gramsci. Hegemony, in the Gramscian sense, means *domination by consent*—in effect, the active participation of a dominated group in its own subjugation, whether a social underclass, say—Gramsci's own principal focus—or a colonized people.[13] The attraction of the concept for postcolonial studies is that it serves to account for the ability of an imperial power to govern a colonized territory whose indigenous population overwhelmingly outnumbers the army of occupation. In such cases (thinking alongside Gramsci), the indigene's desire for self-determination will have been displaced by a discursively inculcated notion of the greater good, couched in such terms as social stability (whether in the form of a *Pax Romana* or a *Pax Britannica*) and economic and cultural

13. See, for example, Antonio Gramsci, *Selections from the Prison Notebooks* (ed. and trans. Quintin Hoare and Geoffrey Nowell Smith; London: Lawrence & Wishart, 1971), p. 12. Hegemony is a recurrent preoccupation in the *Prison Notebooks*.

advancement. The more efficient an imperial administration, indeed, the more it will rely on hegemonic acquiescence and the less it will have recourse to material force in the retention and exploitation of its colonial possessions — in which case the neocolonial empires of contemporary global capitalism would represent a quantum leap in administrative efficiency when measured against the relatively unwieldy empires of the past.[14]

The concept of hegemony usefully illuminates the situation of Roman Asia. The province itself originated not in an invasion but in an invitation: Attalus III of Pergamum bequeathed his kingdom to the Romans. It became *provincia Asia* after his death in 133 BCE, and expanded in increments over the next half-century or so, gradually assuming the form it would take under the Principate. Like any Roman province, the routine governance of Asia depended upon the active cooperation and participation of the local urban elites. The administrative infrastructure consisted of a loose coalition of self-governing cities, each having responsibility for the territorial hinterland attached to it. The mainspring of the complex hegemonic mechanism that enabled Roman governance of Asia, however — economically a jewel in the imperial crown, rich in natural resources, agriculture, and industry — was the intense competition for imperial favor and recognition in which the principal Asian cities were permanently locked (Ephesus, Pergamum, and Smyrna in particular, although the rivalry extended to many lesser cities as well). A vital expression of this competition was the city's public demonstration of the measure of its loyalty to the emperor, the ultimate patron or benefactor in relation to whom the city was a client or dependent, and as such in rivalry with the other client cities of the province for a limited quantity of goods and privileges. And the principal mechanism in turn (the wheel within a wheel) for formal demonstrations of such loyalty was the *imperial cult*: the rendering of divine honors to Roman Emperors, living or dead.

Divus Caesar

Officially instituted in 42 BCE when the Roman senate posthumously recognized Julius Caesar as divine, the imperial cult — to the extent that it can be spoken of in the singular: it was profoundly marked by

---

14. A shift provocatively explored by Michael Hardt and Antonio Negri in *Empire* (Cambridge, MA: Harvard University Press, 2000).

regional variation, as we shall see — infiltrated the religio-political life of every province in the empire during the Augustan and post-Augustan periods (with the hard-won exception of the province of Judea). Whereas in the western provinces the imperial cult tended to be imposed by Rome, in the eastern provinces it was a 'voluntary' affair. It could well afford to be. Ruler worship in the east predated Roman expansion, having been catalyzed in particular by the spectacular conquests of Alexander the Great. Whereas in Rome itself divine honors were offered as a rule only to deceased emperors (impatient exceptions notwithstanding, notably Caligula, Nero, and Commodus), the worship of currently reigning emperors was tolerated and even encouraged in the provinces. What more reassuring token of an apparent willingness to be conquered could a conqueror possibly desire? — even if the provincial imperial cults may, in historical hindsight, also be construed as surreptitious determinations on the part of the emperor's subjects of who and what he was to be for them, thus paradoxically setting subtle limits on his autonomy in the very act of acknowledging his absolute authority.

From an extremely early stage, the local Asian elites enthusiastically embraced the Roman imperial cult, dedication to which became a major vehicle of competition between the leading cities of the province.[15] But it was a highly regulated competition. Delegates of the various civic communities met annually as the Council or Assembly (*koinon*) of Asia in one of the five official provincial cities (Ephesus, Pergamum, Smyrna, Sardis, or Cyzicus) in order to conduct the business of the province, a crucial element of which was the organization

---

15. S.R.F. Price, *Rituals and Power: The Roman Imperial Cult in Asia Minor* (Cambridge: Cambridge University Press, 1984), remains the standard study of this phenomenon. For extended engagement with Price's work in the context of Pauline studies, see Richard A. Horsley (ed.), *Paul and the Roman Imperial Order* (Harrisburg, PA: Trinity Press International, 2004). For an in-depth case study of the imperial cult in one of Revelation's seven cities, see Steven J. Friesen, *Twice Neokoros: Ephesus, Asia and the Cult of the Flavian Imperial Family* (Religions in the Graeco-Roman World; Leiden: Brill, 1993). Diverse attempts to read Revelation in relation to the imperial cult can be found in Thompson, *The Book of Revelation*; J. Nelson Kraybill, *Imperial Cult and Commerce in John's Apocalypse* (Journal for the Study of the New Testament Supplement Series, 132; Sheffield: Sheffield Academic Press, 1999); Howard-Brook and Gwyther, *Unveiling Empire*; Friesen, *Imperial Cults and the Apocalypse of John*; and Allen Brent, *The Imperial Cult and the Development of Church Order: Concepts and Images of Authority in Paganism and Early Christianity before the Age of Cyprian* (Leiden: Brill, 1999). For my own efforts in this vein, see *God's Gym: Divine Male Bodies of the Bible* (London and New York: Routledge, 1996), pp. 117-38.

of the imperial cult. In 29 BCE, a mere two years after Octavian/
Augustus's accession to supreme power, the Assembly of Asia had
requested and was granted the honor of erecting a provincial temple
to Roma and Augustus at Pergamum. The establishment of a cult of
Roma and Augustus in Asia and in the neighboring province of
Pontus–Bithynia became a model for other eastern provinces. The
cult of Roma or *Dea Roma* (the personification of Rome as goddess) is
a particularly telling manifestation of hegemony (again, in the Gramscian sense), since no such cult existed in the capital itself. It was not
imposed nor even modeled by those at the apex of power, in other
words, but was invented by Roman subjects instead (*elite* subjects,
however, a point to which I shall return below). A temple to *Dea
Roma* had existed at Smyrna since 193 BCE, the first such temple in
Asia Minor.

But the Assembly of Asia devised still more extravagant ways to
acknowledge Rome's intimate and apparently irresistible hold on the
destiny and daily life of the province. Early in the Principate, the
assembly, in consultation with the Roman proconsul of Asia, determined to honor *Divus Augustus* by creating a new calendar for the
province that would begin, not on January 1 as in the standard
Roman calendar, but on September 23, the emperor's birthday —
again a signal instance of those nearer the base of the pyramid of
power surpassing those nearer the apex (those elites, that is, in the
capital itself with physical access to the emperor) in the symbolic performance of subjection — a performance all the more remarkable for
the fact that prior to the principate of Augustus the province had
suffered acutely under Roman rule, due to rapacious governors,
crushing taxes, and a disastrously unsuccessful rebellion. The energy
and rapidity with which the province of Asia subsequently set about
deifying the conqueror and sweeping the sordid history of exploitation under the rug of myth testifies to the unprecedented efficiency of
the Roman hegemonic apparatus under the Principate — an efficiency
that would be almost inexplicable were it not for the fact that the
most extravagant expressions of consent to Roman domination of the
region arose from the ranks of the local elites, who stood to gain
infinitely more from ostentatious displays of acquiescence than the
mainly impoverished urban and rural populations whom they
purported to represent. Considerable prestige attached to the priesthoods and other offices of the provincial imperial cults — they could,
indeed, form the pinnacle of a local political career. Major priesthoods
in the imperial cults, moreover — most especially that of Annual

President or Chief Priest (*archiereus*) of the provincial assembly—
could also form crucial stepping stones to a political career in Rome
itself for the select few, or at least for their sons or grandsons.

In due course, therefore, each of Revelation's seven cities, along
with others in the province, erected temples or altars to Roman poten-
tates living or dead: Julius Caesar (coupled with *Dea Roma*), Augustus
(also with *Dea Roma*), Tiberius (with the Roman senate), Vespasian,
Domitian, and Hadrian. The leading cities competed for the coveted
title of *neokoros*, 'Temple Warden/Caretaker', awarded at the discre-
tion of the senate and the emperor to cities containing an imperial
temple with pan-provincial status. And elaborate imperial festivals
became a prominent feature of the religious life of the province,
enmeshing the populace in a communal symbolic articulation of the
omnipresence and immanence of absolute power in the absent person of the Roman Emperor, whose arms encircled the civilized world
by virtue of the *imperium Romanum*.

Catachresis

How best to situate Revelation in relation to the complex matrix of
power relations that determined the religio-political life of Roman
Asia? Consummately counter-hegemonic in thrust (in the special
sense in which I have been using the term hegemony), Revelation
represents a stunning early instance of an anti-imperial literature of
resistance. In shocking contrast to the official prayers offered to the
Greek gods of the Olympian pantheon by priests of the local imperial
cults for the health of the Roman Emperor and the length of his reign
(for prayers on behalf of the emperor were more common than
prayers addressed to his image), Revelation gleefully predicts the
imminent destruction of Rome instead, which it mockingly renames
'Babylon' (14.8; 16.9; 17.5; 18.2, 10, 21), in answer to the counter-
prayers offered by Christians to their own god (6.9-11; 8.3-4; cf. 16.5-
7; 19.1-2). In effect, faithful Christians constitute an imperial counter-
cult in Revelation, a priesthood (1.6; 5.10; 20.6) dedicated to the Christian Emperor and his co-regent, Jesus Christ, in relation to which the
official cult is meant to be seen as a monstrous aberration: worship of
a hideous Beast that derives its ultimate authority from Satan (13.4, 8,
12, 14-15; cf. 14.9-11; 16.2; 19.20; 20.4).

This cunning polemical strategy can be understood as a signal
instance of catachresis. Originally a classical Greek term denoting
'misuse' or 'misapplication', catachresis has been revived and

adapted by Gayatri Spivak, as noted earlier,[16] to designate a process whereby the victims of colonialism or imperialism strategically recycle and redeploy facets of colonial or imperial culture or propaganda. Catachresis, in this sense, is a practice of resistance through an act of creative appropriation, a retooling of the rhetorical or institutional instruments of imperial oppression that turns those instruments back against their official owners. Catachresis is thus also an act of counter-appropriation: it counters the appropriative incursions of imperialist discourse — its institutional accouterments, its representational modes, its ideological forms, its propagandistic ploys — by redirecting and thereby deflecting them. As a strategy of subversive adaptation, catachresis is related to parody, which can be defined in turn as an act or practice of strategic misrepresentation. In the context of imperialist and anti-imperialist discourse, indeed, parody is best regarded as a species of catachresis.

Parody of the Roman imperial order permeates Revelation, reaching a scurrilous climax in the depiction of the goddess Roma, austere and noble personification of the *urbs aeterna*, as a tawdry whore who has had a little too much to drink (17.1-6). The most fundamental instance of catachresis in Revelation, however, is its redeployment of the term 'empire' (*basileia*) itself. In Asia as in any Roman province, the most immediate and most encompassing referent of the term *basileia* would have been the *imperium Romanum*.[17] Revelation, however, far from dispensing with the category of empire altogether in pronouncing upon the divine sphere, retains the imperial model instead (down to its details, as we shall see), but makes certain audacious adjustments to it — most significantly, switching the figure at its center so that it is no longer the Roman Emperor, an exchange which effects a retooling of the entire model, producing a catachrestic realignment of the whole.

God as Caesar

Speculation with regard to the details of this realignment has long been a standard feature of critical scholarship on Revelation. Chapters 4–5, for example, which constitute a notable case in point, have elicited observations such as the following:

16. See p. 37 above (and also note the caveat that attends my definition of catachresis).

17. As remarked earlier (p. 38). Cf. Howard-Brook and Gwyther, *Unveiling Empire*, p. 224.

a. the acclamation, 'Worthy art thou' (*axios ei*), addressed to God or the Lamb by those assembled around the heavenly throne (4.11; 5.9; cf. 5.12), was also employed in Roman imperial court ceremonial to greet the emperor;

b. the title 'our Lord and God' (*ho kyrios kai ho theos hēmōn*), likewise used in the heavenly court (4.11; cf. 4.8; 11.17; 15.3; 16.7; 19.6; Jn 20.28), was also applied to the emperor Domitian (whether or not he himself actually demanded it),[18] under whose reign Revelation achieved its final form, if the scholarly majority is on target;

c. the twenty-four elders around the throne (4.4) correspond to, among other things, the twenty-four lictors who regularly accompanied Domitian (lictors being fasces-bearing bodyguards whose number symbolized — indeed, trumpeted forth — the degree of *imperium* conferred upon a Roman potentate);

d. the elders' gesture of casting their crowns or wreaths (*stephanoi*) before the throne (4.10) corresponds with a form of obeisance frequently offered to Roman Emperors;[19]

e. the reappearance of Jesus in the guise of a Lamb standing in the presence of the Divine Emperor 'as though it had been slaughtered' (*hōs esphagmenon*, 5.6) acquires added semantic clout from the fact that the image of the Roman Emperor officiating at sacrifice was a pious commonplace from the reign of Augustus onwards, almost no one other than the emperor (and his immediate family) being depicted thus in the imperial iconography (sculptures, friezes, coins, and imprinted sacrificial cakes) that proliferated throughout the empire;[20]

and so on.

---

18. On this point, see p. 72 n. 71 above.

19. Any good-sized commentary on Revelation is likely to list some or all of these first four parallels. David E. Aune's is the most exhaustive commentary to date (*Revelation* [3 vols.; Word Biblical Commentary, 52A-C; Dallas: Word Books; Nashville: Thomas Nelson, 1997–98), and is especially illuminating for our topic if read alongside his 'The Influence of Roman Imperial Court Ceremonial on the Apocalypse of John', *Papers of the Chicago Society of Biblical Research* 28 (1985), pp. 5-26.

20. This last is my own contribution to this heady speculative exercise, inspired by Mary Beard, John North, and Simon Price, *Religions of Rome*. I. *A History* (Cambridge: Cambridge University Press, 1998), pp. 350-51.

The multiplication of such parallels by critical scholars has by no means been confined to Revelation 4–5; to a lesser extent, it has extended to the book as a whole. The sheer number of these alleged parallels, taken collectively, probably prohibits their outright dismissal as a product of scholarly mass hallucination: even if any specific parallel can always, of course, be contested, the existence of the general authorial strategy to which they gesture collectively is probably as secure as most fixtures in the gently quaking quagmire of Revelation scholarship. I have relabeled that strategy catachresis here, and noted its intimate relationship to parody. That Revelation's representation of the Roman imperial order is essentially parodic, however, has long been a tenet of critical scholarship on the book. In order to disclose what is really at stake in that tenet, and to rethink Revelation's relationship to empire more generally through the conceptual resources afforded by postcolonial theory, I will turn, once again, to the work of Homi Bhabha.[21] But first a final stage set needs to be wheeled into place.

The New Metropolis

One signal advantage of Bhabha's conceptual categories for a reading of Revelation, as we shall see, is that they enable, indeed impel, us to interrogate the metaphysical and ethical dualism that the book attempts to foist upon us as one of its foundational rhetorical strategies: its construction of the Roman Empire as the absolute antithesis of 'the Empire of God and his Messiah' (11.15). The success of the strategy is evident from the fact that this binary opposition has been endlessly (and unreflectively) replicated even in critical commentaries on Revelation.

Within the book itself, this dualism attains its apogee in the construction of the New Jerusalem, a scene in which Babylon/Rome is both absent (because already annihilated: see 18.1–19.5; cf. 19.17-21) and present (because still required, as we are about to see). The scene concludes with a blessing and a curse: 'Blessed are those who wash their robes, so that they will have the right to the tree of life and may enter the city by the gates. Outside are the dogs and sorcerers and fornicators and murderers and idolaters, and everyone who loves and practices falsehood' (22.14-15; cf. 21.8, 27). Here, then, is the

---

21. For a rather different treatment of parody in Revelation, see Maier, *Apocalypse Recalled*, pp. 164-97. Whereas I (impelled by Bhabha) argue that the parody topples over into mimicry, Maier argues that it slides over into irony.

cartography of paradise (cf. 2.7), an attenuated, absolutely hierar-
chized geography of difference, designed to distinguish a (hyper-
idealized) 'metropolis' — the New Jerusalem — from a (demonized)
'periphery' — that which until recently was designated 'Babylon' in
this book. Revelation's vision of paradise restored (cf. 22.1-2; Gen.
2.10; Ezek. 47.1-12) is thus the logical culmination of the dualism that
has characterized its rhetoric throughout. The cartographic self-
representations of the Roman Empire itself, in which the imperial
territories gradually shaded over into the barbaric, the chaotic, and
the monstrous the further one ventured outward from the metropolis, is here countered with what is, in effect, a catachrestic parody of
imperial cartography: immediately beyond the walls of the Christian
metropolis, absolute alterity begins, with no incremental passage
from sameness to difference to act as conceptual buffer (a binary con-
ceit all the more curious for the contradictory fact that out in the
negative zone entire nations are apparently poised to pay homage to
the new megalopolis: see 21.24, 26). In Revelation's hyperdualistic
cosmos, then, Christian culture and Roman culture must be absolutely
separate and separable (cf. 18.4: 'Come out of her, my people...'). But
are they? This is where Bhabha's strategies of colonial discourse
analysis come into their own.

Ambivalence, Mimicry, Hybridity

Much of Bhabha's *The Location of Culture*, arguably the most influential (and controversial) contribution to colonial discourse analysis
since Said's *Orientalism*, amounts to a critical interrogation of any
conceptual dichotomization of metropolis and periphery, empire and
indigene, colonizer and colonized.[22] Bhabha's enabling assumption is
that the relationship between colonizer and colonized is characterized
by ambivalence instead, which is to say attraction and repulsion
at one and the same time.[23] Basing himself ultimately on the psychoanalytic contention that ambivalence is ubiquitous in psychic
processes,[24] Bhabha's presumption is that the stance of the colonized

22. Homi K. Bhabha, *The Location of Culture* (London and New York:
Routledge, 1994); Edward W. Said, *Orientalism: Western Conceptions of the Orient*
(New York: Pantheon, 1978).
23. See Bhabha, 'Of Mimicry and Man: The Ambivalence of Colonial Discourse', in *The Location of Culture*, pp. 85-92; and 'Articulating the Archaic:
Cultural Difference and Colonial Nonsense', in *The Location of Culture*, pp. 123-38,
esp. pp. 129-38.
24. See 'Articulating the Archaic', p. 132.

vis-à-vis the colonizer is rarely if ever one of pure unequivocal oppo-sition—which, by extension, calls a second dualistic distinction into question, that between the resistant colonial subject, on the one hand, and the complicit colonial subject, on the other. For Bhabha, resis-tance and complicity coexist in different measures in each and every colonial subject. And the complex conjoining of resistance and com-plicity is nowhere more evident than in the phenomenon of colonial mimicry.[25]

Colonial mimicry results when the colonizer's culture is imposed on the colonized and the latter is lured or coerced into internalizing and replicating it. This replication is never perfect, however—the colonized is never simply an exact copy of the colonizer ('*Almost the same but not white*', is how Bhabha wittily phrases the matter)[26]—nor does the colonizer desire that this mimicry be absolutely accurate, in any case, for then the hierarchical distinction between primary and secondary, original and copy, colonizer and colonized, would col-lapse, and with it the linchpin of imperial ideology. Hence the essen-tial ambivalence of the colonizer's injunction to the colonized to mimic him: 'Replicate me/do not replicate me'. This injunction, moreover, is fraught with risk for the colonizer: mimicry can all too easily topple over into mockery or parody, thereby menacing the authority, even the identity, of the colonizer.

The third concept that, together with ambivalence and mimicry, captures the complex psychic interpenetration of colonizer and colonized, for Bhabha, is hybridity.[27] In its 'weak' sense, the term hybridity as used in contemporary postcolonial studies means no more than that the contact between colonizer and colonized is constantly productive of hybrid cultural manifestations. Bhabha, however, has given the concept of hybridity a decidedly Derridean twist, seeing it not as a simple synthesis or syncretic fusion of two

25. 'Of Mimicry and Man' is again the key text. Bhabha's concept of colonial mimicry can be traced to various influences, but prominent among them is V.S. Naipaul's postcolonial novel, *The Mimic Men* (as Bhabha himself acknowledges; see 'Of Mimicry and Man', p. 87). 'We pretended to be real...', Naipaul's pro-tagonist Singh reminisces, 'we mimic men of the New World...' (*The Mimic Men* [London: André Deutsch, 1967], p. 146). Further on Bhabha's appropriation of Naipaul, see David Huddart, *Homi K. Bhabha* (Routledge Critical Thinkers; London and New York: Routledge, 2006), pp. 71-75.

26. Bhabha, 'Of Mimicry and Man', p. 89, his emphasis.

27. See Bhabha, 'Signs Taken for Wonders: Questions of Ambivalence and Authority under a Tree outside Delhi, May 1817', in *The Location of Culture*, pp. 111-22.

originally discrete cultures but rather as an in-between space — or 'Third Space', to use his own preferred term[28] — in which cultures are themselves simultaneously constituted and deconstructed: the identity of any cultural system only emerges as an effect of its differences from other cultural systems, but the infinitely open-ended differential network within which any given culture is situated radically and necessarily destabilizes its identity even as it generates it. In consequence, no culture can be pure, prior, original, unified, or self-contained; it is always already infected by impurity, secondariness, mimicry, self-splitting, and alterity. In a word, it is always already infected by hybridity.

In order to outline Bhabha's theory in brief, I have had to abstract it from its embeddedness in the analysis of disparate colonial texts and histories — most especially those of nineteenth-century British India, the prime catalyst for much of Bhabha's conceptual innovation — and systematize it to an extent that Bhabha himself, in good deconstructive fashion, has studiously avoided.[29] But he has not been able to avoid scathing criticism. As discussed in the previous chapter, his theory has been prodded, probed, and repeatedly contested over such issues as its alleged universalism — its application of 'First World' psychoanalytic categories to 'Third World' psychic processes — and its alleged diminution of agency — its neglect of overt and conscious forms of resistance on the part of the colonized, not least armed resistance, in favor of covert and unconscious forms of resistance. While these are serious criticisms and concerns, I would venture nonetheless to suggest that certain of the supple concepts proposed by Bhabha, used cautiously and creatively, can enable a reappraisal not only of the book of Revelation's relationship to empire, but of Revelation's theology more generally. In what follows, therefore, I will be less interested in proving the theory than in reopening the book.

28. See Bhabha, 'The Commitment to Theory', in *The Location of Culture*, pp. 19-39 (37-39), together with 'The Third Space: Interview with Homi K. Bhabha', in Jonathan Rutherford (ed.), *Identity: Community, Culture, Difference* (London: Lawrence & Wishart, 1991), pp. 207-21.

29. Anybody delving into *The Location of Culture* and expecting to find tidy, systematic expositions of ambivalence, mimicry, hybridity, etc. will be sorely disappointed. For detailed systematizations of Bhabha's essentially untidy thought, one needs to go instead to the various introductions to it, such as those listed on p. 80 n. 11 above.

The Book of Mimicry

The phenomenon of mimicry is endemic to Revelation. The book's representation of the Roman imperial order is essentially parodic, as we have noted, and parody is a species of mimicry: it mimics in order to mock. Do Bhabha's pronouncements on colonial mimicry apply, then, to Revelation's parodic strategy? Yes and no, it seems to me. In contrast to the scenario adduced by Bhabha in which systemic mimicry of the agents and institutions of imperialism perpetually threatens to teeter over into parody or mockery, Revelation presents us with a reverse scenario in which parody or mockery of the imperial order constantly threatens to topple over into mimicry, imitation, and replication. Revelation's implicit claim, as commentators never tire of telling us, is that Roman imperial court ceremonial, together with the imperial court itself, are but pale imitations—diabolic imitations, indeed—of the heavenly throne room and the heavenly liturgy. But commentators also routinely note that the heavenly court and liturgy in Revelation are themselves modeled in no small part on the Roman imperial court and cult (recall our earlier ruminations on Rev. 4–5)—which means in effect that the 'heavenly' order in Revelation is busily engaged in imitating or mimicking the 'earthly' order, notwithstanding the book's own implicit charge that the earthly is merely a counterfeit copy of the heavenly.[30]

The latter observation borders on the obvious, perhaps. Yet the obvious is not without interest in this instance. Revelation's attempted sleight of hand ensnares it in a debilitating contradiction. Christians are enjoined to mimic Jesus, who in turn mimics his Father ('To the one who conquers I will give a place with me on my throne, just as I myself conquered and sat down with my Father on his throne', 3.21), who, in effect, mimics the Roman Emperor, who himself (at least as represented in the imperial cult) is a mimetic composite of assorted royal and divine stereotypes. In Revelation, Christian authority inheres in imitation ('To everyone who conquers and continues to do my works to the end, I will give authority [*exousia*] over the nations, to rule them with an iron rod [cf. 12.5, in which the same Psalmic phrase is applied to Jesus himself]...even as I also received authority from my Father', 2.26; cf. 20.4). But if the

---

30. As Robert M. Royalty, Jr, has recognized; see his *The Streets of Heaven: The Ideology of Wealth in the Apocalypse of John* (Macon, GA: Mercer University Press, 1998), pp. 99 n. 57, 246.

Roman imperial order is the ultimate object of imitation in Revelation, then, in accordance with the book's own implicit logic, it remains the ultimate authority, despite the book's explicit attempts to unseat it.

Mimicry and Monstrosity

On Revelation's own account, of course, it is Rome, the sea-beast, that is the consummate mimic — the mimic monster — with its seven heads and ten horns (13.1; 17.3), in imitation of the great red dragon (12.3, explicitly identified as Satan in 12.9 and 20.2), whose own appearance is in turn an imitation of various ancient Near Eastern mythic proto-types.[31] Furthermore, the unholy trinity of Satan, sea-beast, and 'false prophet' (for the latter epithet, see 16.13; 19.20; 20.10) mimics the holy trinity (strictly lower-case, of course; we are not yet within spitting distance of Nicea) of God, Lamb, and prophetic spirit (for the latter, see 2.7, 11, 17, 29; 3.6, 13, 22; cf. 1.10; 4.2; 17.3; 21.10). In addition to the general structural parallel of two antithetical triads, certain characteristics ascribed to the sea-beast in particular mirror those ascribed to Jesus or God: note especially the Christlike 'resurrection' attributed to the sea-beast in 13.3, 14, also the thrice-repeated declaration that 'it was and is not and is to come' (which crops up twice in 17.8 and again in 17.11, in variant forms), parodying the thrice-repeated acclamation of God as he 'who is and who was and who is to come' (1.4, 8; 4.8). Also notable is the depiction of the land-beast as also a lamb-beast: 'it had two horns like a lamb' (13.11). Revelation is engaging in subtle mockery of Satan and his elect agents here, it would seem, implying that they are best seen as distorted reflections of God and his elect agents.

Yet, as we have just observed, Revelation's deity cannot function as anchor for this mimetic chain, but is instead merely another link in it, because modeled on the Roman Emperor — and we have not even begun to consider the extent to which this deity is also a composite copy of Ezekiel's deity, Daniel's deity, and so on, themselves in turn ultimately constructed on the model of the ancient Near Eastern monarch. If the Roman imperial court is, in Revelation, merely a dim, distorted reflection of the heavenly court, the latter is itself merely a magnified reflection of the former and sundry other earthly courts, so that the seer's vision of heaven occurs in a mimetic hall of mirrors.

---

31. Adela Yarbro Collins, *The Combat Myth in the Book of Revelation* (Harvard Dissertations in Religion, 9; Missoula, MT: Scholars Press, 1976), remains the classic study of this and related themes.

Again, this observation smacks of the obvious, and as such falls short of profundity. Yet the 'obvious' does not always command acknowledgment. The difficulty of effectively exiting empire by attempting to turn imperial ideology against itself is regularly underestimated, it seems to me, by those who acclaim Revelation for decisively breaking the self-perpetuating cycle of empire. To my mind, Revelation is emblematic of the difficulty of using the emperor's tools to dismantle the emperor's palace. The seer storms out of the main gates of the imperial palace, wrecking tools in hand, only to be surreptitiously swept back in through the rear entrance, having been deftly relieved of his tools at the threshold.

The Book of Conquest

More than any other early Christian text, Revelation is replete with the language of war, conquest, and empire — so much so, indeed, as to beggar description.[32] Note in particular, however, that the promised reward for faithful Christian discipleship in Revelation is joint rulership of the Empire of empires soon destined to succeed Rome (3.21; 5.10; 20.4-6; 22.5), a messianic Empire established by means of mass-slaughter on a surreal scale (6.4, 8; 8.11; 9.15, 18; 11.13; 14.20; 19.15, 17-21; 20.7-9, 15) calculated to make the combined military campaigns of Julius Caesar, Augustus, and all of their successors pale to insignificance by comparison. All of this suggests that Revelation's overt resistance to and expressed revulsion toward Roman imperial ideology is surreptitiously compromised and undercut by covert compliance and attraction. Not for nothing is Rome figured in Revelation as a prostitute — indeed, as 'the mother of whores' (*hē mētēr tōn pornōn*, 17.5): what better embodiment, for the seer, of seductive repulsiveness, of repulsive seductiveness? Empire is the site of immense ambivalence in this book.

Bhabha's controversial intimation is that since colonial discourse is inherently ambivalent, and as such internally conflicted, it contains the seeds of its own dissolution, independently of any overt act of resistance on the part of colonized subjects. With regard to Revelation, however, the scenario is again reversed. Because Revelation's

32. I reflect elsewhere on Revelation's war theme, reading it as a discursive (and highly circular) performance of masculinity: war making men making war making men... (Stephen D. Moore, *God's Beauty Parlor: And Other Queer Spaces in and around the Bible* [Contraversions: Jews and Other Differences; Stanford, CA: Stanford University Press, 2001], pp. 171-99).

anti-colonial discourse, its resistance to Roman omnipotence, is infected with the imitation compulsion, and hence with ambivalence, it contains the seeds of its own eventual absorption by that which it ostensibly opposes. (Actually, this too is consonant with Bhabha's theory, since he ascribes ambivalence to the colonized no less than the colonizer. The logical collapse of counter-imperial discourse, however, under the weight of its own internal contradictions, is not the kind of phenomenon that Bhabha tends to emphasize or explore.) In this regard, Revelation epitomizes, and encapsulates for analytical scrutiny, the larger and later process whereby Christianity, in the (post-)Constantinian epoch, paradoxically *became* Rome.

As various colonial discourse analysts from Albert Memmi to Homi Bhabha have argued, the relationship between colonizer and colonized is best conceived as a mutually constitutive one.[33] In terms of identity construction, the flow of effects is not all in one direction; instead, there is a complex circulation of influences and effects between colonizer and colonized. The metropolis's relationship to the colonies, to take a rather basic example, becomes a crucial element in its ideological self-representation, and hence in the communal construction of its cultural identity.

Arguably, the post-Constantinian Christianization of the Roman Empire offers the most spectacular historical example of this phenomenon. As a means through which to conceptualize its own unique identity and destiny, metropolitan Roman culture absorbed and internalized Christianity, originally a peripheral, provincial product (although one to whose emergence Rome had already contributed the crucial catalyst by publicly executing its 'founder'). As though anticipating this astounding act of cooption, Revelation resolutely targets hybridity, and holds up for emulation a Christian praxis that is at once peripheral and pure.

Hybrid Harlotry

The threat of the hybrid is embodied for Revelation in the 'works' and teaching of 'the Nicolaitans' (2.6, 15), the teaching of 'Balaam' (2.14; cf. Num. 22–24; 31.8, 16; Deut. 23.4-5; Josh. 24.9-10; 2 Pet. 2.15-16; Jude 11), and the teaching of 'that woman Jezebel' (2.20; cf. 1 Kgs 16.31; 18.1-19; 19.1-3; 21.23, 25; 2 Kgs 9.22, 30-37). The Nicolaitans are

---

33. See Albert Memmi, *The Colonizer and the Colonized* (trans. Howard Greenfeld; Foreword by Homi K. Bhabha; Boston: Beacon Press, 2001).

otherwise unknown; subsequent references to them in patristic literature seem to depend ultimately on Revelation. The names Balaam
and Jezebel can be presumed to be symbolic. The phrase 'the teaching
of Balaam' would appear to be a synonym for 'the teaching of the
Nicolaitans'. The context further suggests that 'Balaam' is not a code-
name for a Christian teacher at Pergamum, although 'Jezebel' would
seem to be a code-name for an actual Christian prophet at Thyatira —
a Nicolaitan prophet to be precise: the content of her teaching is
described in terms identical to that of the Nicolaitans. Like the names
Balaam and Jezebel, the practice of fornication (*porneusai*, 2.14, 20)
with which the Nicolaitans are charged is probably symbolic, fornication being a common figure for idolatry in the Jewish scriptures.[34]
The Nicolaitans are best seen as Christian 'assimilationists', who, like
their counterparts in the Corinthian church (see 1 Cor. 8.1-13; 10.23–
11.1), took a relaxed or pragmatic view of Christian accommodation
to certain cultural norms, specifically (to cite the practice that elicits
the seer's censure), eating meat in assorted socio-religious settings,
whether public settings, such as regular calendric festivals, including
those of the imperial cult; or (semi-)private settings, such as banquets
or other meals hosted by trade guilds or other voluntary associations
or social clubs; or simply eating temple 'leftovers' — meat that has
been sold in the marketplace after having been sacrificed and par-
tially consumed in the temple cults.

Revelation's stance, then, with regard to Christian participation in
the regular civic life of Roman Asia — exemplified by participation in
the many cultic and semi-cultic meals that constituted an important
ingredient of the 'social glue' of the province — is strenuously anti-
assimilationist. But this is to say that its stance is also counter-
hegemonic (using 'hegemonic' once again in its Gramscian sense).[35]
Christians must not enact, through symbolic means, their own subjection to the Roman Empire by participating in the social and religious rituals that collectively prop up the far-flung canopy of the
empire and enable it to cast its shadow over the day-to-day lives of
the diverse populations under its sway. Revelation enjoins a practice

34. For more detailed presentations of the arguments advanced thus far in this
section, see Thompson, *The Book of Revelation*, pp. 121-24; Aune, *Revelation 1–5*,
especially pp. 148-49; and G.K. Beale, *The Book of Revelation* (The New International Greek Testament Commentary; Grand Rapids, MI: Eerdmans, 1999),
especially pp. 260-62. For an attempt to read Jezebel against larger cultural
tapestries, see Tina Pippin, *Apocalyptic Bodies: The Biblical End of the World in Text
and Image* (Biblical Limits; London and New York: Routledge, 1999), pp. 32-42.

35. See pp. 101-102 above.

of non-violent resistance to empire instead, a symbolic 'coming out' of empire (cf. 18.4: 'Come out of her, my people, so that you do not participate in her sins...') while continuing to remain physically within it—though whether a coming out to form full-fledged counter-communities (systematic antitypes of standard Asian communities) or a more ad hoc, guerilla-style coming out is unclear.

As such, the main pillars of Asian collaboration with Roman domination, the members of the Assembly of Asia, an important aspect of whose function was the organization and promotion of the imperial cult, as noted earlier, are singled out for special condemnation in Revelation—provided that the land-beast of 13.11ff., assigned with the responsibility of 'making the earth and its inhabitants worship the [sea-]beast' (Rome and its emperors: cf. 13.1; 17.3, 9), is to be identified as the priesthood of the imperial cult, as has frequently been suggested.[36] The land-beast derives its authority from the sea-beast, but the latter is said to derive its own authority from the dragon, who is Satan (13.4; cf. 12.9; 20.2).

Revelation's unequivocal condemnation of collaboration with Rome, however—even (or especially?) collaboration conducted through symbolic (i.e. ritual) means—extends, by implication, to all strata of Asian society, as its denunciation of Christian assimilationism makes clear. But why? Is it because the mortar of empire is inevitably mixed with the blood of its victims (2.13; 6.9; 13.15; 16.6; 17.6; 18.24), so that (to shift the metaphor slightly) those who reap the benefits of empire, even when the benefits are meager, are, by extension, guilty of the blood that keeps the wheels of empire oiled (17.1-2, 6)? By this logic, only fatal casualties of empire can be deemed innocent of its systemic injustices.[37] If this is indeed Revelation's central assertion regarding the mechanics and ethics of empire, it is an utterly uncompromising and unsettling one.

In light of such a stance, the consistent demonization of imperial authority in Revelation becomes yet more comprehensible, as does its denunciation of assimilationist Christianity. In order that Revelation's blanket critique of empire acquire full rhetorical force, the distinction between the agents of empire, on the one hand, and the victims of empire, on the other, must be asserted at an absolute, and hence

---

36. The suggestion goes back at least to Eduard Lohse, *Die Offenbarung des Johannes* (Das Neue Testament Deutsch; Göttingen: Vandenhoeck & Ruprecht, 12th edn, 1979), p. 72.

37. John Dominic Crossan makes a similar point about the teaching of the historical Jesus, as he reconstructs it; see his *Jesus: A Revolutionary Biography* (San Francisco: HarperSanFrancisco, 1994), p. 62.

metaphysical, level, and such a distinction is necessarily menaced by
any manifestation of Christian hybridity, however innocuous. Within
Revelation, it is the Nicolaitans, epitomized by 'Jezebel', who most
fully embody the threat of hybridity, as we have seen.

But what is the precise relationship between 'Jezebel' and the
'Great Whore', that other female incarnation of iniquity in Revelation
(beyond the — possibly coincidental — fact that each name evokes an
especially unappetizing fate, that of ending up on the wrong end of
the food chain: the original Jezebel is famously devoured by dogs,
whereas the Whore is devoured by a far more fearsome Beast, 1 Kgs
21.23; 2 Kgs 9.30-37; Rev. 17.16)? In other words, what is the relationship between Christian assimilationism and imperial oppression
('And I saw that the woman was drunk with the blood of the saints
and the blood of the witnesses [tōn martyriōn] to Jesus', 17.6; cf. 13.15;
18.24) in this book? The Whore, it may be argued, represents the
threat to Christianity from without, whereas Jezebel represents the
threat to Christianity from within. The threat from within, however,
represented by the spectacle and the specter of Christian assimilation,
is precisely that the threat from outside is not *purely* external: the
outside has infiltrated and contaminated the inside. Jezebel and the
Whore thus represent but two sides of the same (counterfeit) coin in
Revelation: on the one hand, an inside that has somehow strayed
outside; on the other hand, an outside that has somehow stolen
inside.

The Book of Empire

In its concern to maintain intact the high-walled partition separating
imperial metropolis and Christian periphery, Revelation, though pas-
sionately resistant to Roman imperial ideology, paradoxically and
persistently reinscribes its terms, to the extent that Roman imperial
ideology (like subsequent European imperial ideology) can itself be
said to have pivoted around an interrelated series of dualistic distinctions between metropolis and periphery, civilized and barbaric,
advanced and backward, and so on (that brand of imperialistic dualism that Frantz Fanon aptly dubbed 'Manicheanism').[38] Of course,

---

38. See, for example, Frantz Fanon, *The Wretched of the Earth* (trans. Constance
Farrington; New York: Grove Press, 1968 [French original 1961]), pp. 41, 93; also
Nigel C. Gibson, *Fanon: The Postcolonial Imagination* (Oxford: Polity Press, 2003),
especially pp. 113-17. Abdul R. JanMohamed has developed the concept further:
see his *Manichean Aesthetics: The Politics of Literature in Colonial Africa* (Amherst:

Revelation maintains the metropolis/periphery binarism only in order to stand it on its head: the hierarchical power relations that currently obtain between metropolis and periphery, Rome and Christianity, are soon destined for spectacular reversal: 'The world empire has become the empire of our Lord and his Messiah' (*egeneto hē basileia tou kosmou tou kyriou hēmōn kai tou Christou autou*, 11.15). Were the elements on each side of the binary opposition to be allowed to bleed into each other, a clean reversal of the hierarchy would not be possible. Activities or ideologies that do not conform to the binary separation, therefore (participation of Christians in the imperial cult, for example), are subject to censure or rendered taboo in Revelation. But the inherent instability and untenability of the binary division comes to displaced expression in the elaborate mimicry that, as we saw, characterizes Revelation's depiction of the 'other' empire, that of God and the Lamb, a mimicry that persistently blurs the boundaries between the two empires until it becomes all but impossible to decide where one leaves off and the other begins. For the Divine Empire that Revelation proclaims is anything but independent from the Roman Empire; instead it is parasitic on it.

In due course, however, the host absorbed the parasite, precipitating the host's mutation into the one monstrosity that the seer of Revelation seems incapable of imagining: an empire that is Roman and Christian at one and the same time. But the curious phenomenon of Constantinian Christianity itself bears monumental testimony to the fatal flaw in Revelation's theology, the fact that it counters empire with empire: to proclaim that 'The world empire has become the empire of our Lord and his Messiah' is also to proclaim that 'The empire of our Lord and his Messiah has become the world empire'. More than any other early Christian text (prior to Tertullian, at any rate), Revelation epitomizes the imperial theology that enabled the Roman state effortlessly to absorb Christianity into itself, to turn Christianity into a version of itself, and to turn itself into a version of Christianity—notwithstanding the paradox that Revelation is also ostensibly more hostile to Rome than any other early Christian text. The flaw in Revelation's theology inheres in three mutually reinforcing—and inescapably obvious?—features of the text (although the obvious is always hedged about with obliviousness, and hence never

University of Massachusetts Press, 1983); or, for a digest, his 'The Economy of Manichean Allegory', in Bill Ashcroft, Gareth Griffiths, and Helen Tiffin (eds.), *The Post-Colonial Studies Reader* (London and New York: Routledge, 1995), pp. 18-23.

as inescapable as one would like). First of all, the throne is the paramount metonym for God in this book.[39] Second, the principal attributes of 'the one seated on the throne' are stereotypically imperial attributes: incomparable glory and authority; absolute power; and punitive wrath. And third, the principal activities of the one seated on the throne and those of his elite agents are quintessentially imperial activities: the conduct of war and the enlargement of empire.[40]

To construct God or Christ, together with their putatively salvific activities, from the raw materials of imperial ideology is not to shatter the cycle of empire but merely to transfer it to a transcendental plane, thereby reinscribing and reifying it. The dearth of non-imperial synonyms for the Christian theological commonplace(s), 'the kingdom (or reign, or rule) of God (or Christ)', even in contemporary theological and pastoral discourse,[41] is symptomatic of the extent to which imperial metaphors have maintained, and continue to maintain, a virtual monopoly and stranglehold on the Christian theological imagination — one ultimately unchecked by the cross, I would venture to add, which all too easily folds up to form a throne — creating an imperial divine amalgam or 'essence' that is extremely difficult to dismantle or dislodge.

And yet there is undoubtedly a place for what Gayatri Spivak, in a related context, has termed 'strategic essentialism'.[42] The envisioning of a cosmic Counter-Empire presided over by a Divine Emperor may serve an important strategic function in struggles for liberation from situations of desperate oppression, as work on Revelation such as that of Allan Boesak or Pablo Richard eloquently testifies.[43] Revelation is eminently well-equipped to speak to such situations; to a greater or lesser extent, it was in such a crucible that Revelation itself was forged (not yet a situation of systemic state-sponsored persecution, apparently — but the seer's intuition that such oppression lay over the

39. Richard Bauckham, *The Theology of the Book of Revelation* (New Testament Theology; Cambridge: Cambridge University Press, 1993), is particularly good on this; see especially pp. 31-34, 41-46 *passim*, 140-43.

40. See further Moore, *God's Beauty Parlor*, pp. 175-91.

41. One such synonym, however, would be the neologism 'kindom of God', coined by Ada María Isasi-Díaz in *En la lucha (In the Struggle): Elaborating a Mujerista Theology* (Minneapolis: Fortress Press, 2nd edn, 2003).

42. And which she glosses as 'a strategic use of positivist essentialism in a scrupulously visible political interest' (Gayatri Chakravorty Spivak, 'Subaltern Studies: Deconstructing Historiography', in her *In Other Worlds: Essays in Cultural Politics* [New York: Methuen, 1987], pp. 197-221 [205]).

43. See Boesak, *Comfort and Protest*; Richard, *Apocalypse*.

horizon was entirely accurate). Ultimately, however, if Christian theology is to be intellectually as well as ethically adequate, and as such less luridly anthropomorphic and less patently projectionist, might it not require what Revelation, locked as it is in visions of empires and counter-empires, emperors and counter-emperors, is singularly powerless to provide: a conception of the divine sphere as other than empire writ large?[44]

44. The first full-scale attempt to develop such a conception has appeared since I penned these words, John D. Caputo's *The Weakness of God: A Theology of the Event* (Indiana Series in the Philosophy of Religion; Bloomington and Indianapolis: Indiana University Press, 2006), which I view as an extraordinarily original and profound attempt despite my quibble with it below. 'My idea is to stop thinking about God as a massive ontological power line that provides power to the world', Caputo explains, 'instead thinking of something that short-circuits such power and proves a provocation to the world that is otherwise than power' (p. 13). He claims to find such a way of thinking in the New Testament 'under the name "kingdom of God"...filled in or fleshed out, given a kind of phenomenological fulfillment, in soaring parables and mind-bending para-doxes... You see the weak force that stirs within the name of God only when someone casts it in the form of a narrative, tells mad stories and perplexing parables about it, which is what Jesus did when he called for the kingdom of God... The kingdom of God that is called for in the New Testament is an anar-chized field... In the kingdom, weak forces play themselves out in paradoxical effects that confound the powers that be, displaying the unsettling shock delivered to the reigning order by the name of God' (pp. 13-14). Caputo's Jesus, then (although this is not a book about Jesus; Paul plays a more prominent role in it, and Derrida a more prominent role than Paul), is the world-subverting sage familiar from certain recent strands of historical Jesus scholarship. We never discover what Caputo would do with the other face of the kingdom of God in the Synoptic tradition, the one ushered in with irresistible force by an imperial Christ enthroned on the clouds and attended by angelic courtiers.

Conclusion

It will by now come as no surprise to the reader to hear that I find myself chiefly unconvinced by readings of Mark, Revelation, or other New Testament texts that hold them up as signal instances of unequivocal anti-imperial resistance literature, even while I readily recognize the efficacy, even the necessity, of such interpretations in certain contexts, especially contexts of oppression and marginalization that obliquely mirror those in which many of the New Testament texts, putatively, were produced. What such readings fail to account for, nonetheless, or so it seems to me, is a single inconvenient but colossal fact—namely, that certain honorable exceptions aside, the vast majority of Christian interpreters through the ages have managed to read these same texts as supportive of empire, when not as actual divine warrants for inexorable imperial expansion. Rather than dismiss this incalculably influential interpretive trajectory as the product of systemic misreading on a monumental scale, if not of mass hermeneutical hallucination outright, I have tended instead to assume that this mode of reading, like all modes of reading, is merely selective and exclusive, electing to foreground certain elements of the texts at the expense of certain other elements that recent liberationist exegetes, in particular, have preferred to highlight.

The enigma of how a disparate set of texts written in the margins of the Roman Empire, if not from its underside, eventually became, collectively, the charter document of post-Constantinian, which is to say imperial, Christianity—which is also the enigma of how one Jesus of Nazareth, a Galilean peasant nonentity, became, primarily through the agency of these same unlikely texts, a new Romulus, the founder of a new Rome—is one that each of the exegetical chapters in this book has compulsively (re)turned to sooner or later. My preoccupation with this puzzle, however, has also driven the entire inquiry implicitly more than it has featured in it explicitly. No less significant for the inquiry, meanwhile, has been the contrary fact that these texts also preserve indelibly the marks of their original marginality and resist imperial ideology even while being engulfed in its maw.

Measuring the relative strength of these two opposing forces in relation to three such texts has, at base, been the task this book has taken on.

Another aspect of this pull and tug between resistance and entanglement, and one that the book has pondered at some length, is the relationship of empire to apocalypse in Mark, Revelation, and even John, a text in which apocalyptic is ordinarily thought to play a negligible role, except as 'realized eschatology'. I have argued, however, that the role assigned to Rome in John is essentially an apocalyptic one, Rome rushing in to fill the theological vacuum left by the Johannine erasure of a dramatized parousia, even while Rome is also the veiled object of scathing critique in John. My argument with regard to Mark, so far as it touched on apocalyptic, was that the insistence of its protagonist on returning in imperial splendor, thereby implicitly trumping Rome, but in a game for which Rome has written the rules, stands in acute tension, if not in outright contradiction, with his radical countercultural and counterimperial social ethic. Along similar lines, my reading of Revelation has attempted to call into question the purely oppositional role that previous scholarship has tended to construct for it in relation to Rome, and has argued instead for a symbiotic relationship between Revelation's apocalyptic eschatology and Roman imperial ideology, one that, for all Revelation's ostensible antipathy toward Rome, reduces Revelation to representing the divine sphere as a kind of über-Rome or Roman Empire writ large, and as such compromises its endeavor to shatter the relentless cycle of empire once and for all.

I have been interested throughout, then, in how literary constructions of an Empire of God emanating from early Christianity, especially apocalyptic constructions, attempt, to whatever degree, to stand over against the Roman Empire, but necessarily from deep within it — and so also with it deep within them — so that they end up covertly, and perhaps inevitably, recycling certain of the empire's fundamental enabling values and assumptions even while engaging in overt or covert condemnation of them. The themes of this book, as such, have not only been empire and apocalypse, but also the infinitesimal space that has simultaneously separated and connected the two in the three early Christian texts we have analyzed.

POSTCOLONIAL STUDIES AND EMPIRE STUDIES: AN ANNOTATED BIBLIOGRAPHY*

I. *General*

Adam, Ian, and Helen Tiffin (eds.), *Past the Last Post: Theorizing Post-Colonialism and Post-Modernism* (New York and London: Harvester Wheatsheaf, 1991).

Ahmad, Aijaz, *In Theory: Classes, Nations, Literatures* (London: Verso, 1992).
Contains a scathing Marxist critique of postcolonial theory, epitomized for the author by the work of Edward Said.

— 'The Politics of Literary Postcoloniality', *Race and Class* 36 (1995), pp. 1-20. Reprinted in Mongia (ed.), *Contemporary Postcolonial Theory*.
Ahmad extends his critique to Homi Bhabha.

Ashcroft, Bill, Gareth Griffiths, and Helen Tiffin, *The Empire Writes Back: Theory and Practice in Post-Colonial Literatures* (London and New York: Routledge, 1989).
One of the books that was instrumental in constituting postcolonial studies as a field.

— *Post-Colonial Studies: The Key Concepts* (London and New York: Routledge, 2nd edn, 2001).
An A–Z mini-encyclopedia of postcolonial studies, saved from triteness by the general quality of the articles. An immensely useful resource, especially if used with more conventional introductions to the field.

---

*   For the distinction between postcolonial studies and empire studies (a porous one, to be sure), see p. 19 above, a distinction needed not so much for the 'General' section of this bibliography as for the 'Biblical Studies' section. I have attempted (unsuccessfully, no doubt) to provide a comprehensive listing of works in biblical studies at the time of writing that engage explicitly, to whatever degree, with the field of postcolonial studies. Even the appearance of exhaustiveness is, however, unattainable in relation to what I am calling 'empire studies', its edges being far too fuzzy. I have likewise attempted no comprehensive listing of work in liberation or contextual hermeneutics, even though such work often overlaps with postcolonial hermeneutics (see pp. 14-17 above), while the 'General' section also represents but a selection, needless to say, from the extra-biblical field of postcolonial studies. A final caveat: the New Testament bias of the 'Biblical Studies' section will be readily apparent, and should be put down to my lesser familiarity with the field of Old Testament/Hebrew Bible.

Ashcroft, Bill, Gareth Griffiths, and Helen Tiffin (eds.), *The Post-Colonial Studies Reader* (New York and London: Routledge, 1995).

Eighty-six short essays, mainly abridged excerpts from longer works. The anthology is divided into fourteen parts, each with its own introduction: 'Issues and Debates'; 'Universality and Difference'; 'Representation and Resistance'; 'Postmodernism and Post-Colonialism'; 'Nationalism'; 'Hybridity'; 'Ethnicity and Indigeneity'; 'Feminism and Post-Colonialism'; 'Language'; 'The Body and Performance'; 'History'; 'Place'; 'Education'; and 'Production and Consumption'.

Barry, Peter, *Beginning Theory: An Introduction to Literary and Cultural Theory* (Manchester: Manchester University Press, 2nd edn, 2002).

One would be hard-pressed to name a more beginner-friendly introduction to postcolonial criticism than the relevant chapter in this textbook.

Bhabha, Homi K., *The Location of Culture* (London and New York: Routledge, 1994).

Arguably, this is the book that, more than any other, epitomizes 'postcolonial theory'. The core essays in the collection deal with nineteenth-century India, and expound Bhabha's influential concepts of colonial ambivalence, mimicry, hybridity, 'third space', and 'sly civility'. One of these essays, 'Signs Taken for Wonders', is also an exercise (of sorts) in biblical hermeneutics.

—'Postcolonial Authority and Postmodern Guilt', in Lawrence Grossberg, Cary Nelson, and Paula A. Treichler (eds.), *Cultural Studies* (London and New York: Routledge, 1992), pp. 56-68.

—'Postcolonial Critic: Homi Bhabha', in Patrick Colm Hogan and Lalita Pandit (eds.), *Literary India: Comparative Studies in Aesthetics, Colonialism and Culture* (Albany: State University of New York Press, 1995), pp. 237-53.

An interview with Bhabha.

—'Postcolonial Criticism', in Stephen Greenblatt and Giles B. Gunn (eds.), *Redrawing the Boundaries: The Transformation of English and American Literary Studies* (New York: Modern Language Association of America, 1992), pp. 437-65.

Not as accessible an essay as one would normally expect to find in a textbook, but a useful entrée nonetheless to Bhabha's thought.

—'Postmodernism/Postcolonialism', in Robert S. Nelson and Richard Shiff (eds.), *Critical Terms for Art History* (Chicago: University of Chicago Press, 1996), pp. 307-22.

—'Surviving Theory: A Conversation with Homi K. Bhabha', in Fawzia Afzal-Khan and Kalpana Seshadri-Crooks (eds.), *The Pre-Occupation of Postcolonial Studies* (Durham, NC: Duke University Press, 2000), pp. 369-79.

Like 'Postcolonial Critic' above, one of the more accessible and useful of Bhabha's many interviews.

Bhabha, Homi K. (ed.), *Nation and Narration* (London and New York: Routledge, 1990).
> The essays collected in this volume (not least Bhabha's own 'DissemiNation', which, however, also appears in *The Location of Culture*) variously deconstruct or otherwise interrogate the concept of 'nation'.

Campbell, Jan, *Arguing With the Phallus: Feminist, Queer and Postcolonial Theory. A Psychoanalytic Contribution* (New York: St Martin's Press, 2000).

Childs, Peter, and Patrick Williams, *An Introduction to Post-Colonial Theory* (London and New York: Prentice Hall/Harvester Wheatsheaf, 1997).
> Includes useful chapters on Said, Bhabha, and Spivak.

Desai, Gaurav, and Supriya Nair (eds.), *Postcolonialisms: An Anthology of Cultural Theory and Criticism* (New Brunswick, NJ: Rutgers University Press, 2005).
> Thirty-seven selections, divided into the following parts: 'Ideologies of Imperialism'; 'The Critique of Colonial Discourse'; 'The Politics of Language and Literary Studies'; 'Nationalisms and Nativisms'; 'Hybrid Identities'; 'Gender and Sexualities'; 'Reading the Subaltern'; 'Comparative (Post)colonialisms'; and 'Globalization and Postcoloniality'.

Fanon, Franz, *Black Skins, White Masks* (trans. Charles Lam Markmann; New York: Grove Press, 1991 [French original 1952]).
> Fanon's most influential work, a searing analysis of the complicity of colonialism and racism.

Gandhi, Leela, *Postcolonial Theory: A Critical Introduction* (New York: Columbia University Press, 1998).
> Situates postcolonial theory in relation to poststructuralism, postmodernism, Marxism, and feminism.

Goldberg, David Theo, and Ato Quayson (eds.), *Relocating Postcolonalism* (Oxford: Blackwell, 2002).
> A multi-faceted assessment of the field, with contributions by Said, Bhabha, and Spivak, and substantial essays such as Benita Parry's 'Directions and Dead Ends in Postcolonial Studies'.

Hardt, Michael, and Antonio Negri, *Empire* (Cambridge, MA: Harvard University Press, 2001).
> A much-discussed, and highly controversial, neo-Marxist presentation of globalization as an unprecedented phase of empire without borders.

Harrison, Nicholas, *Postcolonial Criticism: History, Theory and the Work of Fiction* (Oxford: Blackwell, 2003).
> Postcolonial literary criticism applied to assorted works from the African colonial arena.

Hawley, John C. (ed.), *Encyclopedia of Postcolonial Studies* (Westport, CT: Greenwood Press, 2001).
> At 520 pages, considerably more detailed and comprehensive than Ashcroft *et al.*'s mini-encyclopedia, *Postcolonial Studies* (but also far pricier).

—*Postcolonial Queer: Theoretical Intersections* (Albany: State University of New York Press, 2001).

Huddart, David, *Homi K. Bhabha* (Routledge Critical Thinkers; London and New York: Routledge, 2006).

The first book-length introduction to this complex postcolonial theorist.

Lazarus, Neil (ed.), *The Cambridge Companion to Postcolonial Literary Studies* (Cambridge: Cambridge University Press, 2004).

Thirteen essays on such topics as 'The Institutionalisation of Postcolonial Studies'; 'Poststructuralism and Postcolonial Discourse'; and 'Feminism in/and Postcolonialism'.

Lewis, Reina, and Sara Mills (eds.), *Feminist Postcolonial Theory: A Reader* (Edinburgh: Edinburgh University Press, 2003).

The anthology contains selections from such prominent critics as Rey Chow, bell hooks, Audrey Lorde, Ann McClintock, Chandra Mohanty, Adrienne Rich, and Gayatri Spivak.

Loomba, Ania, *Colonialism/Postcolonialism* (London and New York: Routledge, 1998).

A good general introduction, although it provides little in the way of concrete strategies for postcolonial analysis.

Loomba, Ania, Suvir Kaul, Matti Bunzl, Antoinette Burton, and Jed Esty (eds.), *Postcolonial Studies and Beyond* (Durham, NC: Duke University Press, 2005).

A team of contributors from different disciplines (including Daniel Boyarin) critically reflect on the past, present, and possible future(s) of postcolonial studies.

McClintock, Anne, *Imperial Leather: Race, Gender and Sexuality in the Colonial Contest* (London and New York: Routledge, 1995).

Virtuoso analyses of the complex intersections of race, class, sex, and gender in the British Empire and recent South Africa.

McClintock, Anne, Aamir Mufti, and Ella Shohat (eds.), *Dangerous Liaisons: Gender, Nation and Postcolonial Perspectives* (Minneapolis: University of Minnesota Press, 1997).

An important collection that bridges postcolonial and gender studies.

McLeod, John, *Beginning Postcolonialism* (Manchester: Manchester University Press, 2000).

As one reviewer aptly puts it, 'Baffled by Bhabha? Scared by Spivak? Then this is the book for you'.

Memmi, Albert, *The Colonizer and the Colonized* (trans. Howard Greenfeld; Foreword by Homi Bhabha; Boston: Beacon Press, 2001 [French original 1966]).

A seminal work of colonial discourse analysis. Its stress on the psychological interdependence of colonizer and colonized anticipates major currents in contemporary postcolonial theory.

Minh-ha, Trinh T., *Woman, Native, Other: Writing Postcoloniality and Feminism* (Bloomington: Indiana University Press, 1989).

An influential work by a major postcolonial and feminist critic.

Mongia, Padmini (ed.), *Contemporary Postcolonial Theory: A Reader* (London: Arnold, 1996).
Nineteen selections, including several important critiques of post-colonial theory, divided into the following parts: 'Shifting Terrains'; 'Disciplining Knowledge'; and 'Locating Practice'.

Moore-Gilbert, Bart, *Postcolonial Theory: Contexts, Practices, Politics* (London: Verso, 1997).
Dense and demanding, but still, in my opinion, the best one-volume introduction to postcolonial theory. The distinctions drawn in the introduction between postcolonial theory and postcolonial criticism are fundamental, and the lengthy chapters on Said, Spivak, and Bhabha are excellent.

Moore-Gilbert, Bart, Gareth Stanton, and Willy Maley (eds.), *Postcolonial Criticism* (London: Longman, 1997). An anthology of ten excerpts, most of them from 'classic' works in the field, preceded by a 70-page intro-duction.

Parry, Benita, *Postcolonial Studies: A Materialist Critique* (Postcolonial Litera-tures; London and New York: Routledge, 2004).
The critique is leveled primarily at colonial discourse analysis in the mode of Bhabha, Spivak *et al.*

Pratt, Mary Louise, *Imperial Eyes: Travel Writing and Transculturation* (London and New York: Routledge, 1992).
An influential book, best known for the concept of the 'contact zone' that it develops.

Quayson, Ato, *Postcolonialism: Theory, Practice or Process?* (Cambridge: Polity Press, 2000).
Attempts to relate postcolonial studies more fully to political practice.

Said, Edward W., *Culture and Imperialism* (New York: Vintage Press, 1993).
Contains exemplary analyses of both the cultural productions of empire (e.g. the novels of Austen and Conrad, the music of Verdi) and of the resistance to empire (e.g. the literature of Yeats, Achebe, and Rushdie), and in the process introduces the method that Said terms 'contrapuntal reading'.

—*Culture and Resistance: Conversations with Edward W. Said* (ed. David Barsamian; Cambridge, MA: South End Press, 2003).

—*The Edward Said Reader* (ed. Moustafa Bayoumi and Andrew Rubin; New York: Vintage Books, 2000).

—'An Exchange: *Exodus and Revolution*', *Grand Street* 5 (1986), pp. 246-59.
Said responds to Michael Walzer's *Exodus and Revolution*, a study of the political meanings of the exodus narrative.

—*Orientalism* (New York: Vintage Books, 2003).
This twenty-fifth anniversary edition contains a new preface by the author. Originally published in 1978, the book is widely viewed as the charter document of postcolonial studies as an academic discipline. Influenced by Foucault and also by Gramsci, it analyzes 'the Orient' and 'the Oriental' as Western discursive constructs, with particular attention to nineteenth-century Western scholarship and its imperial contexts.

—'Orientalism and Beyond', in Bart Moore-Gilbert, Gareth Stanton, and Willy Maley (eds.), *Postcolonial Criticism* (London: Longman, 1997), pp. 34-73.

—'Orientalism Reconsidered', in Francis Barker *et al.* (eds.), *Literature, Politics and Theory* (London: Methuen, 1986), pp. 210-29.

San Juan, E. [Epifanio], Jr., *Beyond Postcolonial Theory* (New York: St Martin's Press, 1998).

An impassioned critique of postcolonial theory for its alleged detachment from grassroots movements for liberation and social transformation, especially in the Two-Thirds World.

Schwarz, Henry, and Sangeeta Ray (eds.), *A Companion to Postcolonial Studies* (Oxford: Blackwell, 2000).

Twenty-nine essays on such topics as 'Imperialism, Colonialism, Postcolonialism'; 'Postcolonial Feminism/Postcolonialism and Feminism'; 'U.S. Imperialism: Global Dominance without Colonies'; 'Africa: Varied Colonial Legacies'; and 'Spivak and Bhabha'.

Singh, Amritjit, and Peter Schmidt (eds.), *Postcolonial Theory and the United States: Race, Ethnicity and Literature* (Jackson: University of Mississippi Press, 2000).

Spivak, Gayatri Chakravorty, 'Can the Subaltern Speak?', in Cary Nelson and Lawrence Grossberg (eds.), *Marxism and the Interpretation of Culture* (Urbana: University of Illinois Press, 1988), pp. 271-313.

A dense, influential, and controversial meditation on the impossibility of 'speaking for' the marginalized and dispossessed. According to Spivak, postcolonial intellectuals need to 'learn that their privilege is their loss'. Excerpted in Ashcroft, Griffiths, and Tiffin (eds.), *The Post-Colonial Studies Reader*.

— *A Critique of Postcolonial Reason: Toward a History of the Vanishing Present* (Cambridge, MA: Harvard University Press, 1999).

Spivak's *magnum opus*, in which much of her earlier work (including that on the subaltern) achieves definitive expression. The book is, among other things, an internal critique of postcolonial studies from highly nuanced Marxist and feminist positions. A difficult but rewarding read.

— *In Other Worlds: Essays in Cultural Politics* (London and New York: Routledge, 1988).

Certain of the essays in this collection were extremely significant for postcolonial studies in its emergent phase, such 'Three Women's Texts and a Critique of Imperialism' and 'Subaltern Studies: Deconstructing Historiography'.

— *The Post-Colonial Critic: Interviews, Strategies, Dialogues* (ed. Sarah Harasym; London and New York: Routledge, 1990).

— *The Spivak Reader: Selected Works of Gayatri Chakravorty Spivak* (ed. Donna Landry and Gerald M. MacLean; London and New York: Routledge, 1996).

—' "What Is It For?" Gayatri Chakravorty Spivak on the Functions of the Postcolonial Critic', *Nineteenth-Century Contexts: An Interdisciplinary Journal* 18 (1994), pp. 71-81.

Williams, Patrick, and Laura Chrisman (eds.), *Colonial Discourse and Post-colonial Theory: A Reader* (New York: Columbia University Press, 1994).
Thirty-one selections, divided into the following parts, each with its own introduction: 'Theorizing Colonial Cultures and Anti-Colonial Resistance'; 'Theorizing the West'; 'Theorizing Gender'; 'Theorizing Postcoloniality: Intellectuals and Institutions'; 'Theorizing Postcoloniality: Discourse and Identity'; and 'Reading from Theory'.

Young, Robert J.C., *Postcolonialism: An Historical Introduction* (Oxford: Blackwell, 2001).
Arguably, the most impressive introduction to postcolonialism to date; its breadth is unparalleled. Of particular relevance for postcolonial literary (and biblical) criticism are the chapters on colonialism, imperialism, neocolonialism, and postcolonialism, as well as those on 'Women, Gender and Anti-Colonialism'; 'Edward Said and Colonial Discourse'; 'Foucault in Tunisia'; and 'Derrida in Algeria'.

—*Postcolonialism: A Very Short Introduction* (Oxford: Oxford University Press, 2003).

—*White Mythologies: Writing History and the West* (London and New York: Routledge, 1990).
Particularly notable for its chapters on Said, Spivak, and Bhabha, which, while not as full as those in Moore-Gilbert, *Postcolonial Theory*, are also essential reading for anybody interested in these thinkers.

II. *Biblical Studies*

Ahn, Yong-Sung, *The Reign of God and Rome in Luke's Passion Narrative: An East Asian Global Perspective* (Biblical Interpretation Series, 80; Leiden: Brill, 2006).
Engages with the postcolonial theory of Edward Said and Homi Bhabha. Argues that Luke simultaneously contests and is complicit with Roman imperial ideology: 'Perhaps the context of imperialism that dominates Western scholarship on Luke', writes Ahn, 'has encouraged the bifurcated view of the gospel as either pro-Roman or anti-Roman'.

Alexander, Loveday (ed.), *Images of Empire* (Journal for the Study of the Old Testament Supplement Series, 122; Sheffield: JSOT Press, 1991).
Essays on biblical texts in this collection include: Richard Bauckham, 'The Economic Critique of Rome in Revelation 18'; Philip Davies, 'Daniel in the Lion's Den'; Douglas Edwards, 'Surviving the Web of Power: Religion and Politics in the Acts of the Apostles, Josephus, and Chariton's *Chaereas and Callirhoe*'; and Vernon Robbins, 'Luke–Acts: A Mixed Population Seeks a Home in the Roman Empire'.

Avalos, Hector, 'Columbus as Biblical Exegete: A Study of the *Libro de las Profecias*', in Menachem Mor and Bryan F. Le Beau (eds.), *Religion in the Age of Exploration: The Case of Spain and New Spain* (Omaha: Creighton University Press, 1996), pp. 59-80.

—'*The Gospel of Lucas Gavilán* as Postcolonial Biblical Exegesis', *Semeia* 75 (1996), pp. 87-106.
The gospel of the title is a Spanish paraphrase of Luke from 1970s Mexico.

Barclay, John (ed.), *Negotiating Diaspora: Jewish Strategies in the Roman Empire* (The Library of Second Temple Studies, 45; New York: T. & T. Clark International, 2004). Of particular relevance are the essays on Josephus by Barclay and James McLaren, which argue that he employs 'subaltern' tactics, deploying the tools of the 'colonial' culture for the advantage of his own.

Belo, Fernando, *A Materialist Reading of the Gospel of Mark* (trans. Matthew J. O'Connell; Maryknoll, NY: Orbis Books, 1981 [French original 1974]).
Employs Roland Barthes' strategies of reading within a Marxist framework to analyze Mark's resistance to Rome.

Berquist, Jon L., 'Postcolonialism and Imperial Motives for Canonization', *Semeia* 75 (1996), pp. 15-36. Reprinted in R.S. Sugirtharajah (ed.), *The Postcolonial Biblical Reader* (Oxford: Blackwell, 2006).
Situates the early stages of Hebrew Bible canonization during the Persian reign over colonial Yehud.

Boer, Roland, 'Green Ants and Gibeonites: B. Wongar, Joshua 9, and Some Problems of Postcolonialism', in Laura Donaldson (ed.), *Postcolonialism and Scriptural Reading* (Semeia, 75; Atlanta: Society of Biblical Literature, 1996), pp. 129-52.
The work of the *faux* Aboriginal author is ingeniously juxtaposed with the biblical text.

—*Last Stop before Antarctica: The Bible and Postcolonialism in Australia* (The Bible and Postcolonialism, 4; Sheffield: Sheffield Academic Press, 2001).
A stimulating set of interconnected essays that bring selected biblical texts into dialogue with postcolonial studies, postcolonial literature, nineteenth-century explorer journals, and other facets of colonialism's complex legacy. Concludes with reflections on the Bible's role in the production of postcolonialism itself.

—'Marx, Postcolonialism, and the Bible', in Stephen D. Moore and Fernando F. Segovia (eds.), *Postcolonial Biblical Criticism: Interdisciplinary Intersections* (The Bible and Postcolonialism, 8; New York: T. & T. Clark International, 2005), pp. 166-83.
A Marxist critique of postcolonial studies and postcolonial biblical criticism.

—'Remembering Babylon: Postcolonialism and Australian Biblical Studies', in R.S. Sugirtharajah (ed.), *The Postcolonial Bible* (The Bible and Postcolonialism, 1; Sheffield: Sheffield Academic Press, 1998), pp. 24-48.

Boer, Roland (ed.), *Vanishing Mediator? The Presence/Absence of the Bible in Postcolonialism* (Semeia, 88; Atlanta: Society of Biblical Literature, 2002).
Boer's incisive introduction to the volume anticipates 'Marx, Postcolonialism, and the Bible' above. The contributors, literary scholars in the main, range over such topics as Australian Aboriginal hermeneutics, explorer hermeneutics, and missionary conversion and education.

Brett, Mark G., 'The Ethics of Postcolonial Criticism', in Laura Donaldson
　　(ed.), *Postcolonialism and Scriptural Reading* (Semeia, 75; Atlanta: Society
　　of Biblical Literature, 1996), pp. 219-28.
　　　　A penetrating response to the essays gathered in this volume.
—*Genesis: Procreation and the Politics of Identity* (London and New York:
　　Routledge, 2000).
　　　　Informed in part by postcolonial theory, Brett argues that Genesis may
　　be read as a covert assault on the ethnocentrism of the Persian imperial
　　apparatus.
—'Genocide in Deuteronomy: Postcolonial Variations on Mimetic Desire', in
　　Mark A. O'Brien and Howard N. Wallace (eds.), *Seeing Signals, Reading
　　Signs: The Art of Exegesis. Studies in Honour of Antony F. Campbell, S.J., for
　　His Seventieth Birthday* (Journal for the Study of the Old Testament
　　Supplement Series, 415; New York: T. & T. Clark International, 2005),
　　pp. 75-89.
—'Israel's Indigenous Origins: Cultural Hybridity and the Formation of
　　Israelite Ethnicity', *Biblical Interpretation* 11 (2003), pp. 400-12.
Brueggemann, Walter, 'Always in the Shadow of the Empire', in Michael L.
　　Budde and Robert W. Brimlow (eds.), *The Church as Counterculture*
　　(Albany: State University of New York Press, 2000), pp. 39-58.
—'At the Mercy of Babylon: A Subversive Rereading of the Empire', *Journal
　　of Biblical Literature* 11 (1991), pp. 3-22.
Bryan, Christopher, *Render to Caesar: Jesus, the Early Church, and the Roman
　　Superpower* (Oxford: Oxford University Press, 2005).
　　　　Combats what Bryan sees as the excesses of the political and
　　'postcolonial' reconstructions of the historical Jesus, especially Richard
　　Horsley's.
Burrus, Virginia, 'Luke–Acts', in Fernando F. Segovia and R.S. Sugirtharajah
　　(eds.), *The Postcolonial Commentary on the New Testament* (New York: T. &
　　T. Clark International, forthcoming).
　　　　A reading thoroughly informed by postcolonial theory, especially that of
　　Bhabha.
Carroll, Robert P., 'The Myth of the Empty Land', *Semeia* 59 (1992), pp. 79-93.
　　　　'The two myths of the empty land and the impurely occupied land play
　　an important part in the representation of the founding of the Second
　　Temple community'.
Carter, Warren, 'Are There Imperial Texts in the Class? Intertextual Eagles
　　and Matthean Eschatology as "Lights Out" Time for Imperial Rome
　　(Matthew 24:27-31)', *Journal of Biblical Literature* 122 (2003), pp. 467-87.
／ —'Contested Claims: Roman Imperial Theology and Matthew's Gospel',
　　Biblical Theology Bulletin 29 (1999), pp. 56-67.
—'Honoring the Emperor and Sacrificing Wives and Slaves: 1 Peter 2:13–3:6',
　　in Amy-Jill Levine (ed.), *A Feminist Companion to the Catholic Epistles and
　　Hebrews* (The Feminist Companion to the New Testament and Early
　　Christian Writings, 8; London: T. & T. Clark International, 2005), pp.
　　13-43.
—'Imperial Paradigms in the Parables of Matthew 18:21-35 and 22:1-14',
　　Interpretation 56 (2002), pp. 260-72.

—'Matthean Christology in Roman Imperial Key: Matthew 1:1', in John Riches and David C. Sim (eds.), *The Gospel of Matthew in its Roman Imperial Context* (Journal for the Study of the New Testament Supplement Series, 276; New York: T. & T. Clark International, 2005), pp. 143-65.

—*Matthew and Empire: Initial Explorations* (Harrisburg, PA: Trinity Press International, 2001).

Attempts to extend the ancient context against which Matthew is read from the Jewish synagogue to the Roman Empire, arguing that the gospel contains a multifaceted critique of Roman imperial ideology. Carter's reading of the Matthean Pilate is especially interesting, and cuts against the grain of both ecclesial and scholarly interpretations of this character. This book is, in effect, a thematic companion to Carter's *Matthew and the Margins*.

—*Matthew and the Margins: A Sociopolitical and Religious Reading* (Bible and Liberation Series; Maryknoll, NY: Orbis Books, 2000).

Takes the form of a section-by-section commentary on the entire Gospel of Matthew. Argues that this gospel is a counter-narrative designed to turn the followers of Jesus into an alternative community that is resistant to the authorities of both the Jewish synagogue and the Roman state.

—'Matthew', in Fernando F. Segovia and R.S. Sugirtharajah (eds.), *The Postcolonial Commentary on the New Testament* (New York: T. & T. Clark International, forthcoming).

—'Paying the Tax to Rome as Subversive Praxis: Matthew 17:24-27', *Journal for the Study of the New Testament* 76 (1999), pp. 3-31.

—'Resisting and Imitating the Empire: Imperial Paradigms in Two Matthean Parables', *Interpretation* 56 (2002), pp. 260-72.

The two parables are 'The Unforgiving Servant' and 'The Wedding Feast'.

—'Vulnerable Power: The Early Christian Movement's Challenge to the Roman Empire', in A.J. Blasi, J. Duhaime, and P.A. Turcotte (eds.), *Handbook of Early Christianity and the Social Sciences* (Walnut Creek, CA: Alta Mira Press, 2002), pp. 453-88.

Cary, Norman R., '*Christus Mundi*: The Jesus Figure in Postcolonial Literature', *Christianity and Literature* 41 (1991), pp. 39-59.

Cassidy, Richard J., *Christians and Roman Rule in the New Testament: New Perspectives* (New York: Crossroad, 2001).

Includes chapters on the following: the Synoptic Gospels; John; Romans and 1 Peter; Paul's letters from prison; and Revelation.

—*John's Gospel in New Perspective: Christology and the Realities of Roman Power* (Maryknoll, NY: Orbis Books, 1992).

Argues that Johannine Christology is not mere theological theorizing, but a matter of immense political import.

Cave, Alfred A., 'Canaanites in a Promised Land: The American Indian and the Providential Theory of Empire', *American Indian Quarterly* 12 (1998), pp. 277-97.

Chia, Philip, 'On Naming the Subject: Postcolonial Reading of Daniel 1', *Jian Dao* 7 (1997), pp. 17-35. Reprinted in R.S. Sugirtharajah (ed.), *The Postcolonial Biblical Reader* (Oxford: Blackwell, 2006).
   Identifies colonial strategies such as segregation and renaming in Dan. 1, and argues that the text articulates a program of resistance to them.
Cogan, Mordechai, *Imperialism and Religion: Assyria, Judah and Israel in the Eighth and Seventh Centuries BCE* (Missoula, MT: Society of Biblical Literature, 1974).
Collins, John J., *The Bible after Babel: Biblical Criticism in a Postmodern Age* (Grand Rapids, MI: Eerdmans, 2005).
   Of relevance is Chapter 3, 'Exodus and Liberation in Postcolonial Perspective'.
Connor, Kimberly Rae, ' "Everybody Talking about Heaven Ain't Going There": The Biblical Call for Justice and the Postcolonial Response', in Laura Donaldson (ed.), *Postcolonialism and Scriptural Reading* (Semeia, 75; Atlanta: Society of Biblical Literature, 1996), pp. 107-28.
Crossan, John Dominic, and Jonathan L. Reed, *In Search of Paul: How Jesus' Apostle Opposed Rome's Empire with God's Kingdom* (New York: HarperCollins, 2004).
   Crossan's ideas on earliest Christianity and empire, forged in his historical Jesus work, here receive more explicit expression in this co-authored book on Paul.
Donaldson, Laura E., 'Are We All Multiculturalists Now? Biblical Reading as Cultural Contact', in Stephen D. Moore (ed.), *In Search of the Present: The Bible through Cultural Studies* (Semeia, 82; Atlanta: Society of Biblical Literature Publications, 1998), pp. 79-97.
   '[R]eading in general and biblical reading in particular is a site of cultural contact much like the first meeting between the indigenous peoples of the Americas and Europeans'.
—'Gospel Hauntings: The Postcolonial Demons of New Testament Criticism', in Stephen D. Moore and Fernando F. Segovia (eds.), *Postcolonial Biblical Criticism: Interdisciplinary Intersections* (The Bible and Postcolonialism, 8; New York: T. & T. Clark International, 2005), pp. 97-113.
   Uses the postcolonial theory of Gayatri Spivak to reflect on the demon-possessed daughter of Mark 7.24-30 in conjunction with the Medium of Endor of 1 Sam. 28.3-25.
—'The Sign of Orpah: Reading Ruth through Native Eyes', in R.S. Sugirtharajah (ed.), *Vernacular Hermeneutics* (The Bible and Postcolonialism, 2; Sheffield: Sheffield Academic Press, 1999), pp. 20-36. Reprinted in R.S. Sugirtharajah (ed.), *The Postcolonial Biblical Reader* (Oxford: Blackwell, 2006).
   Argues that it is Orpah, Ruth's sister-in-law, who provides an emancipatory model for American Indian women because she embraces her own clan, in contrast to Ruth, the more usual exemplar, who converts/assimilates.
Donaldson, Laura E. (ed.), *Postcolonialism and Scriptural Reading* (Semeia, 75; Atlanta: Society of Biblical Literature, 1996).

The earliest such collection in biblical studies. Main articles include: Jon Berquist on imperialism and canon formation; Musa Dube on the Johannine Jesus' encounter with the Samaritan woman; Jim Perkison on Mark's Syro-Phoenician woman; Hector Avalos on *The Gospel of Lucas Gavilán*; Kimberly Rae Connor on African American spirituals; Roland Boer on Josh. 9 and B. Wongar; Jace Weaver on Native Americans and the postcolonial; and Miriam Peskowitz on biblical tourism.

Donaldson, Laura E., and Kwok Pui-lan (eds.), *Postcolonialism, Feminism and Religious Discourse* (London and New York: Routledge, 2002).
Essential reading on the title topics. It has, however, little to say directly about the Bible.

Draper, Jonathan A., 'Hermeneutical Drama on the Colonial Stage: Liminal Space and Creativity in Colenso's Commentary on Romans', *Journal of Theology for Southern Africa* 103 (1999), pp. 13-32.
An example of Draper's extensive work on Bishop Colenso, nineteenth-century missionary to the Zulu.

Draper, Jonathan A. (ed.), *Orality, Literacy and Colonialism in Southern Africa* (Semeia Studies, 46; Atlanta: Society of Biblical Literature Publications, 2003).
The principal theme of this multifaceted collection is the ways in which indigenous oral traditions in Southern Africa, including but not limited to oral traditions concerning the Bible, are preserved and transmitted over against a literacy that tends to legitimize and promote the dominant colonial culture.

— *Orality, Literacy and Colonialism in Antiquity* (Semeia Studies, 47; Atlanta: Society of Biblical Literature Publications, 2004).
Notable essays in this collection include: Richard Horsley, 'The Origins of the Hebrew Scriptures in Imperial Relations'; Werner Kelber, 'Roman Imperialism and Early Christian Scribality'; and Claudia V. Camp, 'Oralities, Literacies, and Colonialisms in Antiquity and Contemporary Scholarship'.

Dube, Musa W., '*Batswakwa*: Which Traveller Are You? (John 1:1-18)', in Gerald O. West and Musa W. Dube (eds.), *The Bible in Africa: Transactions, Trajectories, and Trends* (Leiden: Brill, 2001), pp. 150-62.

— 'Consuming a Colonial Cultural Bomb: Translating *Badimo* into "Demons" in the Setswana Bible (Matt. 28-34; 15:22, 10:8)', *Journal for the Study of the New Testament* 73 (1999), pp. 35-59.

— ' "Go Therefore and Make Disciples of All Nations" (Matt 28:19a): A Postcolonial Perspective on Biblical Criticism and Pedagogy', in Fernando F. Segovia and Mary Ann Tolbert (eds.), *Teaching the Bible: The Discourses and Politics of Biblical Pedagogy* (Maryknoll, NY: Orbis Books 1998), pp. 224-46.

— 'Jumping the Fire with Judith: Postcolonial Feminist Hermeneutics of Liberation', in Silvia Shroer and Sophia Bietenhard (eds.), *Feminist Interpretation of the Bible and the Hermeneutics of Liberation* (Journal for the Study of the Old Testament Supplement Series, 374; London: Sheffield Academic Press, 2003), pp. 60-76.

— *Postcolonial Feminist Interpretation of the Bible* (St Louis: Chalice Press, 2000). Arguably, the most impressive monograph to date in postcolonial biblical criticism. Provides incisive postcolonial feminist readings of the conquest narrative in Joshua and the Canaanite woman pericope in Matthew; critiques white Western scholars (including feminist scholars) for ignoring fundamental issues of colonialism and imperialism in Matthew; and mediates interpretations of the Canaanite woman episode developed by non-academic women in the African Independent Churches.

— 'Postcolonialism and Liberation', in Miguel A. De La Torre (ed.), *Handbook of U.S. Theologies of Liberation* (St Louis: Chalice Press, 2004), pp. 288-94.

— 'Postcoloniality, Feminist Spaces, and Religion', in Laura E. Donaldson and Kwok Pui-lan (eds.), *Postcolonialism, Feminism and Religious Discourse* (London and New York: Routledge, 2002), pp. 100-121.

— 'Rahab Says Hello to Judith: A Decolonizing Feminist Reading', in Fernando F. Segovia (ed.), *Toward a New Heaven and a New Earth: Essays in Honor of Elisabeth Schüssler Fiorenza* (Maryknoll, NY: Orbis Books, 2003), pp. 54-71. Reprinted in R.S. Sugirtharajah (ed.), *The Postcolonial Biblical Reader* (Oxford: Blackwell, 2006).

— 'Reading for Decolonization (John 4:1-42)', *Semeia* 75 (1996), pp. 37-60. Reprinted in Dube and Staley (eds.), *John and Postcolonialism*.

— 'Savior of the World, but Not of This World: A Postcolonial Reading of Spatial Construction in John', in R.S. Sugirtharajah (ed.), *The Postcolonial Bible* (The Bible and Postcolonialism, 1; Sheffield: Sheffield Academic Press, 1998), pp. 118-35.

— 'Scripture, Feminism and Postcolonial Contexts', in Kwok Pui-lan and Elisabeth Schüssler Fiorenza (eds.), *Women's Sacred Scriptures* (Maryknoll, NY: Orbis Books, 1998), pp. 45-54.

— 'Searching for the Lost Needle: Double Colonization and Postcolonial African Feminisms', *Studies in World Christianity* 5 (1999), pp. 213-28.

— 'Toward a Post-colonial Feminist Interpretation of the Bible', *Semeia* 78 (1997), pp. 11-26.

Dube, Musa W., and Jeffrey L. Staley (eds.), *John and Postcolonialism: Travel, Space and Power* (The Bible and Postcolonialism, 7; New York: Continuum, 2002).

Essays include: Tod Swanson on Johannine Christianity and the collapse of ethnic territory; Staley on vine, mountain, and temple in John; Dube on decolonizing John 4.1-42; Francisco Lozada, Jr, on John 5 and colonial evangelism; Mary Huie-Jolly on Maori reading and John 5.10-47; Jean Kim on adultery and hybridity in John 7.53–8.11; Leticia Guardiola-Sáenz on border-crossing and John 7.53–8.11; Zipporah Glass on nation and John 15.1-8; Adele Reinhartz on John, Rome, and Canadian identity; and Tat-siong Benny Liew on John's community of upward mobility.

Duchrow, Ulrich, 'Biblical Perspectives on Empire: A View from Western Europe', *Ecumenical Review* 48 (1994), pp. 21-27.

Elliott, Neil, 'The Anti-Imperial Message of the Cross', in Richard A. Horsley (ed.), *Paul and Empire: Religion and Power in Roman Imperial Society* (Harrisburg, PA: Trinity Press International, 1997), pp. 167-83.

—'The Apostle Paul's Self-Presentation as Anti-Imperial Performance', in Richard A. Horsley (ed.), *Paul and the Roman Imperial Order* (Harrisburg, PA: Trinity Press International, 2004), pp. 67-88.

— *Liberating Paul: The Justice of God and the Politics of the Apostle* (The Bible and Liberation Series; Maryknoll, NY: Orbis Books, 1994; reprinted Minneapolis: Fortress Press, 2005).
   The first half of this pathbreaking book traces the long tradition of reading Paul's letters to legitimize oppression or maintain the status quo, while the second half attempts to counter-read the letters as anti-imperial resistance literature.

—'Paul and the Politics of Empire: Problems and Prospects', in Richard A. Horsley (ed.), *Paul and Politics: Ekklesia, Israel, Imperium, Interpretation. Essays in Honor of Krister Stendahl* (Harrisburg, PA: Trinity Press International, 2000), pp. 17-39.

—'Romans 13:1-7 in the Context of Imperial Propaganda', in Horsley (ed.), *Paul and Empire*, pp. 184-204.

Fernandez, Eleazar S., 'From Babel to Pentecost: Finding a Home in the Belly of the Beast', *Semeia* 90/91 (2002), pp. 29-50.
   Includes a postcolonial reading of the Babel narrative (Gen. 11.1-9).

Fiorenza, Elisabeth Schüssler, 'The Ethos of Interpretation: Biblical Studies in a Postmodern and Postcolonial Context', in Rodney L. Petersen with Nancy M. Rourke (eds.), *Theological Literacy for the Twenty-First Century* (Grand Rapids: Eerdmans, 2002), pp. 211-28.

Friesen, Steven J., *Imperial Cults and the Apocalypse of John: Reading Revelation in the Ruins* (Oxford: Oxford University Press, 2001).
   Friesen's framing chapter, 'Religious Criticism', has recourse to the postcolonial theory of Edward Said.

Frilingos, Christopher A., *Spectacles of Empire: Monsters, Martyrs, and the Book of Revelation* (Divinations: Rereading Late Ancient Religion; Philadelphia: University of Pennsylvania Press, 2004).
   Like Friesen above, Frilingos also appeals to the postcolonial theory of Said in framing his project.

Gallagher, Susan VanZanten, 'Mapping the Hybrid World: Three Postcolonial Motifs', in Laura Donaldson (ed.), *Postcolonialism and Scriptural Reading* (Semeia, 75; Atlanta: Society of Biblical Literature, 1996), pp. 229-40.
   A highly instructive response essay: 'For some postcolonial literary theorists, several of the essays in this volume would have little, if any, critical validity…'

Gallagher, Susan VanZanten (ed.), *Postcolonial Literature and the Biblical Call for Justice* (Jackson: University Press of Mississippi, 1994).
   The essays, all by literary scholars, treat such topics as biblical concepts of justice in postcolonial fiction; the Walzer–Said exchange on the Exodus narrative; and representations of Jesus in postcolonial fiction.

Gill, David W.J., 'The Roman Empire as a Context for the New Testament', in Stanley E. Porter (ed.), *A Handbook to the Exegesis of the New Testament* (New Testament Tools and Studies, 25; Leiden: E.J. Brill, 1997), pp. 389-406.

Glass, Zipporah G., 'Building toward "Nation-ness" in the Vine: A Postcolonial Critique of John 15:1-8', in Musa W. Dube and Jeffrey L. Staley (eds.), *John and Postcolonialism: Travel, Space and Power* (The Bible and Postcolonialism, 7; New York: Continuum, 2002), pp. 153-69.

Gruber, Mayer I., 'The Ancient Israel Debate: A Jewish Postcolonial Perspective', *Ancient Near Eastern Studies* 38 (2001), pp. 3-27.

Guardiola-Sáenz, Leticia A., 'Border-Crossing and its Redemptive Power in John 7:53 – 8:11: A Cultural Reading of Jesus and the Accused', in Ingrid Rosa Kitzberger (ed.), *Transformative Encounters: Jesus and Women Reviewed* (Leiden: E.J. Brill, 2000), pp. 267-91. Reprinted in Dube and Staley (eds.), *John and Postcolonialism*.

—'Borderless Women and Borderless Texts: A Cultural Reading of Matthew 15: 21-28', *Semeia* 78 (1998), pp. 69-81.

Gundry, Robert, 'Richard A. Horsley's Hearing the Whole Story: A Critical Review of its Postcolonial Slant', *Journal for the Study of the New Testament* 26 (2003), pp. 131-49.

Horsley responds to Gundry's review in the same issue of *JSNT*.

Han, Jin Hee, 'Homi Bhabha and the Mixed Blessing of Hybridity in Biblical Hermeneutics', *The Bible and Critical Theory* 1.4 (2005). Online journal: http://publications.epress.monash.edu/loi/bc.

Herzog, William R., II, *Jesus, Justice, and the Reign of God: A Ministry of Liberation* (Louisville, KY: Westminster John Knox Press, 2000).

An 'historical Jesus' book that charges previous questers (including the Jesus Seminar) with domesticating him, and attempts instead to locate Jesus as a 'prophet of justice' within the socio-political matrix of Roman Palestine.

Horsley, Richard A., 'Feminist Scholarship and Postcolonial Criticism: Subverting Imperial Discourse and Reclaiming Submerged Histories', in Shelly Matthews, Cynthia Briggs Kittredge, and Melanie Johnson DeBaufre (eds.), *Walk in the Ways of Wisdom: Essays in Honor of Elisabeth Schüssler Fiorenza* (Harrisburg, PA: Trinity Press International, 2003), pp. 297-317.

— *Hearing the Whole Story: The Politics of Plot in Mark's Gospel* (Louisville, KY: Westminster John Knox Press, 2001).

A major iconoclastic work that challenges most of the assumptions that have informed Western interpretations of Mark, both scholarly and popular. Argues that Mark is a 'submerged people's history' that tells of a peasant renewal movement pitted against the Roman imperial order and its colonial outworkings in first-century Palestine.

— *Jesus and Empire: The Kingdom of God and the New World Disorder* (Minneapolis: Fortress Press, 2003).

The Jesus of the title is, essentially, that of Mark combined with that of the Sayings Gospel Q, and is a Jesus who not only has the Roman Empire in his sights but the contemporary American Empire as well.

—'The Origins of the Hebrew Scriptures in Imperial Relations', in Jonathan A. Draper (ed.), *Orality, Literacy and Colonialism in Antiquity* (Semeia Studies, 47; Atlanta: Society of Biblical Literature Publications, 2004), pp. 107-34.

— *Religion and Empire: People, Power, and the Life of the Spirit* (Minneapolis: Fortress Press, 2003).
At its core, a prophetic denunciation of the current nexus of US Christianity and US politics and foreign policy, based on the message of the historical Jesus as Horsley reconstructs it.

— 'Submerged Biblical Histories and Imperial Biblical Studies', in R.S. Sugirtharajah (ed.), *The Postcolonial Bible* (The Bible and Postcolonialism, 1; Sheffield: Sheffield Academic Press, 1998), pp. 152-73.
Contains a useful distillation of Horsley's interpretation of Mark and Paul.

— 'Subverting Disciplines: The Possibilities and Limitations of Postcolonial Theory for New Testament Studies', in Fernando F. Segovia (ed.), *Toward a New Heaven and a New Earth: Essays in Honor of Elisabeth Schüssler Fiorenza* (Maryknoll, NY: Orbis Books, 2003), pp. 90-105.
Horsley's most explicit engagement to date with extra-biblical postcolonial studies.

Horsley, Richard A. (ed.), *Hidden Transcripts and the Arts of Resistance: Applying the Work of James C. Scott to Jesus and Paul* (Semeia Studies, 48; Atlanta: Society of Biblical Literature Publications, 2004).
Scott's enormously suggestive study, *Domination and the Arts of Resistance*, is the inspiration for this collection, which ends with a 'dialogue' with Scott himself.

— *Paul and Empire: Religion and Power in Roman Imperial Society* (Harrisburg, PA: Trinity Press International, 1997).
Fourteen essays, divided into the following parts: 'The Gospel of Imperial Salvation'; 'Patronage, Priesthoods, and Power'; 'Paul's Counter-Imperial Gospel'; and 'Building an Alternative Society'.

— *Paul and Politics: Ekklesia, Israel, Imperium, Interpretation. Essays in Honor of Krister Stendahl* (Harrisburg, PA: Trinity Press International, 2000).
Sample essays include: Neil Elliott on Paul and the politics of empire; Horsley on 1 Corinthians and empire; Sheila Briggs on slavery, freedom, Paul and Rome; N.T. Wright on Paul's gospel and Caesar's empire; and Sze-kar Wan on the collection for the saints as anticolonial act.

— *Paul and the Roman Imperial Order* (Harrisburg, PA: Trinity Press International, 2004).
Sample essays include: Robert Jewett on Rom. 8:18-23 within the imperial context; Abraham Smith's postcolonial analysis of 1 Thessalonians; and Neil Elliott on Paul's self-presentation as anti-imperial performance. The volume concludes with a general response by the prominent classicist S.R.F. Price.

Horsley, Richard A., and Neil Asher Silberman, *The Message and the Kingdom: How Jesus and Paul Ignited a Revolution and Transformed the Ancient World* (New York: Grossett/Putnam, 1997).

Howard-Brook, Wes, and Anthony Gwyther, *Unveiling Empire: Reading Revelation Then and Now* (Maryknoll, NY: Orbis Books, 1999).
Employs Revelation's critique of Roman imperial ideology and economics as a model for 'coming out of' contemporary empire, epitomized by global capitalism.

Howard-Brook, Wes, and Sharon H. Ringe (eds.), *The New Testament: Introducing the Way of Discipleship* (Maryknoll, NY: Orbis Books, 2002). A New Testament commentary focused on empire, politics, economics, social justice, and radical discipleship.

Jobling, David, ' "Very Limited Ideological Options": Marxism and Biblical Studies in Postcolonial Scenes', in Stephen D. Moore and Fernando F. Segovia (eds.), *Postcolonial Biblical Criticism: Interdisciplinary Intersections* (The Bible and Postcolonialism, 8; New York: T. & T. Clark International, 2005), pp. 184-201.

Joh, Wonhee Anne, *Heart of the Cross: A Postcolonial Christology* (Louisville, KY: Westminster John Knox Press, 2006). Has recourse to postcolonial theory to argue that the cross simultaneously pays homage to and menaces the forces of empire. 'The cross as a double gesture speaks to those who have shifted from a typical politics of identity to political identities shaped more by postmodern ambiguities of difference.'

✓ Kelber, Werner H., 'Roman Imperialism and Early Christian Scribality', in Jonathan A. Draper (ed.), *Orality, Literacy and Colonialism in Antiquity* (Semeia Studies, 47; Atlanta: Society of Biblical Literature Publications, 2004), pp. 135-54. Reprinted in R.S. Sugirtharajah (ed.), *The Postcolonial Biblical Reader* (Oxford: Blackwell, 2006). Includes incisive comparative analysis of the relationship to Rome embodied in Mark, Luke–Acts, and Revelation.

Keller, Catherine, *God and Power: Counter-Apocalyptic Journeys* (Minneapolis: Fortress Press, 2005). Part 2, 'Of Beasts and Whores: Examining Our Political Unconscious', analyses Revelation and the US Empire jointly from feminist, poststructuralist, and postcolonial perspectives.

Keller, Catherine, Michael Nausner, and Mayra Rivera (eds.), *Postcolonial Theologies: Divinity and Empire* (St Louis: Chalice Press, 2004). The first book on postcolonialism to emerge from theological studies. Several of the essays in the collection intersect with biblical studies.

Kim, Jean K., 'Adultery or Hybridity? Reading John 7:53–8:11 from a Postcolonial Context', in Musa W. Dube and Jeffrey L. Staley (eds.), *John and Postcolonialism: Travel, Space and Power* (The Bible and Postcolonialism, 7; New York: Continuum, 2002), pp. 111-28.

—'Hybrid but Fatherless: Jesus for the "Children of the Dust" ', *Ewha Journal of Feminist Theology* 3 (2005), pp. 30-58. Utilizes the postcolonial concept of hybridity to revisit the thesis that Jesus' father was a Roman soldier.

—' "Uncovering her Wickedness": An Inter(con)textual Reading of Revelation 17 from a Postcolonial Feminist Perspective', *Journal for the Study of the New Testament* 73 (1999), pp. 61-81.

—*Woman and Nation: An Intercontextual Reading of the Gospel of John from a Postcolonial Feminist Perspective* (Biblical Interpretation Series, 69; Leiden: E.J. Brill, 2004). Writing explicitly out of a Korean context, Kim argues that 'John's resistance to Roman imperial power defines and shapes the boundaries of his Jewish nationalism', and she 'examines the role of the Johannine female characters in supporting Jesus' role as a national hero and functioning as continuers of the nation'.

Kim, Seong Hee, 'Mark, Women, and Empire: Ways of Life in Postcolonial and Korean Perspectives' (PhD dissertation, Drew University, 2006).
Draws on postcolonial, feminist, and cultural studies to treat the women in the latter chapters of Mark—the poor widow, the anointing woman, and the women at the cross and tomb.

—'Rupturing the Empire: Reading the Poor Widow as a Postcolonial Female Subject (Mark 12:41-44)', *lectio difficilior* 1 (2006). Online journal: http://www.lectio. unibe.ch/06_1/kim_rupturing.htm

Kim, Uriah Y., *Decolonizing Josiah: Toward a Postcolonial Reading of the Deuter-onomistic History* (The Bible in the Modern World, 5; Sheffield: Sheffield Phoenix Press, 2005).
Criticizes as colonialist the prevailing view of the Deuteronomistic History, and attempts to read it otherwise from an Asian-American perspective informed by postcolonial studies.

Kwok Pui-lan, *Discovering the Bible in the Non-Biblical World* (Bible and Liberation Series; Maryknoll, NY: Orbis Books, 1995).
Keenly attentive to colonial issues in the biblical text and its interpretation.

—'Discovering the Bible in the Non-Biblical World: The Journey Continues', *Journal of Asian and Asian-American Theology* 2 (1997), pp. 64-77.

—'Jesus/the Native: Biblical Studies from a Postcolonial Perspective', in Fernando F. Segovia and Mary Ann Tolbert (eds.), *Teaching the Bible: Discourses and Politics of Biblical Pedagogy* (Maryknoll, NY: Orbis Books, 1998), pp. 69-85.

— *Postcolonial Imagination and Feminist Theology* (Louisville, KY: Westminster John Knox Press, 2005).
Especially relevant for biblical scholars is Chapter 3, 'Making the Connections: Postcolonial Studies and Feminist Biblical Interpretation' (which is reprinted in R.S. Sugirtharajah [ed.], *The Postcolonial Biblical Reader* [Oxford: Blackwell, 2006]).

Lee, Archie Chi Chung, 'Mothers Bewailing: Reading Lamentations', in Caroline Vander Stichele and Todd Penner (eds.), *Her Master's Tools? Feminist and Postcolonial Engagements of Historical-Critical Discourse* (Global Perspectives on Biblical Scholarship, 9; Atlanta: Society of Biblical Literature Publications, 2005), pp. 195-210.

—'Returning to China: Biblical Interpretation in Postcolonial Hong Kong', *Biblical Interpretation* 7 (1999), pp. 156-73.
Lee's text is Isaiah 40–66. The issue also contains responses to Lee by Philip Chia, Kwok Pui-lan, Katherine Doob Sakenfeld, and Fernando Segovia, with a rejoinder by Lee.

Levine, Amy-Jill, 'The Disease of Postcolonial New Testament Studies and the Hermeneutics of Healing', *Journal of Feminist Studies in Religion* 20 (2004), pp. 91-99.
Levine's article opens a 'Roundtable Discussion: Anti-Judaism and Postcolonial Biblical Interpretation' in this issue of *JFSR*, in which Kwok

Pui-lan, Musimbi Kanyoro, Adele Reinhartz, Hisako Kinukawa, and Elaine Wainwright respond to Levine and Levine replies to the respondents. Lawrence Wills then responds to all of the preceding.

Liew, Tat-siong Benny, 'Ambiguous Admittance: Consent and Descent in John's Community of "Upward" Mobility', in Musa W. Dube and Jeffrey L. Staley (eds.), *John and Postcolonialism: Travel, Space and Power* (The Bible and Postcolonialism, 7; New York: Continuum, 2002), pp. 193-224.

—'Margins and (Cutting-)Edges: On the (Il)legitimacy and Intersections of Race, Ethnicity, and (Post)colonialism', in Stephen D. Moore and Fernando F. Segovia (eds.), *Postcolonial Biblical Criticism: Interdisciplinary Intersections* (The Bible and Postcolonialism, 8; New York: T. & T. Clark International, 2005), pp. 114-65.

— *Politics of Parousia: Reading Mark Inter(con)textually* (Biblical Interpretation Series, 42; Leiden: E.J. Brill, 1999).

Draws heavily on literary and cultural theory, especially the postcolonial theory of Homi Bhabha, to argue that Mark's Gospel reinscribes colonial and imperial ideology even as it attempts to resist it, particularly in its apocalyptic discourse and its authoritarian characterization of Jesus.

—'Tyranny, Power and Might: Colonial Mimicry in Mark's Gospel', *Journal for the Study of the New Testament* 73 (1999), pp. 7-31. Reprinted in R.S. Sugirtharajah (ed.), *The Postcolonial Biblical Reader* (Oxford: Blackwell, 2006).

An elegant distillation, in effect, of Liew's *Politics of Parousia*.

Lozada, Francisco, Jr, 'Contesting an Interpretation of John 5: Moving Beyond Colonial Evangelism', in Musa W. Dube and Jeffrey L. Staley (eds.), *John and Postcolonialism: Travel, Space and Power* (The Bible and Postcolonialism, 7; New York: Continuum, 2002), pp. 76-93.

Marshall, John W., 'Postcolonialism and the Practice of History', in Caroline Vander Stichele and Todd Penner (eds.), *Her Master's Tools? Feminist and Postcolonial Engagements of Historical-Critical Discourse* (Global Perspectives on Biblical Scholarship, 9; Atlanta: Society of Biblical Literature Publications, 2005), pp. 93-108.

Masenya, Madipoane (ngwana' Mphahlele), 'Their Hermeneutics Was Strange! Ours Is a Necessity! Rereading Vashti as African-South African Women', in Caroline Vander Stichele and Todd Penner (eds.), *Her Master's Tools? Feminist and Postcolonial Engagements of Historical-Critical Discourse* (Global Perspectives on Biblical Scholarship, 9; Atlanta: Society of Biblical Literature Publications, 2005), pp. 179-94.

McKinlay, Judith, *Reframing Her: Biblical Women in Postcolonial Focus* (The Bible in the Modern World, 1; Sheffield: Sheffield Phoenix Press, 2004). Reads selected biblical women (e.g. Sarah, Hagar, Rahab, Jezabel, the Woman Clothed with the Sun) from the social location of a descendant of white New Zealand settlers.

Meier, Harry O., and Mark Vessey (eds.), *The Calling of the Nations: Exegesis, Ethnography, and Empire in a Biblical Historic Present* (Toronto: University of Toronto Press, forthcoming).

Moore, Stephen D., *God's Beauty Parlor: And Other Queer Spaces In and Around the Bible* (Contraventions: Jews and Other Differences; Stanford, CA: Stanford University Press, 2001).

Chapters 3 and 4, on Romans and Revelation respectively, engage with colonial issues.

—'Postcolonialism', in A.K.M. Adam (ed.), *A Handbook of Postmodern Biblical Interpretation* (St Louis: Chalice Press, 2000), pp. 182-88.

Moore, Stephen D., and Fernando F. Segovia (eds.), *Postcolonial Biblical Criticism: Interdisciplinary Intersections* (The Bible and Postcolonialism, 8; New York: T. & T. Clark International, 2005).

Includes the editors on beginnings, trajectories, and intersections in postcolonial biblical criticism; Segovia on mapping the postcolonial optic; Moore on the postcolonial and the postmodern; Laura Donaldson on Mark 7.24-30 with 1 Sam. 28.3-25; Benny Liew on race, ethnicity and (post)colonialism; and both Roland Boer and David Jobling on Marxism, postcolonialism, and the Bible.

Myers, Ched, *Binding the Strong Man: A Political Reading of Mark's Story of Jesus* (Maryknoll, NY: Orbis Books, 1988).

A pioneering exercise in 'First World' liberationist exegesis that reads Mark as a manifesto for non-violent resistance to empire.

Oakes, Peter, 'Christian Attitudes to Rome at the Time of Paul's Letters', *Review and Expositor* 100 (2003), pp. 103-11.

—*Philippians: From People to Letter* (Society for New Testament Studies Monograph Series, 110; Cambridge: Cambridge University Press, 2001).

Of particular relevance is Chapter 5, 'Christ and the Emperor'.

—'Representations of Empire: Rome and the Mediterranean World', *Journal of Theological Studies* NS 55 (2004), pp. 686-89.

—'A State of Tension: Rome in the New Testament', in John Riches and David C. Sim (eds.), *The Gospel of Matthew in its Roman Imperial Context* (Journal for the Study of the New Testament Supplement Series, 276; New York: T. & T. Clark International, 2005), pp. 75-90.

Compares representations of Rome in 1 Thessalonians, Romans, Mark, Acts, and Revelation.

Oakes, Peter (ed.), *Rome in the Bible and the Early Church* (Carlisle: Paternoster Press; Grand Rapids, MI: Baker Book House, 2002).

New Testament articles include: Steve Walton on Luke's representation of Rome; Walton on the Lukan Paul's reception in Rome; Conrad Gempf on Roman law and society and Romans 12–15; Bruce Winter on Paul's ethnic, social, and gender inclusiveness; and Oakes on God's sovereignty over Roman authorities in Philippians.

Prior, Michael, *The Bible and Colonialism: A Moral Critique* (The Biblical Seminar, 48; Sheffield: Sheffield Academic Press, 1997).

The earliest monograph on the title topic, it examines the ways in which biblical land traditions have been used to legitimize colonization in Latin America, South Africa, and Palestine/Israel.

—'The Bible and the Redeeming Idea of Colonialism', *Studies in World Christianity* 5 (1999), pp. 129-55.

Punt, Jeremy, 'From Rewriting to Rereading the Bible in Postcolonial Africa: Considering the Options and Implications', *Missionala* 30 (2002), pp. 410-42.

—'The New Testament, Theology and Imperialism: Some Postcolonial Remarks on *Beyond New Testament Theology*', *Neotestamentica* 35 (2001), pp. 120-45.

—'Postcolonial Biblical Criticism in South Africa: Some Mind and Road Mapping', *Neotestamentica* 37 (2003), pp. 59-85.

—'Towards a Postcolonial Reading of Freedom in Paul', in Justin S. Upkong *et al.* (eds.), *Reading the Bible in the Global Village: Cape Town* (Global Perspectives on Biblical Scholarship, 3; Atlanta: Society of Biblical Literature Publications; Leiden: Brill, 2002), pp. 125-49.

—'Why Not Postcolonial Biblical Criticism in South Africa? Stating the Obvious or Looking for the Impossible', in Matthew Collins (ed.), *Society of Biblical Literature 2003 Seminar Papers* (Atlanta: Society of Biblical Literature Publications, 2003), pp. 17-44.

Reed, Stephen A., 'Critique of Canaan Banana's Call to Rewrite the Bible from a Postcolonial Perspective', *Religion and Theology* 3 (1996), pp. 282-88.

Reinhartz, Adele, 'The Colonizer as Colonized: Intertextual Dialogue between the Gospel of John and Canadian Identity', in Musa W. Dube and Jeffrey L. Staley (eds.), *John and Postcolonialism: Travel, Space and Power* (The Bible and Postcolonialism, 7; New York: Continuum, 2002), pp. 170-92.

Despite the specificity of the subtitle, includes an excellent general analysis of John's relations to Rome.

Riches, John, and David C. Sim (eds.), *The Gospel of Matthew in its Roman Imperial Context* (Journal for the Study of the New Testament Supplement Series, 276; New York: T. & T. Clark International, 2005).

Ranges more broadly than Matthew or the New Testament. Essays with a New Testament focus include: Peter Oakes on Rome in the New Testament; Sim on Rome in Matthew's eschatology; Dorothy Jean Weaver on Matthew's Roman characters; Riches on Matthew's missionary strategy in colonial perspective; and Warren Carter on Matthean Christology and Roman imperialism.

Ringe, Sharon H., 'Places at the Table: Feminist and Postcolonial Biblical Interpretation', in R.S. Sugirtharajah (ed.), *The Postcolonial Bible* (The Bible and Postcolonialism, 1; Sheffield: Sheffield Academic Press, 1998), pp. 136-51.

Rivera, Mayra, 'God at the Crossroads: A Postcolonial Reading of Sophia', in Catherine Keller, Michael Nausner, and Mayra Rivera (eds.), *Postcolonial Theologies: Divinity and Empire* (St Louis: Chalice Press, 2004), pp. 186-203. Reprinted in R.S. Sugirtharajah (ed.), *The Postcolonial Biblical Reader* (Oxford: Blackwell, 2006).

Rowlett, Lori, 'Disney's Pocahontas and Joshua's Rahab in Postcolonial Perspective', in George Aichele (ed.), *Culture, Entertainment and the Bible* (Journal for the Study of the Old Testament Supplement Series, 309; Sheffield: Sheffield Academic Press, 2000), pp. 66-75.

Runions, Erin, 'Biblical Promise and Threat in U.S. Imperialist Rhetoric, before and after 9/11', in Elizabeth A. Castelli and Janet R. Jakobsen (eds.), *Interventions: Activists and Academics Respond to Violence* (New York: Palgrave Macmillan, 2004), pp. 71-88.

—*Changing Subjects: Gender, Nation and Future in Micah* (Playing the Texts, 7; Sheffield: Sheffield Academic Press, 2002).
   Reads the Book of Micah with Althusser, Lacan, Žižek, and above all Bhabha, suggesting that '(liminal) identifications with the ambiguities of…Micah might reconfigure the readers' own ideological positions'.

—'Desiring War: Apocalypse, Commodity Fetish, and the End of History', in R.S. Sugirtharajah (ed.), *The Postcolonial Biblical Reader* (Oxford: Blackwell, 2006), pp. 112-28.
   Examines the religio-philosophical underpinnings of George W. Bush's public discourse.

—*How Hysterical: Identification and Resistance in the Bible and Film* (Religion/ Culture/Critique, 1; New York: Palgrave Macmillan, 2003).
   Makes use of postcolonial theory, together with other theoretical resources, to cross-read selected films and biblical texts.

—'Hysterical Phalli: Numbers 16, Two Contemporary Parallels, and the Logic of Colonization', in George Aichele (ed.), *Culture, Entertainment and the Bible* (Journal for the Study of the Old Testament Supplement Series, 309; Sheffield: Sheffield Academic Press, 2000), pp. 182-205.

—'Zion is Burning: "Gender Fuck" in Micah', in Stephen D. Moore (ed.), *In Search of the Present: The Bible through Cultural Studies* (Semeia, 82; Atlanta: Society of Biblical Literature Publications, 1998), pp. 225-46.
   Has significant recourse to Homi Bhabha.

Samuel, Simon, 'The Beginning of Mark: A Colonial/Postcolonial Conundrum', *Biblical Interpretation* 10 (2002), pp. 405-19.
   A study of Mark 1.1 informed by Bhabha's postcolonial theory.

—'Postcolonialism as a Critical Practice in Biblical Studies', *Doon Theological Journal* 2 (2005), pp. 97-119.

—*A Postcolonial Reading of Mark's Story of Jesus* (Library of New Testament Studies Series; New York: T. & T. Clark International, forthcoming).
   Writing explicitly out of an Indian context, Samuel draws extensively on postcolonial theory, especially that of Bhabha, to argue that Mark both affirms and disrupts Roman imperialism and Jewish nationalism.

Sawicki, Marianne, *Crossing Galilee: Architectures of Contact in the Occupied Land of Jesus* (Harrisburg, PA: Trinity Press International, 2000).
   Seeks to discover 'the Galilean Jesus' indigenous cultural idiom in its material structures for the negotiation of kinship, the management of labor, the distribution of commodities, and the construction of gender'.

—'Salt and Leaven: Resistances to Empire in the Street-Smart Paleochurch', in Michael L. Budde and Robert W. Brimlow (eds.), *The Church as Counterculture* (Albany: State University of New York Press, 2000), pp. 59-88.

Seesengood, Robert Paul, 'Hybridity and the Rhetoric of Endurance: Reading Paul's Athletic Metaphors in a Context of Postcolonial Self-Construction', *The Bible and Critical Theory* 1:3 (2005). Online journal: http:// publications.epress.monash. edu/loi/bc

Segovia, Fernando F., 'Biblical Criticism and Postcolonial Studies: Toward a Postcolonial Optic', in R.S. Sugirtharajah (ed.), *The Postcolonial Bible* (The Bible and Postcolonialism, 1; Sheffield: Sheffield Academic Press, 1998), pp. 49-65.

—'In the Wake of Liberation: Postcolonial and Diasporic Criticisms', in Guillermo Hansen (ed.), *Los Caminos inexhauribles de la Palabra* (Buenos Aires: Grupo Editorial Lumen, 2000), pp. 91-114.

—*Decolonizing Biblical Studies: A View from the Margins* (Maryknoll, NY: Orbis Books, 2000).

The first part of the book focuses on cultural studies, the second part on pedagogy and cultural studies, and the third and fourth parts on postcolonial studies. Segovia situates postcolonial biblical criticism in relation to the attempts of scholars from the global South and racial/ethnic minorities from the global North to find voice within biblical studies.

—'Mapping the Postcolonial Optic in Biblical Criticism: Meaning and Scope', in Stephen D. Moore and Fernando F. Segovia (eds.), *Postcolonial Biblical Criticism: Interdisciplinary Intersections* (The Bible and Postcolonialism, 8; New York: T. & T. Clark International, 2005), pp. 23-78.

—'My Personal Voice: The Making of a Postcolonial Critic', in Ingrid Rosa Kitzberger (ed.), *The Personal Voice in Biblical Interpretation* (London and New York: Routledge, 1999), pp. 25-37.

—'Notes toward Refining the Postcolonial Optic', *Journal for the Study of the New Testament* 75 (1999), pp. 103-14.

A response to four reviews of R.S. Sugirtharajah (ed.), *The Postcolonial Bible* (The Bible and Postcolonialism, 1; Sheffield: Sheffield Academic Press, 1998), in the previous issue.

—'Postcolonial and Diasporic Criticism in Biblical Studies: Focus, Parameters, Relevance', *Studies in World Christianity* 5 (1999), pp. 177-95.

—'Postcolonialism and Comparative Analysis in Biblical Studies', *Biblical Interpretation* 7 (1999), pp. 192-96.

A response to Lee, 'Returning to China', in the same issue.

Segovia, Fernando F. (ed.), *Interpreting Beyond Borders* (The Bible and Postcolonialism, 3; Sheffield: Sheffield Academic Press, 2000).

This collection merges biblical studies with postcolonial studies and disaporic studies. Sample essays include Sze-kar Wan's Asian-American reading of Galatians; Francisco García-Treto's Cuban reading of Gen. 39–41; and Jeffrey Kah-Jin Kuan on identity politics and race relations in Esther.

Segovia, Fernando F., and R.S. Sugirtharajah (eds.), *The Postcolonial Commentary on the New Testament* (New York: T. & T. Clark International, forthcoming).

Similar in structure to *The Women's Bible Commentary*, it will contain thematic commentaries on each book of the New Testament. It will likely serve to establish postcolonial biblical criticism more than any other volume in this bibliography.

Smith, Abraham, '1 Thessalonians', in Fernando F. Segovia and R.S. Sugirtharajah (eds.), *The Postcolonial Commentary on the New Testament* (New
   York: T. & T. Clark International, forthcoming).

—' "Unmasking the Powers": Toward a Postcolonial Analysis of 1 Thessalonians', in Richard A. Horsley (ed.), *Paul and the Roman Imperial Order*
   (Harrisburg, PA: Trinity Press International, 2004), pp. 47-66.

Staley, Jeffrey L., 'Changing Woman: Postcolonial Reflections on Acts 16.6-
   40', *Journal for the Study of the New Testament* 73 (1999), pp. 113-35.

—' "Clothed and in her Right Mind": Mark 5:1-20 and Postcolonial Discourse', in R.S. Sugirtharajah (ed.), *Voices from the Margin: Interpreting the
   Bible in the Third World* (Maryknoll, NY: Orbis Books, enlarged edn,
   forthcoming).

—' "Dis Place, Man": A Postcolonial Critique of the Vine (the Mountain and
   the Temple) in the Gospel of John', in Musa W. Dube and Jeffrey L.
   Staley (eds.), *John and Postcolonialism: Travel, Space and Power* (The Bible
   and Postcolonialism, 7; New York: Continuum, 2002), pp. 32-50.

—'Postcolonial Reflections on Reading Luke–Acts from Cabo San Lucas and
   Other Places', in Sharon Ringe and Hyun Chul Paul Kim (eds.), *Literary
   Encounters with the Reign of God* (Harrisburg, PA: Trinity Press
   International, 2004), pp. 422-45.

—*Reading with a Passion: Rhetoric, Autobiography, and the American West in the
   Gospel of John* (New York: Continuum, 1995).
   Of relevance is Chapter 5, 'Not Yet Fifty: Postcolonial Confessions from
   an Outpost in the San Juan Basin'.

Stichele, Caroline Vander, and Todd Penner (eds.), *Her Master's Tools?
   Feminist and Postcolonial Engagements of Historical-Critical Discourse*
   (Global Perspectives on Biblical Scholarship, 9; Atlanta: Society of Biblical Literature Publications, 2005).
   The postcolonial engagements of the subtitle are considerably less
   pronounced and pervasive than the feminist engagements, and
   principally find expression in John Marshall's essay on postcolonialism
   and historiography, Madipoane Masenya's essay on African women
   rereading Vashti, and Archie Lee's essay on Lamentations.

Sugirtharajah, R.S., *Asian Biblical Hermeneutics and Postcolonialism: Contesting
   the Interpretations* (The Bible and Liberation Series; Maryknoll, NY: Orbis
   Books, 1999).
   Makes significant use of Edward Said's concept of 'Orientalism' to
   analyze colonial biblical interpretation.

—*The Bible and Empire: Postcolonial Explorations* (Cambridge: Cambridge University Press, 2005).
   Ranges from the gospel retellings of Thomas Jefferson and Raja
   Rammohun Roy, and the mobilization of biblical texts after the Indian
   uprising of 1857, to the Hebrew scriptures in colonial context.

—*The Bible and the Third World: Precolonial, Colonial and Postcolonial Encounters*
   (Cambridge: Cambridge University Press, 2001).
   Sugirtharajah's most impressive work to date. The precolonial and
   colonial encounters range from China and Africa to India and North

America. The book ends with an extended internal critique of liberation hermeneutics from a postcolonial perspective.

—'Biblical Studies in India: From Imperialistic Scholarship to Postcolonial Interpretation', in Fernando F. Segovia and Mary Ann Tolbert (eds.), *Teaching the Bible: The Discourses and Politics of Biblical Pedagogy* (Maryknoll, NY: Orbis Books, 1998), pp. 283-97.

—'Imperial Critical Commentaries: Christian Discourse and Commentarial Writings in Colonial India', *Journal for the Study of the New Testament* 73 (1999), pp. 83-112.

—*Postcolonial Criticism and Biblical Interpretation* (Oxford: Oxford University Press, 2002).

Perhaps the best textbook introduction to date to postcolonial biblical criticism.

—'A Postcolonial Exploration of Collusion and Construction in Biblical Interpretation', in R.S. Sugirtharajah (ed.), *The Postcolonial Bible* (The Bible and Postcolonialism, 1; Sheffield: Sheffield Academic Press, 1998), pp. 91-116.

—*Postcolonial Reconfigurations: An Alternative Way of Reading the Bible and Doing Theology* (St Louis: Chalice Press, 2003).

Further essays on such topics as the collusion of biblical interpretation and colonial expansion; the Bible's role as a chastened yet still potent icon of contemporary Western culture; and the blind spots of indigenous Indian theology and Euro-American systematic theology.

—'Postcolonial Theory and Biblical Studies', in Ismo Dunderberg, Christopher M. Tuckett, and Kari Syreeni (eds.), *Fair Play: Diversity and Conflicts in Early Christianity. Essays in Honour of Heikki Räisänen* (Novum Testamentum Supplement Series, 103; Leiden: E.J. Brill, 2002), pp. 541-52.

—'Textual Cleansing: A Move from the Colonial to the Postcolonial Version', *Semeia* 76 (1996), pp. 7-19.

Sugirtharajah, R.S. (ed.), *The Postcolonial Bible* (The Bible and Postcolonialism, 1; Sheffield: Sheffield Academic Press, 1998).

Includes Sugirtharajah on biblical studies after the empire; Roland Boer on postcolonialism and Australian biblical studies; Fernando Segovia on biblical criticism and postcolonial studies; Randall Bailey on the danger of ignoring one's own cultural bias; Sugirtharajah on the Eurocentric construction of Christian origins; Musa Dube on spatial construction in John; Sharon Ringe on feminist and postcolonial interpretation; Richard Horsley on Mark and Paul; Kwok Pui-lan on the Jesus Seminar; and Bastiaan Wielenga on Gen. 32–33.

—*The Postcolonial Biblical Reader* (Oxford: Blackwell, 2006).

An anthology of twenty essays, mainly reprints, spanning both testaments and authored by most of the expected names (e.g. Laura Donaldson, Musa Dube, Richard Horsley, Kwok Pui-lan, Erin Runions, Fernando Segovia, Benny Liew) along with a few unexpected names (e.g. Werner Kelber, Karen King). The volume is divided into four parts, each with its own introduction: 'Theoretical Practices'; 'Empires Old and New'; 'Empire and Exegesis' (which accounts for nine of the essays); and 'Postcolonial Concerns'.

— *Postcolonial Perspectives on the New Testament and its Interpretation*, *Journal for the Study of the New Testament* 73 (1999).

A thematic issue that includes: Sugirtharajah's introduction; Tat-siong Benny Liew on colonial mimicry in Mark; Musa Dube on translating *Badimo* as 'demons' in the Setswana Bible; Jean Kim on Rev. 17 from a postcolonial feminist perspective; Sugirtharajah on commentarial writings in colonial India; and Jeffrey Staley on 'border women' and Acts 16.6-40.

— *Vernacular Hermeneutics* (The Bible and Postcolonialism, 2; Sheffield: Sheffield Academic Press, 1999).

This collection 'contains practical appropriations of biblical narratives, informed by the vernacular heritage and by the reader's own identity', and 'tries to place vernacular reading among the ongoing critical movements of our time, such as postmodernism and postcolonialism'.

— *Voices from the Margin: Interpreting the Bible in the Third World* (Maryknoll, NY: Orbis Books, 2nd edn, 1995).

A landmark collection that contains much that is of relevance to postcolonial biblical criticism, not least Part 2, 'Re-use of the Bible: Subaltern Readings', and Part 3, 'The Exodus: One Narrative, Many Readings'. A third enlarged edition is in preparation at the time of writing.

Tan, Yak-Hwee, 'The Question of Social Location and Postcolonial Feminist Hermeneutics of Liberation', in Silvia Shroer and Sophia Bietenhard (eds.), *Feminist Interpretation of the Bible and the Hermeneutics of Liberation* (Journal for the Study of the Old Testament Supplement Series, 374; London: Sheffield Academic Press, 2003), pp. 171-78.

Thurman, Eric, 'Looking for a Few Good Men: Mark and Masculinity', in Stephen D. Moore and Janice Capel Anderson (eds.), *New Testament Masculinities* (Semeia Studies, 45; Williston, VT: Society of Biblical Literature Publications, 2003), pp. 137-65.

Explores the intersection of masculinity and empire in Mark, using the postcolonial theory of Homi Bhabha.

Tolbert, Mary Ann, 'Afterwords: Christianity, Imperialism, and the Decentering of Privilege', in Fernando F. Segovia and Mary Ann Tolbert (eds.), *Reading from This Place. II. Social Location and Biblical Interpretation in Global Perspective* (Minneapolis: Fortress Press, 1995), pp. 347-61.

— 'When Resistance Becomes Repression: Mark 13:9-27 and the Poetics of Location', in Fernando F. Segovia and Mary Ann Tolbert (eds.), *Reading from This Place. I. Social Location and Biblical Interpretation in the United States* (Minneapolis: Fortress Press, 1995), pp. 331-46.

Examines what happens when a text produced in the margins of power is appropriated by those at the center of power.

Waetjen, Herman C., *A Reordering of Power: A Sociopolitical Reading of Mark's Gospel* (Minneapolis: Fortress Press, 1989).

Reads Mark as anti-imperial resistance literature.

Walsh, Brian J., and Sylvia C. Keesmaat, *Colossians Remixed: Subverting the Empire* (Downers Grove, IL: Intervarsity Press, 2004).

Sets Colossians against both the Roman Empire and contemporary neo-imperial formations, especially globalization.

Walton, Steve, 'The State They Were in: Luke's View of the Roman Empire', in Peter Oakes (ed.), *Rome in the Bible and the Early Church* (Carlisle: Paternoster Press; Grand Rapids, MI: Baker Book House, 2002), pp. 1-41.
An excellent study of the complex representation of Rome in Luke–Acts.

Wan, Sze-kar, 'Collection for the Saints as Anticolonial Act: Implications of Paul's Ethnic Reconstruction', in Richard A. Horsley (ed.), *Paul and Politics: Ekklesia, Israel, Imperium, Interpretation. Essays in Honor of Krister Stendahl* (Harrisburg, PA: Trinity Press International, 2000), pp. 191-215.
Calvin Roetzl responds to Wan's essay in the same volume.

Warrior, Robert Allen, 'Canaanites, Cowboys, and Indians: Deliverance, Conquest, and Liberation Theology Today', *Christianity and Crisis* 49 (1989), pp. 261-65. Reprinted in R.S. Sugirtharajah (ed.), *Voices from the Margin: Interpreting the Bible in the Third World* (Maryknoll, NY: Orbis Books, 2nd edn, 1995).
An influential Native American reading of the biblical exodus and conquest narratives that identifies with the Canaanites.

Watts, Edward, 'The Only Teller of Big Truths: Epeli Hau'ofa's Tales of the Tikongs and the Biblical Contexts of Postcolonialism', *Literature and Theology* (1992), pp. 369-82.

Weaver, Jace, 'From I-Hermeneutics to We-Hermeneutics: Native Americans and the Post-Colonial', in Laura Donaldson (ed.), *Postcolonialism and Scriptural Reading* (Semeia, 75; Atlanta: Society of Biblical Literature, 1996), pp. 153-76.
Includes analysis of the role of biblical hermeneutics in the European colonization of North America.

West, Gerald O., 'Early Encounters with the Bible among the Batlhaping: Historical and Hermeneutical Signs', *Biblical Interpretation* 12 (2004), pp. 251-81.
Swims against the current of postcolonial studies by refusing to subsume the Bible's reception by this tribe under their reception of Christianity.

—'From the Bible as *bola* to Biblical Interpretation as *marabi*: Tlhaping Transactions with the Bible', in Jonathan A. Draper (ed.), *Orality, Literacy and Colonialism in Southern Africa* (Semeia Studies, 46; Atlanta: Society of Biblical Literature Publications, 2003), pp. 41-55.

—'A Real Presence, Subsumed by Others: The Bible in Colonial and Postcolonial Contexts', *Semeia* 88 (2001), pp. 199-214.

—'Re-membering the Bible in South Africa: Reading Strategies in a Postcolonial Context', *Jian Dao* (July 1997), pp. 37-62.

—'White Men, Bibles, and Land: Ingredients in Biblical Interpretation in South African Black Theology', *Scriptura* 73 (2000), pp. 141-52.

West, Gerald O., and Musa W. Dube (eds.), *The Bible in Africa: Transactions, Trajectories, and Trends* (Leiden: E.J. Brill, 2001).
Africa's colonial history and its aftereffects is a recurrent theme of this collection.

Westhelle, Vitor, 'Multiculturalism, Postcolonialism, and the Apocalyptic', in Viggo Mortensen (ed.), *Theology and the Religions: A Dialogue* (Grand Rapids, MI: Eerdmans, 2003), pp. 3-13.

—'Revelation 13: Between the Colonial and the Postcolonial, a Reading from Brazil', in David Rhoads (ed.), *From Every People and Nation: The Book of Revelation in Intercultural Perspective* (Minneapolis: Fortress Press, 2005), pp. 183-99.

Wicker, Kathleen, 'Teaching Feminist Biblical Studies in a Postcolonial Context', in Elisabeth Schüssler Fiorenza (ed.), *Searching the Scriptures*. I. *A Feminist Introduction* (New York: Crossroad, 1993), pp. 367-80.

INDEXES

INDEX OF REFERENCES

INDEX OF AUTHORS

Printed in the United States
99840LV00002B/56/A